Uganda's Rev
1979-1

How I Saw It

Pecos Kutesa

Crispin Foyser.

Dedicated to ~~Foy~~ ~~George~~ ~~Boyer~~.
Pse read understand what drove
to war what kept us up to
now and whether we are
still on line.

Author 16/06/2016

FOUNTAIN PUBLISHERS
Kampala

Fountain Publishers Ltd
P. O. Box 488 Kampala
E-mail: sales@fountainpublishers.co.ug
        publishing@ fountainpublishers.co.ug
Website:www.fountainpublishers.co.ug

Distributed in Europe and Commonwealth
countries outside Africa by:
African Books Collective,
P.O. Box 721, Oxford OX1 9EN, UK.
Tel: 44(0) 1869 349110, Fax:+44(0)1869 349110
E-mail: orders@africanbookscollective.com
Website: www.africanbookscollective.com

Distributed in North America by:
Michigan State University Press
1405 South Harrison Road
25 Manly Miles Building
East Lansing, MI 48823-5245
Tel: +1 517 3559543, 800 6782120
Fax: +1 517 4322611
E-mail: msupress@.msu.edu
Website: www.msupress.msu.edu

ISBN 978-9970-02-564-0

Dedication

*Dedicated to the memory of all those combatants
who shed their blood in the struggle
to make Uganda a better country.*

Contents

Map of Uganda   vii
Map of Luweero Triangle   viii
Acronyms   ix
Acknowledgements   xi
Foreword   xii

Why the Struggle   1
Search for anti-Amin forces   4
Recruitment and training   6
Advance on Arua   12
Kikosi Maalum and the West Nile   17
Kabamba (The Red Army days)   20

Cadet Training in Tanzania   24
The "grand" reception back home   37

Escape from Nakasongola   49

The First Combat Mission (Kakiri)   60

Attack by TPDF at Katera   73
Reorganisation and preparation for Nairobi   82
Luwero Triangle and river crossing   84

The Nairobi Journey (Seven Men in a Boat)   86
Kisumu   91
Nairobi and its glamour   93

ADC to Two Different Personalities
(Yusuf Lule and Yoweri Museveni)   96
Formation of NRM/NRA   97

Return Journey from Nairobi   105
The UNLA warm welcome   112

UFM Attack on Lubiri   **126**
The Kikunyu-Kalongero bridge   133

Kalongero: A Bridge Too Far for UNLA   **135**
Kakiri II walkover   142
Bukalabi disaster   146
Safari 50   151

The Katonga Bridge: Reconnaissance   **156**

Kabamba, Masindi and Hoima Offensives   **175**
Hoima, June 1984   184
Kabamba III, January 1985   187
Birembo *Moto Wawaka*   192

Diplomatic Offensive Starts: CHC Goes to Sweden   **195**

Birembo: The Battle That Broke UNLA's Back   **199**

Fighting the Okello Regime   **211**
The Katonga bridge   220

The UNLA Surrenders   **232**

The Fall of Kampala   **237**

The final assault   237
Feeling actual fear   239

The War Beyond Kampala   **250**

Postscript   **259**

Index   270

Map of Uganda

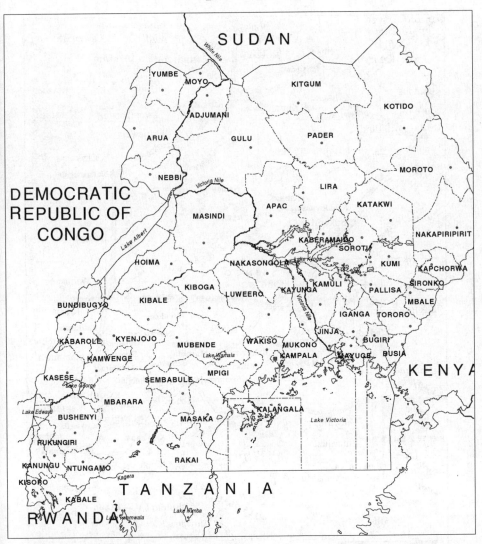

The Luweero Triangle

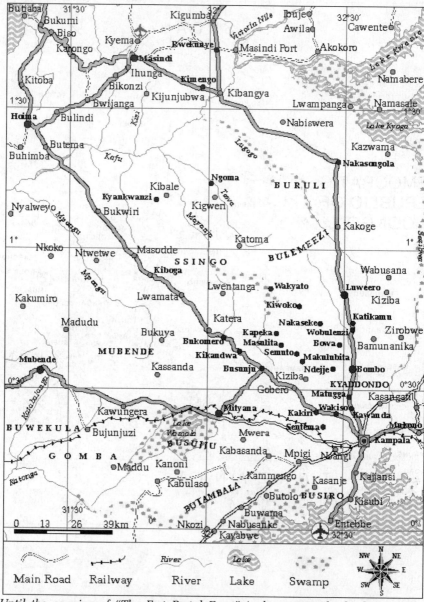

Until the opening of "The Fort Portal Front" in late 1984, the bush war was concentrated in the area between the Hoima and Gulu roads in the districts of Wakiso, Mpigi, Mubende and Luwero. This area was nicknamed "The Luweero Triangle".

Acronyms

ADC	aide de camp
APC	armoured personnel carrier
APM	anti-personnel mine
ATG	anti-tank grenade
AVM	anti-vehicle mine
CA	Constitutional Assembly
Capt.	Captain
CASEVAC	casualty evacuation (procedure)
CHC	Chairman of the High Command
Col	Colonel
COS	Chief of Staff
Coy.	Company
CP	command post
CTR	Chief of Training and Recruitment
CTU	Chio Kuu Cha Taifa Cha Uongozi
DP	Democratic Party
DRC	Democratic Republic of Congo
DS	Directing Staff
FEBA	forward edge of the battle area
FEDEMU	Federal Democratic Movement
FFU	Field Force Unit
FRONASA	Front for National Salvation
FUNA	Former Uganda National Army
GAFSC	Ghana Armed Forces Staff College
GBC	Ghana Broadcasting Corporation
GDP	Gross Domestic Product
Gen.	General
GNP	Gross National Product
GPMG	general purpose machine gun
GSU	General Service Unit
IO	Intelligence Officer
KAR	King's African Rifles
KM	Kikosi Maalum
LC	Local Council
Lt Col	Lieutenant Colonel

Lt	Lieutenant
MMG	medium machine gun
NASA	National Security Agency
NCO	non-commissioned officer
NEC	National Enterprise Corporation
NLA	National Leadership Academy (same as CTU)
NRA	National Resistance Army
NRM	National Resistance Movement
NYA	not yet allotted army number
OAU	Organisation of African Unity
OP	observation post
OR	other ranks
PA	personal administration
POW	prisoner of war
PRA	Popular Resistance Army
RC	Resistance Council
RDF	Rwanda Defence Forces
recce	reconnaissance
RPF	Rwanda Patriotic Front
RPG	rocket propelled grenade
RV	rendezvous point
SAR	semi-automatic rifle
Sgt	Sergeant
SNCO	senior non-commissioned officer
SRB	State Research Bureau
TPDF	Tanzania People's Defence Forces
UA	Uganda Army
UEB	Uganda Electricity Board
UFM	Uganda Freedom Movement
UNHCR	United Nations High Commissioner for Refugees
UNLA	Uganda National Liberation Army
UNLF	Uganda National Liberation Front
UNRF	Uganda National Rescue Front
UPC	Uganda People's Congress
UPDA	Uganda People's Democratic Army
UPDF	Uganda People's Defence Forces
UPM	Uganda Patriotic Movement
UFF	Uganda Freedom Fighters

Acknowledgements

This book would not have been possible without the unreserved support that I received from some people. These include my fellow ex-combatants with whom I cross-checked recollections of dates and events.

It is unfortunate that most of the people I have written about in this book are dead. Nevertheless, comrades such as Gen. Salim Saleh and Gen. Elly Tumwine greatly encouraged me in this endeavour. I also drew much inspiration from H.E. the President of Uganda, Yoweri Kaguta Museveni, whose book, *Sowing the Mustard Seed*, particularly helped me to get the chronology of the revents right. Mr Tim Cooper and Ms Alison Porteous, two journalists who covered the bush war, motivated me by showing a great deal of enthusiasm for the book. Dr Justus Mugaju competently edited the manuscript and commented on the postscript. My publishers constantly cross-checked with me about terms and abbreviations relating to the military as well as bush jargon. This was a team I was delighted to work with. Most important, though, is the enthusiasm everybody showed about the book. I feel I owe all of them a lot of gratitude.

I am also grateful to William Pike and Camerapix for some of the pictures used in the book.

P. K.
December 2005

Foreword

This is the story of the National Resistance Army, a guerilla army that fought and overthrew the government of Uganda in just five years — from 1981 to 1986. The war was unique in that it was home-grown and home-based: it did not enjoy any external assistance and did not have any real external base like most guerrilla wars.

According to Professor Mahmood Mamdani, this was a historical feat; for the first time in the history of Black Africa, civilians became angry enough to shoot the soldiers off the streets of the capital. It was a war that pitted civilians against professional soldiers, and the civilians won.

I was privileged to have participated in this war, right from its inception up to the capture of state power in 1986.

The aim of this story is to share my experiences with those who may have the future and interest of their own country at heart and are concerned enough to fight, not only for Uganda and Africa, but also in any part of the globe.

Every day the print media and the airwaves carry reports of trouble. It seems fighting is in the nature of man and it is going to stay with us for the foreseeable future. While military philosophers agree that the best way to win a war is to avoid starting one in the first place, the reality of life is that since Adam's two sons fought and Cain slew Abel, conflict in human interactions has always been and will always be a fact of life. It is said that the military is one of the oldest professions, second only to prostitution, and I believe that statement stands true today.

It is difficult to explain what goes on in the mind of someone in command when he receives operational orders. Throughout the book, I will try to withdraw myself from the person known as an army officer or a man in combat, and to analyse the body language of officers and men under fire. In so doing, I will attempt to cover all events from enlistment, through training, the first time in combat, to the fears and expectations when planning a mission, and the persona I had to present to my followers. I will also talk about the way we viewed our leaders, the myths we created and the bravado of combatants. These were all aspects of the trials we had to go through bravely at one time or another, not to mention the comedy and the nasty situations like the terror experienced when viewing the gruesome remains of our comrades caught in crossfire or blown up by bombs or mines.

Then comes the end: The exhilaration after a successful mission and the feeling of relief after overrunning targets; the turbulent thoughts caused by defeat; the fear of facing defeated troops; how to report losses to bosses; and all the challenges that face a commander in a war.

I have tried to capture the hope we had in such arduous situations and to imagine the person behind the uniform. In my endeavour to do so, I apologise if I do not spare either my bosses or myself. I may step on my comrades' toes by injuring their inflated egos, but my aim is to teach anyone who, at any given time, finds himself in combat, to know that it is natural and normal to experience fear of loss, or the excitement of success at the end of it all.

A person who does not have any sense of fear is not fit for leadership because he can be dangerous to the people he is leading. The heart to soldier does not grow old, as there is always a sense of romance in all the actions of a soldier. Anybody going into a battle should be able to capture that tone in order to appreciate soldiering, which I believe is a noble profession.

Is it the beat of the war drums that leads men to reach seemingly unattainable heights? Why do others turn into slobbish cowards? How is that beat transmitted to the lower echelons and down to the basic infantry soldiers? What was the magic that made some people heroes? How does the leadership capture that sentiment? Where did people find the stamina to withstand the fear of loss of limbs and thus becoming permanent cripples, which to me is the main fear of a soldier, unlike civilians, who fear death? After all, once you are dead, you have no regrets, I believe.

This narrative is about the experiences of young men of peasant background, some elite intellectuals and many uneducated individuals, all thinking and working in tandem to transform the social and political landscape of their country.

Remember the chants in training marches, the rhythms of marching army boots. Those sounds will always accompany you to battle. In fact, if you listen carefully, you can discern the music in the noise of the guns.

With all the sincerity I can find in my heart, I would like to dedicate this book to the participants in the real combat situations that led to our success in the end. The war was fought for many reasons. I have not tried to justify that, but suffice it to say that my aim is to tell those who will be compelled to wage war in the future, to know what to expect on the battlefield.

The main aim of this book is, therefore, to put in a proper perspective the experience in the field and to demystify the fear of battle, while at the same time trying to show the gruesome face of war – it is an unpleasant business!

"A revolution is not a dinner party", as Mao Tse-Tung said, and there is no limited war. Each battle is designed for killing people on the opposing side. However, as a relatively old hand in the game, what I would like to impart to my readers is the experience of the Nigerians, to allow them to emulate the Nigerian motto after the Biafran civil war. It says: "In a civil war, there is no victor, there is no vanquished. All you have to show at the end of the day are the dead bodies of the same nationality", which would lead to the question, "Who is the enemy in a civil war?"

1

Why the Struggle

Various Ugandans had their reasons for rising up against Idi Amin Dada. Politicians cited lack of democracy, while others cited the deteriorating economy. The superpowers were caught up in the conflicts stemming from the East-West divide and could not care less — what was Uganda to them anyway?

However, at the time some of us were young men caught up in the turmoil of Uganda's political environment. Most of us were not politically conscious enough to envisage what the war would yield. Our main interest was to chase out dictator Idi Amin and his soldiers, and not least Amin's notorious State Research Bureau and Public Safety Unit, which were his most feared security organs.

The first of my many encounters with State Research personnel was in my third year of secondary school. There had been a debating contest between schools in Masaka district, and I had been cited as one of the best speakers; which was a "crime" I would pay for dearly. Those days State Research operatives used to attend all public gatherings and even a school debate was monitored by the state. Among the spectators was one George Nkonge, who had deserted school while in Primary Five. We had been schoolmates in primary school and he had gone on to become a golf caddie. As I left the school gate, Nkonge accosted me and congratulated me on my good English. Jokingly I answered, "But Nkonge, so would you if you had not left school to go chasing golf balls."

I found myself immediately surrounded by rough-looking boys who shoved me into their car and squeezed me into the back seat. Some of the ruffians sat on me. Nkonge, who appeared to be in command, drove the car to the police station. The desk police officer was a big, black, pot-bellied man who sprang to attention and addressed Nkonge as "*Afande* Sir", which implied that Nkonge was someone in authority and known to the police. My shoes were removed and the police sergeant was ordered to administer strokes of the cane to me until morning, and this the police sergeant did religiously. In the morning I was released, and for a week I could not go to school because I was nursing a bruised back. It then dawned on me that Nkonge had joined the dreaded State Research Bureau.

The other incident I recall was when I went to the former Tropic Inn Hotel, to drink a soda with a school-girl friend of mine. Someone standing behind me knocked my glass off the table. I had been introduced to boxing by the then Masaka Boxing Club coach and my reflexes were superb. I wheeled around and hit the thug behind me, sending him reeling to the floor. I sidestepped, doing some nice footwork, but then a hand grabbed me from behind and swung me around. I came face to face with a very tall fellow, who showed me a huge knife and gave me the ultimatum to leave Masaka town in two hours. I was then enjoying in my S.4 vacation, waiting for my O'level examination results. I left Masaka post-haste.

The straw that broke the camel's back, as the saying goes, came when I was really humiliated at a roadblock in Masaka in 1977. I had bribed my way into a bank job. One of the requirements of the bank was to wear a necktie while on duty. The roadblock was located at one of the bends leading to Masaka town. It was positioned in such a way that it came as a complete surprise to motorists, especially to taxi drivers. I was seated in the rear seat of a Peugeot 404 estate car, then very popular.

We just bumped into the roadblock and all of us were ordered out of the car. We were lined up and told to empty our pockets. I had my school identity card on me and a few shillings, which I promptly handed over. It had drizzled, and the soldiers as well as their jeep were covered in mud.

After checking all of us, the soldiers told me in Kiswahili to stay behind. My fellow passengers and the taxi driver were ordered to leave. They got back in the car but did not drive away. Their faces registering concern, sympathy and fear, they waited to see what was going to befall me.

The soldiers asked me in Kiswahili why I was wearing a tie. I answered in English that it was part of the uniform, as I was required to report to my new job at the bank. It was a cardinal sin in those days to answer in English which, to the soldiers of the time, signified contempt for them, owing to their lack of formal education. Secondly, they thought that I equated a tie to their cherished uniform.

"Uniform! Uniform!"one of the soldiers exclaimed in Kiswahili, adding, *"Leo utavaa uniform kama yangu"* (Today you are going to wear a uniform similar to mine), *"Lala chini* (Lie down), *"Viringita"* (Start rolling).

I was rolled in the mud until I was an ochre colour from head to foot. After some time, the soldier told me sarcastically that I was now smart enough to go to work in the bank and then released me. I boarded the waiting taxi but there was total silence inside it until we reached the taxi park. I could imagine what my fellow passengers were thinking; they were grateful that I had survived with so little physical harm.

However, from that moment on, I felt the highest degree of humiliation and indignation. How could such uncouth public servants subject me and many others to such degradation? What did they have that I lacked? Just a gun? I was determined never to endure such humiliation again! What did it take to learn how to handle a gun? Those and similar thoughts occupied my mind until the other passengers had disembarked from the car. I requested the driver to get passengers for the return journey to Lyantonde, since I was no longer in a position to present myself at my new job because of the state of my attire.

Eventually the taxi filled up and the journey back to Lyantonde began. It was an uneventful journey since most of the roadblocks had been abandoned and the soldiers had gone away to look for drinks. One remaining red-eyed ruffian just waved us through.

It was late in the evening when I arrived home, looking, as our people say, "like something the dog has chewed and left behind" (*Eky'embwa yarya ekatsiga).* I had no explanation for, nor answers to, the many questions I was asked, especially by my father.

I had made up my mind to find a way of learning to handle a gun, after which I would return to humiliate that soldier. I had not anticipated that what I had called maximum humiliation would be child's play when I joined the army.

Search for anti-Amin forces

There were rumours that anti-Amin training activities were taking place in neighbouring Tanzania. This rumour persisted and many Ugandans had been aware of the rumour since the 1972 invasion by Tanzania-backed guerrillas. Now, in 1977/78, the rumours reached fever pitch.

The morning after my roadblock experience, my cousin, the late Benjamin Muhanguzi (who later was to play a significant part in the PRA/NRA war against UNLA) and I decided to go to Bukanga near Tanzania and try and trace the people who handled recruitment. Bukanga is on the Tanzania-Uganda border. It was a free zone for the people of the neighbouring areas, the cattle-keepers who had many relatives on both sides of the border.

We set off on foot, and as we travelled we stayed with relatives. Within one week we had reached the Kagera Salient. We spent the nights with the families of relatives, on our last night arriving in a place called Kakunyu. We were apprehensive about telling anybody the aim of our visit, so we disguised ourselves as job seekers and businessmen. There was a lot of smuggling into and from Tanzania by people on both sides, since the people at the border did not respect the boundary between the two countries. The local community shared a common language, albeit with minor differences between dialects.

The Tanzanian community was much more security-conscious than our Ugandan community, so we were warned not to wander around, as we could easily be arrested, even by civilians, and handed over to Field Force Units (FFU), locally known as *Fanya Fujo Uwone*, literally meaning, "You just cause problems and you will see". We kept underground, behaving like visitors, for about a week.

During that time an Indian firm was constructing the Kagera Sugar Factory in the Kyaka area and there was widespread recruitment of manpower. This offered us opportunities to get out and integrate into society. We approached the Indian firm and we were immediately recruited as manual labourers.

The Indian foremen were finding it difficult to communicate with local Tanzanian workers. My knowledge of English was soon recognised and I was made the head of the working groups. I began sub-contracting pieces of work like digging trenches and foundation pits, then started hiring people to do manual work. Payment took place at the end of the week, and each worker was paid according to what he had done. Although I did not realise much gain, I was always able to fulfil my contract by paying the workers as agreed and ended up slightly better off than my fellow labourers.

All this time we were trying to contact any one of the groups fighting Idi Amin. The Tanzanian government system was so well established and entrenched that Tanzanians loved their government and the president so much that anyone who so much as thought of anything anti-establishment was frowned upon by young and old alike. We stayed in Tanzania for three months but failed to contact anybody remotely connected with anti-Amin activities. We became convinced that all the talk in Uganda was just rumour created by State Research operatives.

We were by now a miserable and dejected pair, as we crossed the border back into Uganda. Little did we know that we had just missed a flurry of activity related to the very reason that had taken us to Tanzania in the first place. Ironically, just twenty days after we left the Kagera sugar plant, Idi Amin attacked Tanzania.

The war which everyone had wished for, so that Idi Amin could be eliminated, had started, and it was up to those who wished to find a way of joining the side they wanted, to do so.

My cousin, Benjamin Muhanguzi, had gone to his maternal uncles in Nyabushozi and I had gone back home in Lyantonde, Kabula. Each of us set off from where we were, determined to join the war. Soon we were recruited and started training.

Recruitment and training

I walked from my home in Ryakaihura, Kabula county, to Mbarara town, a distance of 150 km following shortcuts. I met FRONASA scouts on the way. Although Lyantonde had not yet fallen, the mood of the people there was as if the war had already been won.

At the main roundabout (*aha mahembe g'ente*) where there is a concrete sculpture of a cow, I was received by Chefe Mwangisi and others. "Chefe", a pseudonym adopted for security reasons, means "Chief" and was used by FRONASA officers who went to train in Mozambique. I was asked whether I wanted to join the war, and my answer was in the affirmative.

Nobody asked for my identity card, reasons why I wanted to join the army, my background, physical fitness status or the other routine queries a new recruit usually has to answer. I was just told to join a group of men lazying around on the verandahs of the shops. That was around 3.00 p.m.

At 4.00 p.m. Chefe Makosa came in a Land Rover and addressed us. He told us that we would be taken by truck to Kakoba, which had been turned into a training ground. At around 6.00 p.m., a semi-trailer truck without number plates but splashed with mud and covered with tree leaves, came and we were told to jump onto it. I was now a soldier! We arrived at the Kakoba training ground at twilight and the place was awash with young men, each wearing his own clothes. There was no dress code since each individual had come as the urge arose in him to join the struggle. Anybody familiar with a village flea-market can get a rudimentary picture of what the new liberators, as we were popularly known, looked like; only we looked worse.

We were predominantly male and our ages ranged between 12 and 70 years. There were also a few young women among us. The medium of communication was an accepted version of the Tower of Babel, if such a language was ever recorded; and this spelt total confusion.

We idled around in tree shades in clusters and spoke whatever language we felt comfortable with.

Later, a gong was sounded, precipitating a stampede for food. Though some of us had spent quite a bit of time without a solid meal and we were able-bodied civilians with no sense of discipline, we were expected to queue for food in an orderly manner. What a joke!

To complicate matters, there were no plates. Each person had to improvise a container for his block of *posho* and a ladle of half-cooked beans. The human mind is very innovative when driven by physical needs. Very soon, every scrap of metal, plastic, helmets, and even newspaper had been turned into plates.

Seeing people making a fuss about clean plates and cutlery, one realises how deceptive life is. We wolfed the meal down in a few minutes, and soon more than ten drums of food were empty. By drums I mean 200 litre fuel containers, which had been converted into saucepans.

The next difficult task that befell our beleaguered instructors was to maintain order and to try and keep this rabble of peasants quiet. In his book, *Sowing the Mustard Seed*, Yoweri Museveni writes of how difficult it is to keep peasants quiet. However, his experience was with peasants on the run — fugitives. He should have experienced real, raw peasants, who were on the giving end and not in hiding.

The Tanzanian instructors had to use their psychological warfare skills on us. They told us with stern faces that Amin's MiG-21 bombers could hear our voices and would bomb us. That worked for some time, but after an hour or so with no MiG zooming over us, the hubbub resumed. However, by midnight, nature did for the Tanzanians what their threats could not do. It was really cold. Kakoba lies in a sort of valley near the River Rwizi, so the yapping recruits started huddling together in search of some warmth. By 2.00 a.m. the noise had changed from exclamations of heroism and what one intended to do to Amin's thugs, to the gentle buzz of snoring. Try to imagine the combination of thousands of snoring throats mingled with the croaking of the frogs and toads in River Rwizi. It must have been a good orchestra to listen to, only that I was also part of the chorus, making my own contribution to the music.

Mine was a sleep justified. It came from a combination of fatigue and a sense of satisfaction for joining fellow fighters. The meal of posho and beans lulled us into dreamless sleep, only to be rudely awakened by a loud shout of *Ndege! Ndege!* (Plane! Plane!).

We jumped up from our slumber in the same disorderly fashion as we had fallen asleep. Beady-eyed, we looked up at the sky and tuned our ears to the expected roar of MiGs, only to be ordered by a big voice to fall in line. *"FOLEN!"* shouted the instructors.

I wished at that time that there was someone who had the sense to film two thousand raw peasants trying to line up at dawn in such an unfamiliar setting! We rumbled around like wild elephants on the rampage, but trust the Tanzanians: in only two hours we had been arranged a semblance of a military formation. We were told to line up three abreast and each group of 108 people were called a "coy" (company), which was composed of three platoons, with each platoon consisting of three sections of twelve people each. Each "coy" was assigned a Tanzanian instructor. I fell in F company and our instructor was Lance Corporal Paki, who seemed to be of mixed race.

The next problem was the language. While we Ugandans had always prided ourselves on being "superior" to our neighbours, we did not have a national language, a fact which posed a very big problem. Now, imagine a Tanzanian lance corporal addressing one hundred people, each with his own language and dialect. Incidentally, most people had little or no education, and the Tanzanians were too proud of their Kiswahili to even try a few words in English. The problem for F company was solved by my rudimentary knowledge of Kiswahili, which I had acquired during my stint at the Kagera sugar plant. I was immediately made company commander and armed with an SAR (semi-automatic rifle) but without bullets.

We set off on a route march after a mug of porridge. The muddling horde that we became while trying to run in step must have tested our Tanzanian instructor's patience. However, being the soldier he was, he tried and was able to cope with us. By 10.00 a.m. the natural law of elimination had taken its toll.

What had started as a stampeding mob was now reduced to a few staggering groups of ten to twenty people.

By midday, when the instructor called for a five-minute break, I could count only 27 of the original one hundred plus people I had set off with. Lance Corporal Paki mocked me, "Coy commander, *askari wako wapi?*" (Where are your troops?). Of course, I did not have the energy to answer. I just flopped down. I had the extra burden of carrying a bullet-less rifle, which was in itself a big punishment. Now here was this *Afande*, as we called him, asking me to account for the rest of the group!

We staggered back to the camp, picking up the outpaced members of our company along the way, and arrived back in time for the midday meal. After the meal, we expected at least a rest, so that our stomachs could digest this otherwise unpalatable food. But this was not to be. "Recruits, fall in line!" shouted the instructors in the hot afternoon sun. We were told to form up. We trampled the grass and staggered while trying to remain in line, with the instructors barking and kicking at our heels. After we had formed an unimpressive semblance of a parade, the instructors stood before us and told us that the next lesson involved teaching us to walk! I could barely suppress a smile as I translated to my charges what the instructor wanted to teach us. Imagine, here were people older than twelve years, who had been walking since they were toddlers, and now a Tanzanian wanted to teach us how to walk, after running with us for more than ten kilometres; moreover, some of us had walked far just to join! Well, we all kept quiet and watched as we thought the instructor was making a fool of himself. *Kwanza onasimama, alafu onatoa mugu yakushoto mbele...* (First you stand straight, then move your left foot forward...). Now, that may appear nonsensical, but one needs to have been there to see what a mess we made of those simple instructions. When the order was given to move forward, what transpired was a fiasco. Imagine hippos, giraffes and ducks trying to move in one line.

After we had taken a few ungainly steps the instructors shouted, "*Hima!*" (Halt! "*Munanuka!*" (You stink!) "*Viringita*" (Roll!).

We were subjected to the same treatment I had undergone at Idi Amin's roadblock. We were forced to roll on the ground for a long time. However, this time, instead of feeling humiliated and degraded, I felt a sense of curiosity. This was my first lesson in soldiering. I had watched a number of Western films and I had started imagining myself as an armed hero crawling under enemy fire. However, that euphoria evaporated when we were forced to crawl into the storm drainage near the road. The drains were really stinking and few of us had a change of clothing. The shirt and trousers we had on were the only clothes we had brought to the army. By 8.00 a.m., as we scrambled for our evening meal, we were stinking to high heaven. This treatment continued for the next few days. However, by then we had learned how to walk!

After one week we were introduced to the stripping and assembling of the SAR and we started what is known as dry firing, that is, holding and aiming a gun. Up to this time, apart from an occasional escape to the river for a quick dip or being drenched by rain showers, we had not had time for any form of ablution.

The third week was devoted to the range ground and most of us fired live bullets for the first time. In the fourth week we were declared fit for battle, but more training was needed.

We spent a total of seventy days in Kakoba before we were deployed on guard duty around Mbarara town. My sector fell in Ntare School and as a "coy" commander, I commandeered the school library, which I made into my residence and command post. I really enjoyed the library despite its dilapidated state. A lot of looting had taken place in the town and everything was in a shambles. However, there were enough books to provide a good mattress, materials for reading and good paper to roll cigarettes. One of the bad habits I had acquired on joining the army was smoking. In my naivety, I had thought it showed that I was macho enough to be a soldier, which makes me guilty to have contributed to ruining the Ntare School library.

Advance on Arua

The crash programme, training and familiarisation with the gun took us about two months. We spent the time in Mbarara town and the suburbs, when we were introduced to most of our future commanders who had been to Mozambique with the future leader, Yoweri Museveni. One cannot really describe the awe in which we held these handsome young men. These were young men who had been trained in guerilla commando tactics and leadership and they were renowned martial arts experts.

They were dressed in tight-fitting combat uniforms and had a commanding presence. We were mesmerised by people like Fred Rwigyema (RIP), Salim Saleh, Makosa, Pipino, Ivan Koreta, Chefe Ali and others. To us, they looked like aliens from outer space. The way their uniforms fitted them, the way they walked and the commanding authority they oozed when addressing us, their juniors, was absolutely mesmerising.

The FRONASA (Front for National Salvation), to which we belonged, did not have a regular formation of battalions, brigades, etc. Instead it had columns and we were put in the Mondlane column. This column expanded as recruitment went on. There were many columns, as Yoweri Museveni points out in his book, *Sowing the Mustard Seed*. Other columns were Mwesiga, Rwaheru, and others, all named after fallen liberation fighters.

Our column was under the TPDF Brigade 206 KJ. After Mbarara, we advanced on Fort Portal. We always moved behind the Tanzanian troops and did not experience any combat. The Amin soldiers were routed from their positions and were simply fleeing from the Tanzanian army bombings.

At Kakoba some instructors and commanders had tried to lure me into joining the military police. In fact, I had been detailed to do so and, indeed, I had escorted two buses from Mbarara to Kampala. Those were the days when Yusuf Lule was president and he had just been voted out of office. Kampala was full of crowds and people were chanting, *"Twagala Lule oba tufa tufe"* (We want Lule whether we die, we die). I had spent the night in Kibuli with my cousin, Winnie Rwabutiti, sister to Dampa. In the morning, I was supposed to report to Republic House (now Bulange) where the army headquarters was. The taxi driver was at first excited about taking a soldier who could speak Luganda and who was willing to pay the fare. However, when we got near the taxi park he got cold feet. He told me he could not continue because the roads were blocked, and indeed the road to Republic House near Blue Room Hotel in Mengo was blocked by people who were dancing, drumming and shouting anti-government slogans. I paid my fare to the taxi man and got out as he wished me luck. Here I was in a new Tanzanian army camouflage uniform with a brand-new AK-47 with 30 bullets, but I had never experienced any fear, although this was a potentially explosive situation, as I was to find out later.

At that time, all of us new recruits felt on top of the world. What with a uniform and a gun, we felt that there was absolutely nothing beyond us. Civilians were also pampering our egos. We were the liberators who had chased away the *Anyanya*, a term used to refer to Amin's soldiers of foreign origin.

I was soon spotted by the mob, who mistook me for a Tanzanian soldier. However, just for the fun of it, they ordered me to carry my rifle high and join them in their chants of *"Twagala Lule"*. This I did, to their amusement, and they let me pass. I reported to Republic House and I was assigned another vehicle which needed an escort to Mbarara.

When I reported back to Kakoba, I was informed that I had been selected to lead the Military Police and so should prepare to be stationed in Mbarara. My immediate reaction was to reject the idea but instead I complained to Fred Rwigyema. He summoned me to his office. With trepidation, I stood in front of Chefe Fred. He was my idol and here I was ready to disappoint him. He was relaxing in his commander's chair when I entered and he greeted me with a warm smile. He asked me why I was disobeying orders and I explained that my aim in joining the war was to be able to fire the biggest gun there was. Tanzanians had shelled Masaka and Mbarara towns, and the combination of BVM 21s, 122 mm howitzers and 106 mms had created an exhilarating impression in the minds of young adventurous people like me, who joined to fight Idi Amin. The legendary idol, as I envisaged Fred then, just laughed and said, "Okay, go back and command your coy." That was the best order I ever heard.

The advance on Fort Portal was uneventful. When we debussed we were greeted by many ululations, hugs and even kisses from Toro belles. We felt we had really arrived. The barracks (Mountains of the Moon) was besieged by people offering free drinks and edibles. Our commanders were very strict. We marched into our positions, leaving all that excitement behind, but consoled ourselves that that was the army discipline that one had to uphold.

After a week in Fort Portal, an order was given that we move to the frontline, as it was then known. Instead of fear and nervous anxiety we were excited and jubilant. There was euphoria among us, since we believed were now going to fire our guns without hindrance and to show those Amin soldiers the stuff we were made of.

All this time, firing a bullet, even by accident, attracted heavy punishment. We reasoned that nobody would punish us for firing bullets at the frontline. After all, that was what we were armed for in the first place. But this was not to be. We never got a chance to fire indiscriminately as we had hoped. The march was very orderly and strictly disciplined.

We set off on foot, with a water tanker and a few trucks and Land Rovers following.

We reached the Murchison Falls National Park and camped a few times to rest and eat. Otherwise there were no shouts announcing that the enemy had been sighted. The only excitement we had was when Chefe Fred killed a buffalo calf. The soldiers spotted it and started shouting at it. The scared animal was surrounded and did not know where to run, so it stood still while people fired at it from all directions. If Idi Amin's soldiers had witnessed our display of marksmanship, I think they would have come and disarmed us all, as we were good at spending bullets with no visible effect. The animal was wounded but it still stood on all four legs. Then Chefe Fred ordered everyone to cease firing and tried to demonstrate to us what we ought to have done. Now an AK-47 is not a hunting gun and its stopping power is not that much. Not that it does not cause permanent damage. However, unless it is a direct head shot, a person who is hit will stagger forward until he gets cover because the bullet will just pass through him. I witnessed this many times.

Fred must have been hitting the target. However, it took half a magazine of fifteen bullets before the buffalo toppled down from the anthill on which it stood.

We rushed over with excitement to share in Fred's kill. The animal was a net of bullet wounds, having taken more than fifty bullets. We, the recruits, were denied any share of the game, since the order to advance was called immediately. The carcass was thrown into the command Land Rover, and that was the last time we saw or heard of it.

The advance through the national park was otherwise uneventful or 'Nothing to Report', as the army puts it. We could hear the distant rumble of heavy artillery far ahead and more from the easterly direction. It was feared that the Pakwach bridge would be blown up but Amin's people either did not want or did not have time to do it. We crossed the bridge and entered West Nile after crossing Lake Albert by ferry.

We continued our trek till we entered Arua town towards evening. The town was bustling with activity. There were more Tanzanian troops there than civilians. The Tanzanian troops went ahead to secure the borders with both Zaire (now DRC) and the Sudan. Again, we were assigned the duty of guarding the town and its suburbs. Our group, now calling itself "The Red Army" at the instigation of Chefe Salim Saleh, covered the town. My "coy" occupied Tanganyika village. Arua had villages named after countries neighbouring Uganda. There was Kenya, Tanzania, Zambia, etc.

My company was the first to occupy Idi Amin's house, which we found totally empty. However, as our people say, "a rich or old man's home can never be completely empty". I picked up a bundle of five thousand shillings in five-shilling notes. But the main prize was the Citroen Maserati. This is the car Idi Amin drove during the OAU conference in Uganda in 1975 when, owing to public demand, he married his wife Sarah "once more again for the second time", as he so aptly put it. As the company commander, I immediately commandeered the former head of state's prize car. However, apart from offering me a very warm and comfortable bed, there was nothing more that its beauty could offer me. The car was computerised and the keys were not available. Those fancy cars have a bad habit of defying the common Ugandan's limited knowledge of electronics. The car had been parked and the body had settled down, almost touching the tarmac. The whole company tried to push it, but it just sat there unbothered! The few of us who had had more exposure to cars tried to open the bonnet but nobody could find the lever to pull or push.

We looked at the beautiful car and it seemed to stare back at us. It seemed to be looking at us in contempt owing to our ignorance. Nobody could bring himself to vandalise such a masterpiece. Luckily the doors were open, so for two days it became my camp bed. On the third day *Afande* Saleh heard of the car. He came and claimed it as his own. I left it to him. However, he could not move it even an inch either, even when a Tata lorry was used to try to tow it. The chain used damaged the body of the car instead of moving it. The wheels were locked.

I left the car with my boss Saleh and continued with my work. Saleh had the car for about ten days. When the Tanzanian general who was the sector commander laid claim to it, he could not do much with it either. It stayed where we found it until we left Arua for reorganisation in Kabamba.

I forgot all about the car until we landed at Arusha International Airport in Tanzania on our way to Monduli for training, when I saw the same car among the junk looted cars which the Tanzanians had taken home. We were informed that the car had been airlifted and dumped at the airport. By the time we left Tanzania, the car was still parked there.

Kikosi Maalum and the West Nile

In an operation lasting just eight months Tanzania managed to capture and occupy Uganda. Throughout the time it took to chase Idi Amin's soldiers the groups of Ugandan liberators were distinctly divided. There were many Ugandan fighting groups hanging on the apron strings of the Tanzania People's Defence Forces (TPDF). Yoweri Museveni, in *Sowing the Mustard Seed*, describes what transpired in Moshi, Tanzania. When Ugandans opposed to Amin tried to form a government-in-waiting, chaos ensued. There were a number of groups known by acronyms, but the most effective groups combat-wise were Kikosi Maalum and FRONASA.

Kikosi Maalum was composed of former Uganda Army personnel who had escaped to Sudan and later to Tanzania after Amin's coup in 1971. It was effectively under the command of former president Milton Obote and former senior officers of the former Uganda Army.

The next effective group was the Front for National Salvation (FRONASA) under Yoweri Museveni and other intellectuals opposed to Amin. These two groups never saw eye to eye. The relations between the two groups were characterised by pathological fear, hatred and mutual suspicion. Those feelings had their roots in the historical differences among Ugandan peoples. While politicians may blame it on the colonialists' divide-and-rule policy or prejudices of the Ugandan population, the truth of the matter was and still is that the political North has failed to adjust to the ways of the political South and vice-versa.

From the beginning, these two groups, Kikosi Maalum and FRONASA, lived a cat-and-mouse life. The new soldiers belonging to FRONASA were given guard and policing duties in the whole of West Nile. I think the leadership wanted to prevent the Kikosi Maalum soldiers from Acholi and Lango from exacting revenge against the population of West Nile, whom they accused of the atrocities that Amin's army committed against their kith and kin. To the members of Kikosi Maalum, anybody from West Nile, the home district of Idi Amin, whether young or old, was responsible for what had befallen the Acholi and Langi during Amin's regime. It was the duty of the now armed, although not so well-trained, youth from Acholi and Lango to exact revenge against the people of West Nile. At the onset of Amin's rule, most Langi and Acholi soldiers in the Uganda Army had been rounded up and slaughtered, and this contributed to the tension and desire for revenge.

It is also true, as documented in many writings, that the Acholi and Langi bore the brunt of Amin's reprisals after the deplorable Tanzania-backed attack by Ugandan guerrillas on Amin's regime in 1972. Up to the last days of Amin's rule, these people were debased, killed and traumatised by his regime.

However, what we witnessed in West Nile in 1979, especially for us young people who had had a rather protected life compared to our compatriots from the North, was unthinkable. Most of us had never envisaged such ferocious hatred by one group for another.

The Acholi and Langi soldiers hated with untold intensity anything related to Amin and Aminism. This meant anything Lugbara, Madi, Kakwa, etc. and not only the people but even livestock. Is it possible that the slaughter by Amin of Langi and Acholi could have precipitated this? One can hardly believe that a soldier can fire an antitank grenade at a chicken. Those and more bizarre acts were committed in West Nile while we watched. We used to arrest these unruly ruffians and punish them heavily. They were all hardened in their hatred. Their cry was always *"Ata ukiwuwa mimi, wengine watamaliza hawa madui"* (Even if you kill me, others will come and finish these enemies).

After leaving Amin's compound and the comfort of his state-of-the-art vehicle bed, I camped near a school. A little distance away from my camp lived a couple of about my parents' age. This couple belonged to the same religious sect as my parents, a sect known as *Bazukufu*, a born-again or revolutionised version of the Church of Uganda. This group is well represented in most of East Africa and even abroad. These are people who profess puritanism in the Protestant church. Their way of life is exemplary and their contribution to social development is widely acknowledged countrywide. The couple had a lot in common with my parents. They had married in a similar church. The priesthood was familiar to me and, in fact, their wedding photograph had an uncanny similarity to the photograph of my dad and mum, which I had grown up seeing hanging on the wall of our living room. I developed a special feeling for this couple, and the lady of the house welcomed me like a son.

Some evenings, I would visit this family, taking them dry rations, biscuits and beef, and I would enjoy good evening tea as we talked about what *okulokoka*, as they call the conversion to this sect, had done for Uganda. That tranquil atmosphere did not last long because, one evening, while visiting my new-found mother, I underwent one of the worst experiences I had ever had in my life.

The Kikosi Maalum attacked and ransacked the place in the morning. The house was in a shambles, but the worst part was the bodies of the gentle old couple. The old lady had been gang-raped, then bayoneted repeatedly around the lower abdomen. There she lay stark naked in death. It was a revolting and pathetic sight. The man's head had been cut off clean and placed on a chair facing the doorway. I do not remember how I left that scene. All I know is that up to now I have failed to understand how beastly man can be. We were later to witness similar and worse scenes in Luweero Triangle. However, I do believe that the incident weaned me of any romantic fantasies I used to have about war.

After some time we were withdrawn back to Kabamba for reorganisation and formation of the national army.

Kabamba (the Red Army days)

All Ugandan combatants were reorganised at the Kabamba and the Mubende training wings under the command of our own leaders and the Tanzanian instructors. The control of Kampala and other sensitive positions was under the Tanzanians. The Kikosi Maalum were based at the Mubende training wing and the Front for National Salvation were assembled at the Kabamba training wing. There was little or no activity as we awaited our fate from the army headquarters in Kampala. It was from these groups that the first officer corps of the new army, the Uganda National Liberation Army (UNLA), as it was then called, was to be selected.

The mood in the country was in favour of renewal – a new government, a new leadership, but most importantly, a new army. The Kikosi Maalum group had made a mistake in failing to recruit during their advance on Kampala. Although they passed through the biggest part of the country, having entered Uganda through Masaka, they refused to recruit new and more educated people because they felt that the people from the area they were passing through were either unfit for military service or, more importantly, they would not accept their leadership. The latter was true because, for most of the people of central and western Uganda, there seemed to be no difference between Amin's fleeing soldiers and the advancing Kikosi Maalum soldiers, chiefly composed of northern Ugandans.

The army leadership was having its problems, as every group in the Uganda National Liberation Front (UNLF) was fighting for control of the army. The view of most Ugandans was that all the fighters, that is Kikosi Maalum, FRONASA, UFM, etc. should be merged into one national army. However, the Kikosi Maalum felt that soldiering was meant for people from the northern part of Uganda, a notion that had been instilled into many by the British colonial administration. This belief can be traced back to the colonial days, when people from northern Uganda were recruited en masse into the army because of their physique and height, while other ethnic groups were recruited into other areas and callings.

The idea being mooted, that everyone should have access to and knowledge of the gun, was alien and was vehemently opposed by other groups for unknown reasons. Nevertheless, FRONASA went ahead and put it into practice. FRONASA had recruited massively in western and central Uganda where it passed.

All sorts of tricks were employed to make members of the other fighting groups, especially those of FRONASA, desert the army. They tried to starve us, harass us, abuse us and generally make life difficult for us, but we persevered.

The next trick was related to the issue of nationality. Some political youth wingers who had somehow ended up on the verification committees, started referring to us in FRONASA as non-Ugandans, therefore as Rwandese. It is an ironical fact that the person who first alleged that I was a Munyarwanda and who was pursuing my dismissal on the grounds of my being a non-Ugandan, later ended up with me in the Popular Resistance Army (PRA) and is still with me in the UPDF, and he is a real comrade. However, then, when he still wielded the power to decide whether I could stay in the army or be disgracefully discharged, I had to ask him if the book, *Abagabe ba Ankole*, about the Ankole kingdom, in any way mentioned his grandfather's name! Mr Onesmo Rwabyoga, my grandfather, was mentioned in that book. The issue of nationality was adhered to religiously. In fact, none of the future NRA officers who deserted and went back to Rwanda later to form RDF, had been to Monduli, the Tanzanian military academy for cadets. Thus, they did not belong to the first core officers of UNLA.

The next stage was at the officer cadet selection. The criteria were drawn up: Ugandan citizenship, good health, a certain level of education, physical fitness and success in the oral examination. It was a really tense moment for many candidates. However, I do vouch for the fairness of the interviewers. The people who were selected were in one way or another the cream of those interviewed and I still believe they did a good job.

Those of us who were selected in August 1979 were taken to Jinja Military Academy where we met many intellectuals and people with tertiary education. The young men who had been selected from schools and other places of work included lawyers, engineers, teachers and other highly-educated youth.

All this time there was in-fighting for control of this first group of cadets from the UNLA who would form the backbone of the new army, not only among the political and higher army leadership but also amongst us, the cadets. Instead of building up comradeship, having been privileged to be selected from among many Ugandans, we started bickering. There was an unexplained degree of animosity among us, the chosen leaders of the new Uganda Army!

A degree of rivalry would have been healthy, since we were all just young men from different backgrounds, but ours was more intense, dangerous and divisive. Where people would be arguing about academic or physical feats, our arguments were full of threats about what we would do to each other, given the chance.

One officer cadet, Angwella Wod Onyango, was very abusive about my light complexion. He claimed that, since people from the East (he was from the Tororo area) ate finger millet bread, they were better than people from the West, who fed on milk and bananas. His reasoning was that, since grinding stones are used to grind finger millet, the particles that wear off during grinding collect into the knees and bones of the millet eaters, while people like me were just liquid-boned (*mwili teke teke*) or jelly-bodied. I vowed to always beat him at field exercise, and every time he broke down during a route march, I would taunt him about his stone-boned knees. Later we became good friends. Although he is in exile in Sweden as I write this book, I am sure that, as a person, he bears no grudge against me.

The Angwella type of teasing was not harmful, but some of our fellow officer cadets promised to finish off those non-army-material officers. The mistrust and suspicion stayed on until the end of the 10-month course in Tanzania.

2

Cadet Training in Tanzania

From Jinja we were driven to Entebbe International Airport, from where most of us were to travel aboard a plane for the first time in our lives. This was in August 1979. There were many funny incidents on board. There was airsickness. There were also solemn, fearful faces, and those know-it-all types who tried to impress us by demonstrating what the numerous gadgets were used for. All in all it was a hilarious but safe maiden flight for us.

When we landed at Kilimanjaro International Airport in Tanzania, we were welcomed by a group of Tanzanian army officers and men. We did not follow the usual route, but instead, we were bundled onto one bus and two lorries. One of the lorries carried the inscription "Masaka Growers Cooperative Union", a sure embodiment of the fruits of the Tanzanian army's war in Uganda.

We drove to the National Leadership Academy located in Monduli, which is about 80 kilometres from Arusha town. At the quarter guard we were told to disembark. It was about 5.00 p.m. and we were immediately surrounded by a horde of Tanzanian instructors. *"Cadet chuchuma chini"* (Cadets squat), we were ordered, *"Ruka kichura, Cadet"* (Frogjump, Cadet). We were frogmarched from the quarter guard to the parade ground, a distance of half a kilometre. Some of us were in uniform and

24

the rest in civilian clothes. The civilians from Jinja had new uniforms compared to the soldiers from Kabamba and Masindi. Each of us had to get off the vehicle with all his personal property. Most of the soldiers had no personal property, but our intellectual civilian comrades were well equipped with what they thought were the basic necessities for travel. They were a comical sight as they held their heavily-stocked suitcases and sleeping bags on their heads. That was the introduction to the camp, and the rules were immediately read out to us as we stood in a ragged formation, which we imagined was a parade. We were exhausted, gasping for breath and sweating.

Rule No. 1
For the next six weeks any movement from point A to B should be in formation of threes and on the run or trotting. No more walking.

Rule No. 2
Every step on the move should be accompanied by an exclamation, UP! UP! UP!

Rule No. 3
Everybody now should be addressed as Officer Cadet.

Rule No. 4
Every instructor should be addressed as Staff.

Rule No. 5
When called upon, a Cadet should answer with number, rank and name, in that order. For example, when a Cadet is called by a Staff, he should answer 'UD0001 Officer Cadet Muguma Musulumali Owekabamba, Staff' and so on. (This would appear ridiculous to some civilians but it made a lot of sense, even to the most accomplished of army generals.)

The Ugandan contingent was composed of three hundred men. Later we were merged with 150 Tanzanian officer cadets, and four officer cadets from the Seychelles. By random selection we were divided into four companies – A, B, C and D. Each company was allocated a dormitory, each dormitory had three floors – the ground, first and second floors – and each floor could accommodate one platoon. I ended up in Platoon 1, Section I, D "coy". Our hall was called Mirambo. The halls were divided into cubicles and each cubicle could house two cadets. My cubicle-mate was Officer Cadet Santansio Constantine Otoo, who later died from natural causes immediately after the war against the Okello regime, which had ousted Obote.

From the parade ground we were led to our respective dormitories chanting up! up! up! This was when we started to appreciate the efficiency of the military as an institution. Every room bore the names of its two occupants and the locations of the beds were well demarcated. In a short time everyone knew where he belonged, or so we thought.

At 6.00 p.m. prompt, the bell for supper was rung and up! up! up! we went chanting to Machage, the cadet officers' mess.

We were soon through with the meal, and that was when the feeling of being hassled started to set in. I do not think many of us remember the menu. Personally, I cannot remember, not with the Tanzanian corporals hounding us, kicking at our heels and barking at us. It was not a meal to savour.

Soon it was up! up! up! to our rooms, where the question of orientation became a big task. The rooms looked the same, two people would be arguing as to who was the occupant of which bed, when a third person would rush in, asking whether the two contestants for the beds had not read that he was the bona fide occupant of the room. Grim-faced, we would all move out and read the names, only to find that none of the three belonged to the said room and then the search for the right tag on the right door would start all over again. It is distressing to realise that few of my dormitory-mates and even coursemates will be able to read this old soldier's ramble, for most of them are now dead, unfortunately.

The search for the right rooms was concluded at about midnight, and by 1.30 a.m. we were all sound asleep. At 3.00 a.m., after only two hours of sleep, every one of us jumped out of his bed, which was not made, since nobody had the time for such a mundane routine as making beds. Each one was back on his feet. We thought the academy was under enemy attack when the Tanzanian instructor shouted "Cadet, fall in line", each word punctuated by a kick or a wooden staff being banged on the doors. We were a miserable lot when we were jostled onto the parade ground. Most of us were at different stages of dressing in unbuttoned shirts and trousers, loose belts and, of course, unfastened shoelaces. However, trust these "staffs", as they liked to be called, they made the "Afande Cadets" form up in the shortest possible time. At about 4.30 a.m. we set off on our first morning run as officer cadets of Monduli, Tanzania's National Leadership Academy, *Chio Kuu Cha Taifa Cha Uongozi* (CTU). The morning run was not long but few of us were used to running in the middle of the night. We thought that was not the right time for running and we were not prepared to run in bathroom slippers, which some of us were wearing. The route, which followed the perimeter fence of CTU, was unfamiliar. All in all it was a rambling mob shouting up! up! up! That running around the fence, or *kuzunguka ukuta* as it was called in Kiswahili, was to be with us for a long time. For every slight mistake the instructor would just shout "Cadet!" or *"Afande zunguka ukuta!"* It became such a regular practice that, by the time we left Monduli, most of us knew the perimeter fence inch by inch. We also had to study this fence for extracurricular activities like sneaking in and out of the camp, though that was not part of the official training programme.

We assembled at the mess at 8.00 a.m. for our first breakfast of black tea with too much sugar and a slice of bread. After here, up! up! up! to the parade ground, we sang. Now, to take hot tea in an aluminium mess tin needed one to have a fridge for a mouth and tongue, and while you were taking the hot contents the instructor would order you to pour and *"folen"*, meaning fall in line.

From the parade ground we marched to the quartermaster's stores where we were issued with the accoutrements of a cadet. These ranged from uniforms, boots, mess tins, spade, needles, parkas, to blankets and all sorts of accessories, and we did not know the use of most of them.

This exercise took most of the morning, and by the time we dumped our luggage in the dorms it was already lunch time. We rushed to the mess, and from the mess it was again up! up! up! to the parade ground. This was after a meal of posho and beans, so we were not particularly alert. The next stage was supposed to be class but I would be telling a lie if I said that I knew what the lesson was about or whether it was interesting. As soon as we entered the classroom, everybody started dozing. The instructor must have had a lot of patience, but I do not think anybody could really hold our attention. The potential officers were heard snoring in chorus from all corners of the classroom. The rate at which the time was flying in those first days was unbelievable. Soon it was "fall-in Cadets". Up! up! up! went the song, and to the parade ground we trooped. It was 2.00 p.m., which was the appointed time for the afternoon run. Directly opposite the quarter guard was a hill known as Nangungu. No graduate of NLA/CTU can forget it. That is where we were directed to climb in formation. Whoever invented the art of soldiering and military science must have been a past master at malice aforethought. The hill, which appeared low, was shaped in such a way that it sapped the climber's energy step by step. It was tough enough getting to the top (if at all possible in that hot sun). Coming down was Chinese torture. We had not yet heard of things like dead ground, so when the instructor, with a sneer, told us to run up to the top and back in thirty minutes we set off, not knowing what awaited us. From D company Officer Cadet Allen Marrie from Seychelles reached the top of the hill in the time of one hour, but we later learnt that he was a national marathon race champion for his country. The rest of us were not even halfway up when he passed us on his way down. By the time the assembly was called at the parade ground, almost three-quarters of the cadets, myself inclusive, had not reached even halfway up. We were all dead tired.

It was close to supper time when we lined up in formation with our mess tins. The Tanzanian cooks started slapping slices of posho and ladles of meat stew into our mess tins at such a fast rate that it was just by luck that one retained even as little as half of the ration. We gulped down the meagre meal and rushed to the water taps to wash our hands and mess tins and to fill our empty stomachs with tap water.

"Fall in line!" shouted the instructors. We rushed to the now-hated parade ground, and staggered while everyone tried to find his formation.

By 9.00 p.m. we were all assembled and accounted for. In our ignorance we thought we had earned a day's rest. However, this was not to be! *"Leo tuna anza kipindi cha nyimbo"* (Today we start the programme of singing), one of the instructors said. You can imagine the curses the instructors received, inaudible as they may have been. "Sit down, start clapping," the same instructor ordered. We sat down and started clapping in such an unmelodious discord that the instructor had to block his ears with his palms. *"Simama juu"* (Stand up) he shouted, *"Chapaa mgu"* (Mark time), he ordered. We started tramping on the ground, each one at his own pace. The instructor became quite angry. *"Lala chini"* (Lie down) he shouted. *"Viringita"* (Roll) he added. We rolled and crawled all over the parade ground till after midnight, when we were ordered to go and bathe and make our beds and rest. We rushed into the dorms, fought over the few bath tubs and tried to make our beds. Just then we heard "Folen Cadets!" with its accompanying pandemonium of banging doors and boot kicks. We rushed back to the parade ground. That was day number one or two, depending on one's memory, but it seemed to us that for the next six weeks, day and night blended into one and Monday to Friday had no gaps in between. It was just a continuation of up! up! up!, rolling, crawling, frogmarching, parades, Nangungu hill, the perimeter wall, and graduating into climbing Lashaine hill, which is a very prominent physical feature that is seen from as far away as Arusha town.

In between these hassles, we were taught how to make our beds. The funny part of it is that we never used those well-made beds till towards the end of the course. A well-made cadet bed can serve as a centrepiece for an art galley or boutique showroom. The method of making the bed is as bizarre as most military endeavours are. First, one had to lay the bed cover on the bed, then put a mattress on top, then the blanket and the bed sheets on top of the mattress. One had to iron the bed sheets such that there were no creases left in them, then put one's highly polished boots at the foot of the bed and one's polished helmet at the head of the bed. When people talk about polishing or brushing shoes, few know what they are talking about. If you cannot see your face clearly reflected when looking in the toecap of a cadet's shoes, then the cadet is wanting in smartness. The last thing a cadet needed was a comb, because in the course of introduction to the camp, the cadet's hair was always the first casualty.

In those six weeks a lot of things had transpired in Kampala. As cadets, we were not really bothered about the political turmoil at home yet; we were more interested in how to grab a few minutes of sleep. The biggest torture one can undergo is being denied sleep. If a normal human being is kept awake for five days running there is no doubt that, no matter how resilient he may be, he will break down. Our instructors were bent on breaking us down and they went about that business quite effectively.

After a vigorous dawn-to-midnight exercise, one's body tends to demand rest. That was the precious time during which our instructors would order us to start singing while polishing our shoes. One can imagine what type of music we created. There time we would be dozing under the watchful eyes of the corporals while trying to polish our shoes, which were expected to shine so brightly in the morning sun that the instructor could use them as a shaving mirror if he so wished.

The only interesting news from Uganda that reached us in those days was when Hon. Yoweri Museveni, time the then Minister of Defence, visited us. Brigadier David Oyite Ojok (RIP), who was the Chief of Staff, accompanied him. The difference between these two prominent persons was that, while Museveni gave us a lecture on the history of Uganda and what the nation expected of us as the future army leaders, the Chief of Staff approached Mwalimu Julius Nyerere (RIP), the then president of Tanzania, requesting him to ensure regional balance, or rather ethnic balance, in this officer corps in the making. Oyite Ojok's argument was that officer cadets from western and central Uganda outnumbered those from the other parts of Uganda. Nyerere was perplexed by the reasoning of the Ugandan Chief of Staff. He answered in Kiswahili, "*Ndugu COS hiyo ayiwezikane, kwetu Tanzania hiyo mwiko, nitawezajje, mimi kama rahis kwamulisha makadet kutoka Uganda kusimana kwa mistari kwanzia kabila zao, eti Wasoga simama hapa, Wakiga simama hapa, wa Acholi simama hapa. Ayiwezikani ataa hapa kwetu, hawa, wote ni nawaona kama makadet Waganda.* "(Comrade COS, that is impossible. For us in Tanzania that is taboo. How can I as a president line up cadet officers each from his tribal area? That Basoga line up here! Bakiga line up here! Acholi line up here! That is never done at all, all these are officer cadets from Uganda.") That was the end of the Kikosi Maalum machination to get rid of FRONASA-based officers in Tanzania. However, that was just the postponement of a war, which was later to be fought in Uganda.

I cannot forget the day President Godfrey Lukongwa Binaisa dismissed Oyite Ojok. It was a night of jubilation in the FRONASA camp. However, the dismissal lasted only 24 hours before it was annulled by the Kikosi Maalum group of Oyite Ojok. Paulo Muwanga and our leader, President Binaisa, were removed from power. My cubicle-mate, Santansio Otoo, had had a bad time the previous night. Now he rushed into the room in an ecstatic mood and demanded, "Eh Pecos, what have you got to say now?"

I was lost for words, as I did not know what he was talking about. I asked, "Say about what?"

"Eh, eh, your man *ame bulo* (he has blown), gone bust," he cried excitedly.

"Which man? Make sense Otoo! What are you saying?" I asked.

"Your President Binaisa has been overthrown."

"What are you talking about?"

"Don't you listen to BBC?" he asked.

I told him that I had not had time to listen to any radio. Then he told me there had been drastic changes in Uganda and "my President has lost out." He was jumping up and down in excitement. I heaved a silent sigh of relief and asked him what had happened. He told me that *my friend* had grabbed a tiger by the tail and the tiger had bitten off his head.

After six weeks, which seemed like sixty years to us, we were allowed to go on pass leave. We were all very excited; incidentally we had just received our first pay in the army. We searched our packs for any civilian clothes we could find, and we were ready to paint Arusha town red.

The day we hit Arusha town after the six-week introduction to camp will always be memorable to us. After six weeks of vigorous training, we were really fit young men who felt like unleashed dogs after a long time of confinement. Add that feeling of freedom to the few dollars we had in our pockets. It was a really exhilarated group that hit Arusha town that Saturday morning. We tried to appear as ordinary as everybody else but our clean-shaven heads were a complete giveaway. No Tanzanian could fail to notice groups of young clean-shaven men who resembled recently released prison inmates. Since it was our first time in Arusha, the town touts had a field day directing us to what, to them, appeared to be ordinary places like banks, hotels and shops. The commodities most in demand among us were suitcases, clothes, watches and radios. Here the sense of fashion of each group was displayed.We were free to dress the way we liked, so we bought a collection of clothing that would have shocked many. Blood-red shirts with deep-green ties, deep-blue trousers and purple shoes. Combined with yellow socks, what a combination of striking colours these made! A circus troop manager would have envied us our ingenuity.

Apart from our bizarre wardrobe, the music systems we bought easily betrayed our upbringing and backgrounds. We bought huge hi-fi tape recorders. As a result, the journey back to the academy seemed endless to most of our comrades who wanted to reach their rooms and test their gadgets. Arusha town offered us the real feeling of the Tanzanian people. They are very hospitable and humble compared to Ugandans. Even the streetwise youth were more respectful than their Kampala counterparts. There were also many ladies of the night or day, depending on one's choice. The people of Tanzania are very security-conscious and they love and respect their soldiers, and being foreigners, we were highly esteemed. A Ugandan cadet with about $150 to spend was very much in demand by the shopkeepers, hotels, bars, and nooks selling illegal brew (*konyagi*).

We won instant sweethearts, whom we forgot as soon as it was time to board the buses back to the academy. We boarded the buses with our luggage. Anyone seeing us board could have mistaken us for refugees, only that there were no women and children in tow.

It was a really jolly group of cadets who now reported to the loved/hated CTU at around 8.00 p.m. Very few of us reported to the mess as most of us had gorged ourselves on food and drinks in Arusha town.

We were informed that it was now time to clean up our dorms, wash our clothes and complete all other PAs (personal administration). The next day was a Sunday, and it was to be for rest and recreation. We rushed to our rooms, and now the loud music and discotheque we had missed in Arusha town was transferred to our cubicles. Now, everyone who had bought music equipment tried to outcompete all the others by playing it at the highest volume. The fracas that was created might have raised the ghosts, if there were any in the academy. However, since the army and superstition never go hand in hand, it was only our eardrums which suffered.

One memorable example of our folly was that involving an officer cadet called Godwin Onenche, who was Cadet Officer Steven Kashaka's cubicle-mate. The young man turned up his music system full blast. He had closed all the windows and was wearing headphones. The whole dormitory rose up in concern and summoned Cadet Officer Kashaka to come and rescue his roommate, whom they suspected was under threat. Later, when Kashaka persuaded his roommate to open the door, there was Cadet Onenche with the two detachable loud speakers glued to his ears and he was responding to the music. Such and other uncanny behaviour characterised the crop of future army leaders of Uganda. Officer Cadet Godwin Onenche was expressing his appreciation of the wonders of technology and of its ability to give him pleasures he had never dreamt of and the army's ability to put his wish within his grasp.

The dress code, the choice of music, and how we trod the ground, showed the euphoric amazement with which we treated the army as an institution and our position as future leaders of that establishment. We felt on top of the world.

Our training in Tanzania took nine months, during which we were introduced to fieldcraft, military tactics, some strategic thinking and many other things. However, the experience that turned out to be most useful to us later was that of endurance. As cadets we were trained to work under all sorts of arduous conditions, which we later found useful in actual combat. One thing that the army taught me was never to lose my temper. We were abused and humiliated by the instructors to the extent that I have developed the kind of patience which makes it very difficult for anyone to make me lose my head.

An abusive instructor would stand with arms akimbo and with one foot on your back as you crawled in muddy water and ask you, "Who invited you here, Cadet?" Then he would go on: "I never sent you a love letter; I don't know you from Adam. You and I just found ourselves here because of our duties!" Which, though ironical, was true. For if it had not been for my quarrel with Amin's State Research boys, where would I have met Corporal Mpalu of TPDF, who made me sing love songs while sweating, sometimes with tears rolling down my cheeks while holding a rifle high in the air and marching to his beats of "One Two, One Two, Halt!"?

One can only make sense of what transpired when one is in one's trench freezing in the cold at the front line. That is when you really appreciate what your instructor was trying to impart to you using his crude ways.

What the army does to a person is to first break down that false self-confidence of youth to the point where if one is asked to jump up, one does not ask "why?" but "how high?" One reaches a stage where an instructor's cough elicits a spontaneous "yes Staff" response. It is from that state of very low self-esteem that the army re-builds one's confidence based on actual reality.

It is only when the so-called mummy's or daddy's boy meets other men that the reality of life sets in. Respect, so they say, is a double-edged sword. As you use it, it replicates itself. One thing we learnt as cadets is that every human being is an individual who should be treated as she or he deserves to be treated.

By the time we finished training, we liked our "former enemies", meaning the instructors, so much that no one can tell the high esteem in which we hold them, even after thirty years. Cadet training is a stage of transformation, from what you thought you were, into what is acceptable about you. You come up with a clear idea about the realities of life and your niche in the social order. Through what seemed to us as recruits to be unrelated sadistic episodes, the Tanzanian trainers moulded us into effective future combat commanders.

We did not know that *Towa nyimbo* (Start singing), which we thought of as harassment, would correspond with the marching tune, the drum, trumpet, bomb blasts, whizzing of bullets, the looping of mortar bombs and the marching of an infantry soldier. We discovered that these have a lot in common with the songs we learned as cadets.

What we called hardships and punishment – climbing Lashaine and Nangungu hills, running for hours on end, digging and filling up trenches and foxholes – contrary to our earlier belief, endeared the Tanzanian instructors to us.

We appreciated the experience and became conditioned to the extent that, at the end of the course, we did not easily break down. There was always that feeling that if one accomplished such and such a feat, why not accomplish this one also?

In Tanzania we came in contact with the local Maasai, and some cadet officers even indulged in their local brews called *changa'a* and *mbege*. There were isolated cases of indiscipline among us, but nothing alarming. At the peak of our training we had a chance to climb Mt Kilimanjaro. Some of us who were tall wished we were short in stature because as you climb higher you get less oxygen and lose a lot of energy. People like Cadet Officer Frank Guma had a field day, while those of us of average height and those who were really tall had it quite rough. Air at this altitude is thin and therefore one's height affects one's breathing proportionately. Maybe that is why the Bakonzo and Bamba of Mt Rwenzori survive so well on the mountain.

At the end of the nine months of training we boarded the plane back to Uganda. We had been passed out by Mwalimu Julius Nyerere, the President of the United Republic of Tanzania.

We had all pledged to defend the constitution and the population of Uganda and to protect the president. It is ironical when one recalls that only a few months later some of us would be taking up arms against the very government of Uganda that we had vowed to defend.

The "grand" reception back home

Our disillusionment when we landed back at Entebbe International Airport in July 1980 on our way back home from Tanzania can only be compared to the way American GIs felt when they returned home from Vietnam. We had anticipated a grand reception, not only by the army brass band but also by our civilian relatives and friends. What we found at Entebbe compared well with a poor, old widow's funeral. Not only were the civilian population not informed, but they lacked interest in us, and even the army leadership were conspicuously absent. It seemed nobody from the army headquarters had been detailed to receive us. We were left languishing at the airport with no sense of direction. Our luggage was just dumped in the

departure lounge as we wandered aimlessly around in the hope
of identifying someone who might help us.

Being in the army had denied us our individuality and, I
would say, initiative. We had been so acclimatised to taking
orders that nobody thought of hopping into a taxi and going
to Kampala, just 34 kilometres away. Nobody knew where to
report and whom to ask permission. We were all equals and
equally confused. We had landed at noon but until 2.00 p.m.
we just loitered around the airport.

At 4.00 p.m. one Captain Obot from general headquarters
arrived with four lorries. Here we were, dressed in our
supposedly "Sunday best" with all our brand-new suitcases,
music systems and other valuable property, only to be ordered
to jump onto the lorries. What shocked us more was how the
captain addressed us, as cadets and not as officers. There were
cries of "We are officers sir. We are officers and no longer
cadets!" We shouted back in vain. He completely ignored our
pleas. "Cadets," ordered Captain Obot, "jump onto the lorries,
Cadets!" All pretence to dignity was lost and we succumbed
to the orders. It was a miserable group which was driven from
Entebbe Airport to Republic House, the army headquarters.

It was here that the real resentment the army leadership
harboured towards us showed. As I stated earlier the older
army officers felt threatened by this group of new officers who,
apart from anything else, were young and more educated, who
not only posed a threat to their job security but whose political
inclination was not tailored to the UPC political ideology.
We were also viewed as creating an imbalance in the ethnic
composition of the army leadership.

I have already referred to the divided group we had been
before and during training in Monduli. The division had calmed
down during those nine months because of the tight training
schedule and Tanzanian control. We had become comrades
because of shared hardships. Now the divisions flared up into
unmistakable hostility.

Splinter groups started to take shape on the basis of ethnicity, region or political affiliation. The better educated young men had already been infiltrated and divided according to ethnic or linguistic origins or political affiliation. We were assembled in Bulange's Lukiiko Hall (Buganda's parliament), where Captain Obot started harassing us: "You Cadets," he shouted, and we reiterated that we were officers. "You Cadets," he went on, "within six months half of you will be dead and the other half will be in Luzira Maximum Prison." What a grand and heartening welcome to the future leaders of the Ugandan national army! True to Captain Obot's words, that very night, Second Lieutenant Mugisha, who had a twin brother who was also a cadet, was killed mysteriously. That was one officer less out of the 266 who had graduated; the other 34 had failed the course. One officer was dead on the day he ought to have been celebrating his homecoming from a cadet course, and for now that was our reception.

We were later bundled back onto the lorries and driven to the dilapidated former senior non-commissioned officers' mess in Mbuya barracks. This was an NCO mess, not an officers' mess, and it had not been in use since Amin's army had been routed in 1979. We were handed half-inch mattresses and told to make ourselves comfortable, and that food would be ready soon. When the food came it was totally unappetising. It was half-cooked yellow-maize bread and half-cooked beans infested with weevils. This yellow maize, we later learnt, was meant to be animal feed, a donation from the USA to Uganda, a country that is supposed to be capable of feeding itself because of its climatic conditions, geographical location and the fertility of its soils.

One advantage we had was that these political groupings started to take care of their own particular interests. The second lieutenants belonging to the UPC, such as the late Kagata Namiti, were already armed and driving posh cars, and yet the new officers had not been armed officially. However, the Namitis had pistols and bodyguards and they were already posting us. We were all supposed to be second lieutenants but Namiti and company were regarding themselves as majors.

The late Sam Magara, the late Seguya and the late Sam Katabarwa had immediately taken over the leadership of the FRONASA group, so I was not surprised when a car was driven to the NCO mess and I was told to leave those unbecoming surroundings for a better place. Magara drove me to International Hotel, where I was given a room and introduced to Rev. Father Okoth, who was in charge of finances and who later became a member of UPM (Uganda Patriotic Movement), one of the parties that contested in the infamous 1980 general elections. Through Father Okoth's influence, I obtained a self-contained room for myself. He also had a well-stocked bar in his room. That night I started contacting my relatives and friends. Although there was no nationally organised welcome in Kampala, many parties were thrown as relatives received their sons who had returned from Tanzania. The other ranks (OR) that we had left in the country had also finished their recruit training and had already been posted to different units. Whether by chance or design, most of us were posted to the Bugolobi flats, which originally belonged to the Ministry of Housing but which had been turned into a barracks during Amin's days. The Kikosi Maalum and former Uganda Army personnel predominantly occupied the army general headquarters in Mbuya. Inevitably there was hostility between the two groups, so the land stretching between these two barracks was subsequently named Middle East, a name still used today. The soldiers from Bugolobi (FRONASA) were a bit more streetwise and smarter than their counterparts from Mbuya. While the Kikosi Maalum boys were rough and trigger-happy and used brutal force to get anything from drinks to girls to money, the FRONASA boys were more subtle and cultured in their approach. Not that they were honourable, but they were more pleasant to the population in their dishonesty. This, coupled with the language factor, made the Kampala population identify more with FRONASA than with Kikosi Maalum.

The Bugolobi soldiers, who formed the bulk of other ranks and even officers in the subsequent struggle, welcomed us with open arms and briefed us on what was going on in the country. They were more informed about the political atmosphere of the country than the officers were. They already knew where the country was headed. While our heads were full of ideas about the appearance of the soldier and so on, as well as about projecting the national character of the army comprising officers and gentlemen, they just laughed at us and told us to prepare for war.

A rumour had been circulating that the Kikosi Maalum group planned to blow up one of the planes flying back from Tanzania, but Tanzanian intelligence had intercepted the plan and changed the seating arrangements. It was not easy to decide which plane to blow up since the people in Kampala did not know which officers were on which of the two planes. Whether the rumour was true or not, there was no need to convince us, since the hostility was quite visible. Just two weeks before we were given pass leave two good young officers, one of them a personal friend of mine, were killed.

Second Lt. George Gift Kalenzi was gunned down in broad daylight by Captain Ageta "The Terrible" at what is now the Kabaka's roundabout, that is the roundabout on Kabakanjagala road between the then Lubiri barracks (Kabaka's palace) and Republic House (Bulange). After shooting Kalenzi, Ageta dared anybody to come to this young man's help and nobody risked doing that. Young Kalenzi took about five hours to die as everybody just looked on helplessly. The other officer was Second Lt. Onyait. This young man was from Nebbi District, an Alur with the light complexion of a Southerner, and he was moving from the Luzira area to Bugolobi on foot. A group of soldiers from Mbuya barracks were drinking at Silver Springs

Hotel. Nobody knows what their conversation was about, but as soon as they saw Onyait in his smart uniform with a pistol strapped to his waist, they shouted *"Ndiyo hawa"* (Those are the people). They all started shooting, and before long Onyait lay dead on the tarmac of the Luzira road. Therefore, when the Bugolobi boys told us to forget about the national army's pride and think about our and their own survival, they were preaching to the converted.

We got our week's pass leave and each of us went back to his home. The reception in the villages was really impressive. In my case, a special church service was arranged for me. The congregation paid tribute to me and I felt "myself grow wings", as the saying goes. The village belles wanted to associate with me, the young men wanted to walk in step with me. The village drinking places wanted to offer me free booze. And, at the same time, my parents wanted to conduct more prayers with their *balokole* born-again group. I was the centre of attraction and I felt needed and honoured by each and every one. I put on my uniform and really stepped out.

It may sound petty to many people but it felt good to, for once, be celebrities in our home villages. Apart from viewing us as local heroes, Ugandan society was proud of having their own homebred army officers. To the people, especially from southwestern and central Uganda, we embodied the answer to the "foreign" northern army – a legacy left by the colonial power. People started identifying with us. It was not by chance that the first name of our resistance army was Popular Resistance Army (PRA). The army had changed its reputation from "hostile foreign army" to "our boys".

These sentiments did not go down well with the army leadership, which was still controlled by the Kikosi Maalum/ UPC faction comprising the old guard with the discreet support of TPDF. TPDF army officers believed that the answer to Amin's reign of terror was Dr Apollo Milton Obote, whom they claimed had changed after eight years of tutoring by President Julius Nyerere. The Tanzanians could not see why the army should be divided along political and tribal lines but they did not know the history of the country. The TPDF officers may have been right because, in Tanzania, thinking along tribal or regional lines was, and to a certain extent still is, taboo.

The deliberate manipulation of the army commander, Chief of Staff and other army leadership by the UPC and the opinions of the TPDF officers regarding Ugandan politics is what influenced our postings when we had to report to work after our pass leave ended.

Most of the officers who were known to be associated with FRONASA were posted far away from the capital city. We were posted to West Nile, where the war against Amin's former soldiers still raged, and to Karamoja, where cattle rustlers had always been a menace, and to military training wings. Posting to these areas made us unable to influence any events in the capital.

The stage was being set for Obote's takeover. I was posted to Nakasongola Training Wing as a recruit regiment instructor under Lt. Col. Mwakipesire, an old, fatherly TPDF officer.

Many of us were averse to wearing our uniforms while in Kampala. Apart from trying to avoid being associated with the mayhem the Kikosi Maalum soldiers were wreaking on the populace, we were legitimate targets for the Agetas of that time. Captain Ageta had created a group of unruly ruffians whose mission was to terrorise the stubborn Baganda and Westerners into submission. Among those targeted were the new officers from "unfit-for-military-service" communities, with the murder of the two second lieutenants being just the beginning. The capital city had become hostile and most of us had to keep a low profile.

Shootings in the city at all times of the day, and the murder of prominent people, were the order of the day. Heavily armed, drunken and drugged soldiers roamed the streets. Anyone with any sense of decency would not have wanted to put on the camouflage fatigues of the UNLA. That camouflage *madowadowa*, or spotted army dress, signified fear, terror, death, rape and theft of anything, from pens, radios to cars and television sets. The Tanzanian soldiers only added coal to the fire. After finishing with Amin's army, they took it upon themselves to relieve Ugandans of all their personal property.

The Tanzanian soldiers, who had come as humane, soft-spoken liberators, suddenly turned into smiling but sadistic killers. Cases of people being gunned down in broad daylight just for a wristwatch or a radio cassette recorder were rampant. A Tanzanian soldier would accost a civilian and smilingly demand all the money he had plus his watch. If there was any hesitation the soldier would laughingly open fire and the civilian would be dead the very next minute. The Tanzanian soldier would help himself to the loot while whistling *Nyenya akabina, Solome* (Shake your bum Solome), a popular song in those days.

Owning sunglasses, watches, television sets, radios and other gadgets became death sentences for many Ugandans. It was in the midst of this consternation that Apollo Milton Obote arrived in the country to contest the presidency. The day Obote landed in Bushenyi, western Uganda, will always be memorable. The reactions among the people were so mixed that it is difficult to find words to express them. There was jubilation among the Kikosi Maalum soldiers and UPC chairmen. There were wails of outrage from the people of central Uganda at the apparent betrayal by Tanzania by allowing Obote to return. Many could not imagine living under another Obote regime. For example, Mzee Kaganda, a former personal hunter for Sir Edward Mutesa, the Kabaka of Buganda, simply collapsed and died when he heard on Radio Uganda that Obote had landed back in the country. Brigadier Andrew Lutaya was a witness to this sad event.

Obote arrived in the country and hit the campaign trail immediately. All pretence of the so-called accepted procedures for national general elections was abandoned. Obote, who was only one of the candidates, was accorded full presidential privileges. Escort vehicles, motorcycle outriders and all the privileges of a president were available to Obote, while the other candidates were harassed and humiliated at roadblocks. An example is the time Yoweri Museveni, then the de facto number two in the hierarchy of the regime, being the vice chairman of the Military Commission, was humiliated with his family at a roadblock at Kireka, on the outskirts of Kampala City. Here was the vice chairman of the ruling body in Uganda being ordered to kneel on the tarmac, together with his wife and children. Only the intervention of Second Lt. Salim Saleh, who learned about the incident by chance, saved Museveni and his family.

As for the civilian population, it was a nightmare. I was at my post at Nakasongola Training Wing when I received the information that Obote would be coming to campaign in the town and that I had been detailed to arrange his security. I was given a platoon of Tanzanian soldiers and I set up the security of Nakasongola town and community centre.

The commander, Lt. Col. Mwakipesire of TPDF, was well aware of my views about Obote and had given me this task to test my impartiality as an army officer. After deploying the security personnel and guards, I went back to report to the commander, who was sitting in the lounge. On the commander's left was Obote. I saluted my commander and reported that I had finished the assignment. The commander told me in Swahili to salute the big man who was seated next to him. I told him that the big man's time for receiving official salutes had not yet come. I told him that the big man should wait till after the elections.

My commander just laughed and dismissed me. Later, when we were having lunch, I sat directly opposite the "big man". He was at the top of the table and I was at the foot. It was not a comfortable meal for either of us. When I looked up from my plate he would be looking at me. Then he would divert his gaze to his plate, and I would do the same whenever he gazed at me. After some time I got up as if I was going to check on the security. Outside I met Second Lt. Mugumya Magulumali, now a retired major. I knew Magulumali's sentiments about Obote were the same as mine. While chatting away to pass the time, I asked him if he would be able to give me covering fire if, for example, I decided to shoot Obote. He thought about it but pointed out that there was no chance of us surviving. The bodyguards covering Obote outnumbered us and they could outgun us quite easily. He also asked a pertinent question: Where would we run to?

I had not thought about what would happen next. I naively thought that by killing Obote, we would be solving the problems that Uganda would face during his second term. When you are young, you think of quick solutions to problems without necessarily considering the consequences. I thought the answer to Uganda's problems would be the removal of Obote. Later, when I joined the resistance war, I learned that the assassination of an individual, no matter how bad, turns the victim into a hero. I knew that killing Obote would have changed the course of the history of Uganda, but I would have become a hunted outcast and people who still had hope in him would not have witnessed his full absurdity. I heeded Magulumali's advice, went back to lunch and continued my prandial gymnastics with the "big man" until the meal was over.

Some time later my commander called me for counselling. He asked me why, at my age, with a seemingly bright career, I was involved in politics. Did I not know that, with Obote as president, I could be a major in just four years since the Tanzanian troops were leaving the army to us Ugandans? I answered him thus: "Sir, instead of being a major in Obote's army, I would rather be a civilian." Now, the biggest insult to any soldier is to be called a civilian. In fact, if a corporal instructor wanted to insult a cadet he would say, "You Cadet, you are not even fit to be a civilian," which to a soldier is the lowest status of all. My commander looked at me straight in the eye and I think he must have felt some sympathy for such deep feelings. He gave me ten days' extra duty, and that was our last discussion regarding politics.

The presidential election campaign was on and I do not know how many of us new officers managed to cast our votes. I for one did not vote since I was supposed to be on standby twenty-four hours each day for the duration of the exercise.

However, some officers and I used to abscond and go to Kampala. There was a clinic in Bwaise, a suburb of Kampala on the Gulu road, whose owner, a Muganda doctor, was friendly with me. I used to come in military vehicles in my full uniform, with a briefcase where I kept my credentials. I would then get off the truck in Bwaise and go to the doctor's changing room to change into civilian attire, leaving the uniform behind. Then I would board a taxi to the city. There were many soldiers and intelligence people moving up and down, so security was easy to breach by blending with the population, since nobody would risk asking for identification. Every young man could pose as an intelligence operative. Brigadier Oyite Ojok's operatives were young men of my age group who were willing to share in the pickings of power associated with knowing the Chief of Staff. During that time Rev. Fr Okoth also maintained some rooms in Nile Hotel and International Hotel, the current Sheraton Hotel. Somehow I acquired two fully furnished rooms in International Hotel. Up to now I do not know who was footing the bills, but I had fun there for more than five months.

In those days discos and night clubs used to close at 12.00 noon, since shootings would inevitably start around 3.00 p.m. and go on until the next morning. The whole city was unsafe, the only safe places being where "big people" stayed and the two prominent hotels – the Nile Hotel and International Hotel – although soon the former was turned into a slaughterhouse by security and intelligence operatives.

I would be in my room by 3.00 p.m., then go out and swim in the only usable swimming pool. While I was assured of the best accommodation, food and drinks from the good cleric's fridge, I had to foot the bill for any other form of entertainment. I needed money to keep up with the group I was moving around with; otherwise I would have seemed out of place. The soldiers from Bugolobi came in handy, as I stated earlier. They were more streetwise and knew how things worked around the city. People like the late Dampa (aka Private Benjamin), and Privates Kagina, Kamomo, Rwabantu (now colonel), the late Patrick R. Lumumba and many others, helped me to make ends meet. They would frequently take me out to introduce me to the many supporters who were underground.

Soon I also started sabotaging the government, as we liked to call it. Tanzanian soldiers were looting tiles, doors and window frames from the very dorms they were sleeping in. Now, Nakasongola was supposed to be one of the biggest airfields in East Africa. However, when Idi Amin fell out with the Israelis, it was abandoned. Among the many things going to waste were construction iron bars. The Tanzanians did not know about the presence of the bars, but the civilians who had worked with the Israelis did; soon they approached me for help. I would come to Kampala, hire semi-trailer trucks and use recruits to load the iron bars from Nakasongola, and sell them in Kampala, thus earning money to spend.

3

Escape from Nakasongola

The poor excuse for a general election of 1980 passed and real work began. The UPC government, with its Kikosi Maalum faction of the national army, with the Tanzanians' blessing, started to consolidate itself. The rest of the country was in an uproar. The deadly hunt for political opponents intensified. Unruly soldiers gunned down many prominent people, while others had to flee back to the very exile from which they had returned following the fall of Idi Amin.

The struggle within the Uganda National Liberation Army (UNLA) intensified. Any officer or man identified as a FRONASA supporter was marked. We lost many of our comrades in West Nile when a group of former Ugandan Army soldiers opposed to the Obote II regime attacked Bondo barracks in West Nile, near the Sudan border. The attack was a multi-pronged onslaught in which five army detaches were attacked simultaneously.

The young officers, fresh from cadet training, were trying to perform the daily routine of morning muster parade, which is good in peace time but disastrous in war time. It was a demonic act on the part of the Uganda Army group since there had been no formal declaration of war. However, we learnt later that what we had been taught in textbook training was never applicable in actual warfare. We never realised that soon some of us would be using such underhand methods as the accepted *modus operandi*.

The soldiers of Bondo barracks had started falling in line at 6.30 a.m. and by 7.30 a.m. the new platoon commanders had taken up their positions in front of their troops. The administrative officer, or adjutant, called the parade to attention and turned about smartly to salute; the Commanding Officer was armed only with his swagger stick. Then all hell broke loose. The enemy had taken up positions in ambush as early as 5.00 a.m. Now, they crawled into firing positions and opened fire.

It was a debacle that no soldier would wish to experience, especially if one happened to be on the receiving end. The soldiers had only their weapons with few or no bullets, the officers had only their pistols and parade swords, and here were well-armed, well-positioned, trained ex-soldiers picking them off like sitting ducks.

It was utter massacre. This was an attacking soldier's dream and an attacked soldier's nightmare. The killing was a magnificent military feat for the former Uganda Army soldiers and a catastrophe for the young, newly passed-out recruits and their newly commissioned officers.

Even today those who survived that massacre remain traumatised in one way or another. In that infamous battle we lost a number of comrades, among them Second Lt. Muntu, a close relative of mine. One of the officers who survived is a personal friend, now Major Mujuni, nicknamed *Macho Inne* (Four-Eyed) because he always wore glasses. Mujuni performed a feat which those who know him still tease him about today. He withdrew from Bondo and reorganised in Nakasongola, a distance of more than two hundred kilometres, non-stop day and night in two days. The attack took place on 8 October 1980. Mujuni, a lanky six-foot-two man, must have flown over cliffs and ridges. We now tease him that his withdrawal was in the same league as that of the famous 6,000 km Mao Tse-Tung march or, in the Ugandan case, Andrew Lutakome Kayiira, who attacked Lubiri barracks in Kampala, failed to overrun the objective and tactfully withdrew in order to reorganise in Washington DC, USA, a tactical withdrawal of more than 7,000 miles.

The UNLA, in its wisdom, positioned military police personnel on all roads leading out of West Nile to stop withdrawing soldiers from fleeing. At the same time, many military posts started succumbing to the onslaught of the Former Uganda National Army (FUNA).

The whole country was in turmoil! More than 20 groups declared war against the UPC regime and most soldiers as well as many able-bodied young men started looking for one group or other to identify with.

Nakasongola barracks is on the Kampala-Gulu-West Nile highway, and I was chosen to man a roadblock on this road to stop soldiers from escaping from the battle front.

On 6 February 1981, a group led by Museveni attacked Kabamba Training School, adding to the confusion in the country. This group also declared war on the UPC regime.

All this time I was being monitored and I kept looking for the best way to desert. I had maintained good relations with the traders of Nakasongola, especially the drivers of pick-up trucks that transported fish from Lwampanga to Kampala.

On 21 February I had just come from the roadblock where I was commanding a platoon of Tanzanian soldiers when the regiment signal officer came running to me. This young man, Sergeant Emirio, had received a message from general headquarters addressed to the administrative officer, Kabamba Training Wing. The message, both in Kiswahili and English, read: From GHQS (Republic House) to C.O. NAKASONGOLA TRAINING WING INFO ALL UNITS. D O 215 2ND LT. KUTESA O. PECOS SHOULD BE ARRESTED AND BROUGHT TO GHQS UNDER GUARD AAA///. INFO ALL UNITS.

The young signaller gave me the message book to read and told me that he was going to take it to the Commander in two hours, so I had better find a solution pretty fast. This young man was from Soroti, eastern Uganda. He may not have shared the same political views but as a comrade he felt obliged to help me, and in that respect I owe him my life. Most of the officers and men who were the subject of such messages are now dead. Only a few exceptions, such as Salim Saleh and others, managed to escape from UNLA prisons. Most of the rest never lived to tell the tale.

I had just had a bath and I was relaxing on my bed with only a towel wrapped around my waist when I received that message. I thought fast. I put on my uniform and holstered my pistol immediately, packed a shirt, a pair of trousers and a pair of civilian shoes in my briefcase, walked around my room, and saw nothing else worth taking except a James Hadley Chase novel that I had not yet read. I left my room, and did not even bother to close the door. I deserted the army.

The fact that I was deserting my post did not bother me. I had no sense of belonging and no regrets. I moved at leisure across the barracks, up the hill and through the small gate up to the murram road, up to Lwampanga fish landing site, where I boarded the first Peugeot 504 pick-up truck going to Kampala. All the drivers knew me as a regular traveller to and from Kampala, so there was no problem. I sat in the cabin with the driver and another person. The other passengers sat on top of the pile of fish at the rear of the truck. When we reached the roadblock at the Nakasongola junction the Tanzanian soldiers just saluted me and jokingly asked what I would bring them back from Kampala. They were used to my construction materials racket and they knew I always had money to spend, so they were very friendly. The journey to Kampala was uneventful, and soon I was in Bwaise, changing my clothes again.

That day, 21 February 1981, I became a deserter from the army and a fugitive. Instead of being afraid or feeling remorse, I felt exhilarated. At least I was going to do something for my country instead of belonging to a group, the UNLA, that I abhorred and held in contempt because of what they were doing. I set out to find an alternative. The day Kabamba Training School was attacked, I had started seeing myself as a traitor. I was at a crossroads. While I was willing to fight any group affiliated with the former Uganda Army or Amin's people, as we called them, I did not know whose side I would take if armed Ugandans unhappy with the government attacked my unit. Now the opportunity had presented itself to me. I was now a free person to join whatever group I chose, provided it was anti-government. There were quite a number of options. However, my heart still belonged with FRONASA.

Although I had not voted in the elections and the Democratic Party (DP) had a large following as a party because of their religious affiliation, most of us knew that the future of Uganda lay in the hands of those who held guns. Few of us were politically conscious, as the politically correct people of those days described us. Nobody was concerned about the GDP, GNP and all those high-sounding economic terms. To some of us, even words like "democracy" did not mean much. However, what we had in common was anger about what we saw as a threat to our people.

We did not need any political brainwashing, something that most people think rebels need. We were not after pay, since we had left salaries and the comfort of towns and barracks behind. Our major motivation was survival. The most effective means of surviving was to get rid of the threat to our lives. In military terms, the best form of defence is offence. We were in the offensive mood.

The chief campaign manager and mobiliser for the anti-UPC regime was UPC itself. There was no need for anybody to tell us to hate the regime nor was there need to tell the peasant population to hate UPC. The in-built ethnic, religious, regional and language differences, as well as the brutal actions of the UNLA, forced people to rebel. In fact, the name "resistance" signifies the anatomy of rebellion. Ugandan society was rebelling against the status quo or what Commonwealth observers called "a fair poll given the circumstances". What these observers did not address were "the circumstances" and we were the result of those "circumstances".

When I arrived in Kampala, I first wanted to go back to my rooms at International Hotel, only to find that they had been commandeered by the NASA operatives. National Security Agency (NASA) was the regime's internal intelligence unit.

It was by chance that I met a young man called Ssebadduka who had known me for some time. He whisked me away before I presented my face at the counter of the hotel. Ssebadduka, one of the streetwise kind, just told me, "Hey, man, things have changed. Do not even appear anywhere near these hotels. You are wanted!" I asked him how he, a civilian, knew about my status, how could he even dare accost me, an officer in the national army, and tell me that I was wanted? He simply looked at me apprehensively, seeming to wonder at my ignorance, before informing me that, by the mere fact that I was a new officer from Tanzania, as we had been branded, there were some places that were no-go areas for the likes of me. Those no-go areas included all the good hotels, bars, restaurants and even some shopping places. I had to keep as far away from the town centre as possible if I wanted to stay alive.

It was then that the sense of being "wanted" started settling in. Most of my comrades were in the same predicament. The problem was that none of us, the "wanted", could identify with each other, the rationale being that if one of us was compromised the others would remain safe. That was why the people who organised the attack on Kabamba barracks succeeded – because of the simple adage of "need to know".

There were big numbers of people sympathetic to the cause of rebellion but the organisers had to keep it secret; otherwise the resistance would have been nipped in the bud.

The only contacts for most of us were our relatives or friends and, accordingly, most of us who were on the "wanted" list ended up staying with our relatives. That is how I ended up in Bugolobi barracks, where our departed comrades Dampa, Mondo, Lumumba and others were stationed. The barracks was under actual siege. The whole establishment had singled out Bugolobi barracks as a hostile zone. The soldiers of Bugolobi had also built up a defence mechanism. Their actions were all done clandestinely; they had developed a network of coordination with civilian sympathisers. It was the civilians who had the material means, while the soldiers had both the military and technical means.

Kampala city was like a game of chess. Each team moved its pieces in the best way possible in an effort to win. The goal was survival, and the destruction of the opposition.

Captain Ageta's team was one of the toughest players in this chess game and the soldiers from Bugolobi barracks were his checkmate. It was both exciting and dangerous to be a wanted person in Kampala. The Bugolobi boys (former FRONASA) were giving us away, though. So it was decided that I should get in touch with the famous Benjamin Dampa, who was not only suicidal in his operations but a bit more sophisticated than Captain Ageta's boys.

There were many supporters of the anti-UPC regime and most of them were looking for a way to desert UNLA. However, the most organised group was the Popular Resistance Army (PRA), which had set up a sophisticated clandestine system for receiving, scrutinising and ferrying the deserting soldiers and civilian volunteers to their mobile bases. Matayo Kyaligonza, now a retired brigadier, had a smoothly operating team comprising Dampa, Shaban Kashanku (a former Mozambique-trained cadre) and Joy Mirembe, a lady who was instrumental at the beginning of the struggle. These people had set up a number of safe houses in and around Kampala. How they outwitted the intelligence system of UPC, NASA, the network of government informers and even the sympathetic but untrained and, therefore, recklessly talking Kampala crowd, deserves to be mentioned. While it is difficult for an ill-equipped guerrilla force to operate against a government army, operating in a hostile city is even more scary and dangerous. In the city the biggest problem is the identification of the enemy. There are no marked front lines. Anything, even a family tiff among the supporters offering you sanctuary, or a landlord demanding his rent, can expose a well-established cell. Some of us were only trained in conventional warfare. It was, therefore, quite unsettling to move around armed enemy soldiers while unarmed, or at best, armed only with a pistol or a hand grenade.

There was also the question of secrecy. Once more than four young strangers started frequenting a house, people became curious and suspicious about what was going on in the neighbourhood, which posed the highest danger to the operatives and their supporters.

All in all, I did not enjoy urban operations, first because I was not trained for them and, secondly, because they were very demanding. The people among whom you are supposed to be operating are mostly ignorant or innocent bystanders. Any scuffle in the street could draw the wrath of the beastly government soldiers who would shoot indiscriminately at any living thing, or blow up the houses in the vicinity. An urban operative is not in a position to offer any sort of security to the people because he is one of the people being hunted by the government forces anyway.

It was during those days that I was introduced to urban guerilla warfare by Kyaligonza and Dampa. The other anti-UPC groups were also very active, and groups such as the UFM of

Andrew Kayira had started attacking drinking places that were frequented by members of the government forces. One place in particular, known as Kisementi, situated in the Kampala city suburb of Kamwokya, was a very tempting target, for it was frequented by the then Chief of Staff, Brigadier Oyite Ojok, and many other members of the UNLA top brass. There were a number of skirmishes at Kisementi. We even lost a comrade, Private Kanyungutuzi, in one such encounter. Somehow Oyite Ojok escaped unscathed, and though he knew that he was the target, he was brave enough not to show this.

One of the missions I carried out was an attempt to blow up an Agip fuel depot. These tanks were all built in one location at Namuwongo. I did not know what the intention of the city planners was but all the main petrol depots in Uganda were located in this one suburb. If we had succeeded in blowing up the Agip tank, then Shell, Caltex and Total would all have caught fire. As luck would have it, the tank was empty. We had crawled up near enough and Dampa struck the depot with a direct hit with an anti-tank rifle grenade. A bright flame went up and the fire alarm sirens went off. A message was thus sent to the authorities that there had been an attempt to set the city on fire.

It was just the three of us: Kyaligonza, Dampa and myself. However, from the reaction we elicited from the government troops, one would have imagined that the city was under heavy attack. The soldiers were armed at all times, and soon RPG shells, bullets, rifle grenades, hand grenades, machine guns and all sorts of weapons were on display. The three of us simply jumped into our getaway car and Kyaligonza drove calmly to Nkrumah Road where we were staying. The flat we lived in was adjacent to Uganda House, the UPC headquarters. The Nile Grill, a pub at Uganda House, was the de facto headquarters of the NASA operatives. We used to mix with them during the day and play the deadly hide-and-seek game with them during the night. This was Kampala, a city of bullets, bombs and dirty, drunken and drugged soldiers, who were heavily armed and set against the population.

After the fuel tank attack, we were planning to blow up the Kampala water reservoir in Muyenga, but our leader, Museveni, discouraged us from such a course of action. His reasoning was that, if we blew up the Muyenga reservoir, the whole town would be deprived of water, and the worst affected place would be Mulago Hospital, the biggest government hospital used by people from all parts of Uganda. It would be self-defeating for us as freedom fighters to harm our own people, the very people we were seeking to liberate.

All this time, Kyaligonza, Joy Mirembe, Shaban Kashanku and Andrew Lutaya were clandestinely ferrying people to the bush. On the day I was leaving for the bush myself, I came upon a group of soldiers guarding a shop which belonged to Bazilio Olara Okello, the then commander of the Central Brigade. I looked at them and immediately knew they would follow me. I approached their leader and asked him if he was willing to go to the bush with me. He must have thought that I was mad. Here he was with his group on official duty and was being approached by this civilian and told to betray his nation. However, as he told me later, he saw someone who looked serious and either courageous or foolhardy enough to talk of treason in broad daylight. He told me that he was going to consult his comrades and that I should come back after lunch. One will wonder at the unsophisticated and reckless way in which I was operating. However, that was the order of the day. True to the commander's word, when I came at around 3.00 p.m., he, together with his group of about seven, were ready to go. They had collected their heavy coats, ponchos and some magazines and grenades. Kyaligonza was driving the pick-up. I was in front with my uniform and the pips of a second lieutenant next to my friend Frank Katatumba, a former NASA operative, who was staying with us and opted not to be left behind when his friends were leaving for the bush. Frank later became a major and was in active service till his death in 2002.

My troops and I got on the truck and drove off from Nkrumah Road, in the middle of the city, in broad daylight to go to the bush. So much for NASA's security measures: We drove through the town towards the Gulu road and passed through four roadblocks. At all the roadblocks the soldiers saluted me and nobody asked where we were going. I had two IDs, an identity card for a Makerere University Law student and the UNLA identity card. I would flash either of the two, depending on the type of security personnel who asked. Ten miles further on Bombo Road, at Mabanda, we turned off the main road to the left onto a murram road and continued for just half a mile from the main road. Then we got out of the vehicle and continued on foot.

4

The First Combat Mission (Kakiri)

I joined my fellow combatants on 30 March 1981. This day is therefore very significant to me. I was convinced I was doing the right thing. I had regained my initiative, which had been suppressed by the rigid educational system and the straitjacket culture characteristic of most Ugandans.

The Ugandan way of bringing up children and its educational system make one comfortable with certain norms, and that may be why the culture of innovation is very poor in our society. We are taught to follow orders, right from childhood up to old age. We learn to cram information about things done years ago in the Western world and parrot it to achieve high academic grades, but never to put what we have learnt into actual practice. Even the military training some of us attained had denied us the decision-making initiative, as shown earlier regarding our lack of action when we were neglected by the army leaders at Entebbe Airport after our training in Tanzania. Now here was a chance for me to put all the training that I had received into practice, but with the added pleasure of knowing that I would be practising it on what I thought of as an unpopular group in power. I was going to prove that the art of war was not a predestination of only some people in Ugandan society, and that anyone angry enough and with a justifiable cause can make war.

After abandoning the vehicle, we continued our advance to the bush on the footpath. We met someone at the observation post (OP) about one hundred metres away. The news of our arrival had already reached the headquarters.

We had a few packs of greatcoats and personal weapons that we had managed to collect. I was armed with a pistol and the other soldiers had their AK-47s, a few magazines and two or three anti-tank grenades. Although we were only nine in number, to the guys in the bush we were a very big reinforcement. I had two cartons of Benson and Hedges cigarettes in my bag, which I had to throw away because I knew that I had to dispense with such luxury in the meantime. We were escorted into the thicket and there we met our comrades. Yoweri Museveni, the "big man", was among them.

I cannot describe the feeling that engulfed us when we arrived, and the sense of belonging when I met some of the fighters I had known some time before. The "big man" shook my hand while looking straight into my eyes and telling me the name of my father and some other personal information that he had gathered about me. I was later to learn that that is one of the best ways to convert a person to one's cause. In my political campaign as a Constitutional Assembly (CA) delegate candidate I employed the same tactic, for individuals want to be identified with a group they have joined. Being personally known by the leader is an added bonus. During the CA campaign I would identify young persons in the crowd, call them by name and talk about their parents. Immediately such persons would become my campaign managers. It feels good when a "big person" recognises you within the crowd and talks to you in intimate terms. You feel you are not just a statistic but a valued individual. The leader of this group, which was the nucleus of the current Ugandan army, was a master of this human trait. Up to the day we captured Kampala city on 26 January 1986, and even today, that sense of being an individual human being who belongs to the group has persisted and it has helped us to overcome many problems.

The fact that we did not see each other as statistical numbers but as valuable individuals enhanced our *esprit de corps*. That is why we never shied away from talking about our casualties. We would know and let it be known to all our soldiers and supporters that so-and-so, who was a commander or a combatant of such and such a unit, had fallen to the enemy. It nurtured a unique fighting spirit among our soldiers.

The fear and shame of letting down one's comrades turned even the timid by nature into ferocious fighters. If a soldier showed cowardice during a firefight, at night during briefing and recollection of what went wrong or right during that particular battle, the particular soldier would face a lot of teasing and even isolation. In subsequent battles that soldier would try his best to redeem his name, thus sometimes performing some otherwise unattainable feats.

The total number of army men whom I had joined was below fifty, and half of them were unarmed. However, we set out to fight against a whole national army – the UNLA – plus the supporting better-trained and better-armed Tanzania People's Defence Forces.

I had no doubt that we would win the battle. Whether it was ignorance, naivety or the reckless attitude of youthfulness, we were all so sure of winning that even the songs, the language and the way we walked, all exuded absolute confidence.

During the first night we, the new arrivals, started mixing with our comrades. The oldies told stories of their battles at Kabamba 1, Karuguza and Nsunga police stations, and a tale of when they were attacked by Tanzanians at Bukomero. The famous feat was that of Anthony Kyakabale (now a rebel) using the only RPG shell they had to blow up a lorry full of Tanzanian soldiers at a place called Kyekumbya. From that day on, Anthony Kyakabale was known as Kyakabale RPG.

We were supposed to be totally concealed and all conversations were to be in whispers, but the excitement was too high for us. We were like little boys left in a class by a teacher who told them to keep quiet. A conversation would start as a whisper and then we would break out into suppressed laughter. The leaders had a hard time trying to keep this group of excited young men quiet, especially when they had that feeling of mischievous secrecy, not unlike that experienced by boys in a neighbour's orchard. We did not feel like traitors; rather we felt we offered the only solution to Ugandan's problems and were entitled to do what we were doing.

While in Kakoba in 1979 we had been happy to belong to a group that was going to overthrow Amin, and this was under the auspices of the Tanzanian army. Now we were the group that was going to overthrow Obote and his Tanzanian cohorts. Keeping us quiet was really an uphill task.

No fires were allowed, and no smoking either, and the chilly breeze of pre-dawn hours found us huddled in our personal clothes. The first rays of the sun were a welcome occurrence. While the birds sang, the frogs croaked and the mosquitoes buzzed as we welcomed the new day, we were in hiding from sunset at 6.00 p.m. to around 11.00 p.m. and that was when everything settled down. The crickets, birds, animals and even humans, stopped moving, so there was no noise. The second phase between midnight and 3.00 a.m. of the next day was the time for real rest. All jungle life went to sleep then. It is only man, who has always defied the law of nature, who can be active at such an unholy hour. It is then that the anti-social elements start their work. Law-breakers and mischief-makers such as thugs, prostitutes, boys sneaking into the neighbours' houses to see the neighbours' daughters and people involved in all sorts of activities which are frowned upon in daylight are usually at large at that time. So it was not by accident that the leaders in our group had to be on maximum alert at that time.

The third phase is between 3.00 a.m. and 6.00.a.m. There is something strange about 3.00 a.m. I do not know if it only applies to the tropics or East Africa, but at exactly or slightly before or after 3.00 a.m. the cocks crow, and this reminds one of the Biblical story of Simon Peter, Jesus' apostle. That is the time to be on high alert, but usually the body clock betrays the person keeping vigil. That is why the leaders have to check on the soldiers on guard. This checking on the guarding soldiers correlates well with the cadet training, where one is woken up at that unholy hour to go for the morning run.

Daybreak in the African jungle comes at 6.00 a.m. religiously, and that is the precise time for a dawn attack. Every soldier in combat is supposed to be in his trench or firing position on stand-by class one. To some of us who had just come from military training, this sequence of the night activities did not affect us much, our body clocks were already accustomed, but our civilian counterparts found this regime very taxing.

Daybreak came and there was no enemy attack. That was 31 March 1981. This was my first day in the bush as a guerrilla, a bandit, a terrorist or a revolutionary fighter, depending on one's stand in politics at that time. The whole day we met the other members of our group and introduced ourselves to one another casually. There were a few people who were new to me, but as for the majority, we had met both at the Kabamba Training Wing and in FRONASA. Others were civilian sympathisers. However, the most treasured to me were my fellow officers, with whom I had trained in Monduli, Tanzania. Here I met Sam Magara (who later became PRA Army Commander and died in 1982 at the hands of the UNLA in Kampala) Hannington Mugabi, a personal friend, who died in a pistol accident in the middle of the war; Jack Muchunguzi, now working for a private security firm in Kampala; Elly Tumwine (now full general, presidential advisor and Member of Parliament). Among them were also the famous Fred Rwigyema (who in 1990 led the attack on the

Habyarimana government and died on the first day of the war), Paul Kagame, now president of Rwanda, and many others whom you will read about further on in these pages. These last two never went to Monduli because of their nationality but were always with us in the struggle.

When we arrived in the bush, plans for the attack on the Kakiri UNLA detach were well under way. I was assigned Section Two of the five sections which were to carry out the attack in two days. We were being prepared and briefed while Museveni, who was the leader of the platoon, was harmonising reconnaissance on the enemy.

On 4 April 1981, we set off from our hideout to undertake what was to be my first military action against the UNLA. This operation, which was termed a major victory by our group of insurgents, was carried out by only 53 people. This group constituted more than 90 percent of the total number of the army that was undertaking the task of overthrowing the established government of the Republic of Uganda, heavily supported by the soldiers of Tanzania People's Defence Forces. When we reflect on this adventure with my colleagues, we sometimes question our sanity at that time. However, there was no insanity among us, but neither was it a foolhardy, harebrained scheme. It was instead a well-thought-out scheme, a well-calculated move, which we were sure would succeed.

The 53 of us formed a platoon, with Yoweri Museveni as the platoon commander, divided into five sections: Section One under Sam Magara, Section Two under myself, Section Three under Jack Muchunguzi, Section Four under Hannington Mugabi and Section Five, the rear section, where the platoon commander was, under Fred Rwigyema. These five sections were each comprised of ten people. When one decides to become a guerrilla, one must also learn to be a nocturnal animal. Daylight is the time for rest and hiding; actual work starts at night. This was to become our *modus operandi* for the next four years.

We set off from our hideout in Kikandwa at around 11.00 p.m. on 4 April and moved to our objective target. Kakiri would not have been very far if we had used the main route, but we could not afford to travel the way other people usually travelled. We were concealed and thus using footpaths that were rarely used by other people. We travelled in single file, criss-crossing obstacles, crawling under thickets, trying to make as little noise as possible. So a journey which would ordinarily take three to four hours, took us six hours. By daybreak of 5 April we had entered a thicket on the boundaries of an old lady's house. Her name was Nalongo — we later nicknamed her Brigadier. She became one of our supporters. She hid us well, gave us food and we hid there the whole day. We did not talk, did not smoke and did not make any unnecessary movements as the local people went about their normal business. Regular life begins at daybreak and work and movement go on till sunset. The people at the OP watched as people went on their way on the main road, by bicycle, on foot, sometimes even in vehicles, less than half a kilometre from where we were hiding.

At around 10.00 p.m. on 5 April, we left Nalongo's house and advanced to Kakiri. When we arrived within striking distance of Kakiri, we halted. Our aim was to stay there throughout the day till evening arrived, and then we would attack during the evening muster parade, the method which was used earlier by FUNA and which had wreaked havoc upon our people in Bondo. The area we were hiding in happened to be near a village water well. It had rained during the night, so we had left visible footprints. We knew that people coming to the well in the morning would easily spot us and raise the alarm, so the platoon commander called us and we agreed to attack immediately. We moved into position: with Section One of Sam Magara leading, my Section Two following and with Section Three, Four and Five as the rearguard.

The signal for attack was anti-tank grenade fired by one soldier belonging to the first section. This would be followed by a hail of sustained fire. Our concept was always a sharp swift battle, not a war of long duration, the rationale being that because of our limitations, in terms of personnel, weaponry and ammunition, we could not afford to sustain a long battle. The answer was always *surprise* and it usually worked. The reaction time of most African soldiers is slow. This was made worse by the fact that the UNLA soldiers were very undisciplined. At the time of attack, most of the soldiers had abandoned their positions to go drinking and looting in the villages and town centres.

After five minutes of firing we ceased fire, in order to assess the situation. The enemy had dispersed. However, we moved with speed and caution. I can vividly recall the trained soldiers such as Lumumba, Taban, Godfrey Katumbuza, Kamwana Mwana — those of Section One — who were in the front row. They maneuvered obstacles and covered the enemy trenches.

Our major objective was to capture as big a quantity of weapons and military equipment as possible. After charging the enemy camp, I started pulling the captured booty to the rear, where Section Five and the platoon commander were. The platoon commander also had a camera and was taking photographs of the battle. One enemy soldier who was reporting from a drinking spree bumped into us. This soldier, nicknamed Mapengo because he had lost most of his teeth, was known by the soldiers from Bugolobi who were in Section One. Our soldiers started pleading with him to put down his rifle and surrender. The enemy soldier was, however, disoriented. He pointed his rifle loaded with an anti-tank grenade at me while I also pleaded with him to surrender. Rather than surrender he just fired his grenade in the air, threw his gun down and fled. In the meantime, one soldier in my section, Paul Kagame, fired at him. When I recall Kagame with thick eyeglasses imitating how the bullets flew around Mapengo, I cannot suppress a smile. Who could believe that one day Paul Kagame would be His Excellency! But such is life.

While we were preparing to withdraw, a truck carrying a Tanzanian major and a few Tanzanian soldiers coming from Busunju bumped into us. Being used to indiscriminate firing by UNLA soldiers, the Tanzanian officer jumped off the truck and tried to call the undisciplined soldiers to order. He shouted *"Wacha risasi! Tena hini vita gani!"* (Stop firing! What type of war is this?). The poor man did not know that he had just entered the middle of an actual war in the making. I remember Commander Fred Rwigyema standing and using a tree as cover and firing at the Tanzanian major. Fred was calm, composed, smart as usual and firing like a rifle drill instructor. Later we learnt that the Tanzanian major and a few of his soldiers had died. One cannot be sure, but it seems those Tanzanians were the only casualties of that battle of 5 April 1981.

The withdrawal from Kakiri town to the forest was orderly. We had not lost a single person and we had captured more weapons than we had hoped for. We had captured a heavy machine gun, two mortars, lots of ammunition, bombs, uniforms and other military accessories plus a manpack radio set. After withdrawing a few kilometres into the middle of the forest, we reorganised and started sharing our loot. We were only fifty-seven, and in our quest for weapons we had hauled off more than we could carry.

It soon started raining heavily, and to make matters worse, safari ants attacked us. We were quite a grim lot trying to find our way out of the heavy undergrowth in Kakiri forest. The Tanzanian group at Busunju immediately started organising to pursue us. They started lobbing mortar shells into the forest. Another group with an armoured personal carrier (APC) tried to block the Masulita-Kikiri road. This was a misconception on the part of the Tanzanians. We did not need to use the road. We had followed footpaths, and it was footpaths that we wanted to use.

The APC got stuck in the mud and its continuous revving only announced the Tanzanians' presence, but being of peasant origin, most of us experienced extreme fear. It seemed that the mere fact of the APC's rumbling meant the Tanzanians knew our location.

We started sending people to try and find our route so that we could leave the forest. More than four times these messengers would come running back, totally scared, and inform us that the whole place was surrounded.

It is an arduous task trying to move bent almost double in the thick undergrowth of a rain forest while carrying a heavy weight on your back. We were not sure where we were going and because of the rain the whole forest was dark. It was "darkness at noon", in its actual sense and not the Russian metaphor in Koestler's novel.

We kept moving round and round in circles trying to break out of the forest till around 6.00 p.m., when we came upon the Kakiri-Masulita road. The Tanzanians and their APC were about five miles from where we happened on the road. Here our guides reoriented themselves and we started moving back to our base in Kikandwa. It would be a lie to say that all the loot survived the forest debacles. Many soldiers would throw away their heavy burden if they realised that the commanders were not watching, and most of the loot would not have been of immediate value to us anyway. We had many 82 mm mortar shells while the two mortars we had captured were 60 mm calibre. The manpack radio set was also only good for show since we were not communicating with anyone. It was like having a phone set with no one to ring or to call you. However, this radio would later come in useful when we recruited soldiers from the defunct Uganda Army. Meanwhile, we took pictures with our loot. I remember posing with the earphones of the manpack radio and many young officers and men posturing with heavy machine gun bullets wound around their bodies. Such photographs are typical of guerrillas when they want to make an impression in the media. Of course, one cannot fire a heavy machine gun with the bullet chain wound around one's body. However, to a layman it cuts a really intimidating picture.

We had little time to rest and appreciate our success as the Tanzanian troops continued lobbing mortar shells into the forest. Also, because of the rain and the persistent safari ants, the leader issued an immediate order to move.

Crossing the Kakiri-Masulita road was a military feat of its own since we did not know how the enemy had deployed. Every person we sent came back with a more horrifying story of the strength of the enemy than the one before him. One of the most interesting reports came from Sam Wasswa, a young vigilante, later to be known as Wasswa Balikalege because his reports always stated that the enemy was in Kalege. Kalege was one of the trading centres nearest to our bases. Wasswa, now a brigadier, came running, panting, and informed us that he had seen the enemy troops patrolling the road in full parade formation. It was the three-by-three chest formation of the parade ground ceremonial format. One had to sympathise with poor Wasswa. The only troops he had ever seen were on the parade ground on national television, so any group of people in uniform conjured up that image.

Only a few of us, the trained soldiers, could find Wasswa's report hilarious, but the rest of the group became quite despondent. Some of us knew it would not be possible to go on combat patrol in parade formation. At the end of the fiasco, one of our people, someone born in the area named Kakebe, got in touch with a local herdsman. This herdsman of Rwandan origin was one of those who looked after cattle belonging to the Baganda. The Baganda are the indigenous inhabitants of the area. However, they were cultivators by inclination, so if any of them acquired cattle they would always hire a Rwandan national to look after the cattle for them. These *Balaalo*, as they are called, had no political inclinations. They felt that the war being fought did not concern them. When this lone herdsman was approached by Kakebe, however, he showed some excitement. When he was introduced to our leader, who happened to have been born near the Uganda-Rwanda border in Ntungamo, where the ethnic and tribal totems are shared, he was simply overwhelmed. Consequently he became a dependable guide. The Bahima of Uganda have a lot in common with the Batutsi of Rwanda. When this herdsman told our leader that he was of the Benekihondwa clan, instant rapport was established between them.

This Rwandan herdsman of the Beenekihondwa clan was the one who took the risk of going ahead of all the armed people to look for a way out. He went and scouted the route and reported back that it was safe to cross the road. We crossed the road about two kilometres from the stranded TPDF armoured personnel carrier.

We arrived back at Nalongo's home at dawn on 6 April. We rested, ate and stayed in concealment until 5.00 p.m., when we set off again for our camp in Kikandwa. We arrived back tired but excited. We were very jubilant because we had added a number of guns to our armoury, plus two 60 mm mortars, a general purpose machine gun (GPMG) and a lot of other army matériel. The group we had left behind with Elly Tumwine was waiting for us with food. The whole camp was highly elated. However, we had to refrain from making noise for fear of exposing our camp. The leaders had a very hard time trying to keep the triumphant mob quiet. I have earlier talked of the Tanzanian instructors' problems in Kakoba, Mbarara, while we were recruits. Now I was among the people asked to maintain a semblance of order in a jubilant group of soldiers and civilians who had successfully overrun a government army detachment.

It was not an easy task since even we, the officers, could hardly suppress the feeling of joy at our victory. We had attacked, charged and withdrawn with enemy weapons and other loot without any casualty on our side; to all intents and purposes it was a major victory.

5

Attack by TPDF at Katera

After reorganisation in Kikandwa we divided into two groups; the aim was that we should operate on two fronts. One group was to operate on the Gulu road while also contacting our people in Kampala. The other group, under Commander Tumwine, was to operate on the Kampala-Hoima road. I belonged to the latter group and we were to carry with us all the heavy weapons which were not of immediate use. So we had to carry the two mortars and their shells, the GPMG and the other weapons that we had captured in Kakiri. Our group of about 10 soldiers and 20 civilian recruits started moving on the night of 12 April, that is after five days of rest. As had become the norm, we moved at night. Our experience of night movement was, however, still lacking, our coordination poor and we had to struggle to cover the kinds of distances that we were later able to do easily. Our guide was an old peasant with a bicycle. We piled most of our loot on his bicycle and pushed it along. All in all we did not cut a picture of troops on the march; rather we resembled villagers migrating. Although we tried to minimise noise, we were still a trampling group of heavily loaded people who left a very visible track in our wake. Because of our bicycle and the machine gun we were dragging along, we did not cover a long distance before dawn. When dawn arrived, we just crept into the first thicket and fell asleep.

73

We had a very scanty guard. However, nothing happened to us that first day. The next night we pushed on, and by morning we were approaching the Lwamata hills in Kiboga on Hoima road. We arrived at the farm of a supporter where we rested from 15 April until the evening of 17 April, when we set off towards Lwamata. Our aim was to stay at the foot of the hills so that we could cross the road the next day and camp in the Kasejjere area. That was not to be, however.

All this time the Tanzanians had been trying to trace us and we had made their job quite easy. The Tanzanians finally attacked us on the day we arrived at the foot of the Lwamata hills at a place called Katera. We arrived at around 4.00 a.m. and immediately set up camp. We positioned ourselves in a semi-circle facing the valley with the hill behind us. We dug some foxholes and rested.

The Tanzanians started taking up positions around 6.00am. I think they were a little apprehensive because, judging from the track we had left behind, one could have put our size at between one and two companies, which is about 200 people, instead of the 40 half-armed men that we were. Around 7.00am we started sending people to scout around for food and also to get to know the neighbourhood.

One of the people we had sent to the OP came flying into the camp and addressed the commander, Tumwine. He shouted: *"Jambo, Adui! Afande emefika quarter guard"* (Hullo, enemy, the boss is at our quarter guard). It was only later that we could afford to joke at the mistaken reporting. Right now, however, all hell broke loose. We scrambled into our foxholes, ready to repulse the enemy. Because of lack of preparedness, both of our mortars, as well as the machine gun, were still tied in bundles, ready only for carrying but not for use. They were just luggage and not weapons at that time. The only person I saw trying to respond to the enemy was a young man called Kazahura who had just joined us. He was an intellectual and had had rudimentary weapons handling lessons. I doubt if he even managed to cock his gun as the rest stampeded up the hill. I took up a position behind a rock waiting for orders to fire. None came. We were at the foot of the hill and the only withdrawal route was uphill. The Tanzanian soldiers started shooting at us as we climbed. I do not remember how the time passed as I stayed under cover imagining that all my comrades were waiting for the enemy to come into the clearing so that we could shoot. The Tanzanians, who were about one company, quickly overran our empty camp and collected the abandoned weapons. The casualty was only the young man, Kazahura, who had tried to put up some form of resistance. When he was killed, the rest of us fled. As it started raining, I just froze in cover. After taking a few potshots at my fleeing comrades the Tanzanians soon gave up and left. I stayed there till afternoon, when it stopped raining and there was no sign of any movement. I peeped around my cover and shouted "Bullet!" then let off two bullets. I did not get any response, either from the enemy or my comrades. It was then that I realised I had been abandoned in the battlefield. Cautiously I crept out of my cover to where I had seen Commander Tumwine take up position, but the place was deserted. I looked from tree to tree and behind every rock, where any defending person ought to have taken up a position, but I found not a single person there. I started climbing up the hill, following my comrades' footsteps. The track they had left behind was very visible. It started raining again and I continued calling out my own name and shouting in the local dialect, pretending to be a herdsman in search of my lost cattle.

My comrades heard me, but at first they feared that I might have been captured by the enemy and was being used to trace them. Most of my comrades had taken random directions. We had not arranged any rendezvous point (RV) and everyone was on his own, something reminiscent of a later UFM debacle at Lubiri.

It was a very unnerving situation I found myself in. My greatest fear was that all my comrades had been killed. Secondly, how was I going to report to my bosses? That is, if at all I was going to be able to trace them. I started counting the losses. The funny thing is that after unfreezing from the initial shock, I no longer felt any fear. I was only concerned about the loss of our comrades and the weapons.

After some time, a group of my comrades asked me to join them. We had been scattered into many clusters and I had bumped into one of them. This group was composed of my former comrades who were trained soldiers, such as the late Katumbuza, the late Kashoma and others. Each of them started recounting his own version of the battle. Most of the tales were about how fast each person had run away. Katumbuza's case was classical. A Tanzanian corporal had spotted him and had tried to use him as a moving target. The hill was very steep and so Katumbuza could not run fast. His slow climbing figure dressed in a wet and shoddy poncho must have presented the corporal with a tantalising target. However, he never scored a hit. Whenever Katumbuza tripped and fell the Tanzanian would shout *"Nimeliweza hillo!"* (I have finished that one!) only to see Katumbuza get up and continue his trek. The corporal would shout in wonder *"Jameni mbona aki alife?"* (Gentlemen that thing does not die. Why?) There were similar stories of narrow escapes by most of us. Interestingly, none of us bragged about firing even a single bullet at the attacking Tanzanians.

That was the second time I was in live action in a span of 20 days. In less than a month I had been involved in a victorious skirmish and in a humbling rout. We never gave up hope because, apart from comrade Kazahura, we had lost no one and we knew that the rest of the weapons were safe. Slowly we started moving up towards the top of the Lwamata hills. The Lwamata ranges overlook a vast savannah flatland known as *lukoola*, a Luganda term for barren or uninhabited land. This *lukoola* is crisscrossed by the tributaries of River Mayanja. However, most of it is flatland with a few shrubs. This flatland is not good for agriculture, especially in the Ugandan case where irrigation is not yet widely used by the peasants. Nevertheless, it is very good for animal husbandry. Even then the cattle population in this area was one of the highest in the country.

Seen from the top of the Lwamata hills, the *lukoola* looks like a great green carpet with a few trees sprouting here and there. Unless someone is born in the area, it is very easy for them to lose their bearings if they tried to cross this *lukoola*; there are not many geographical landmarks there. There are no hills to use as reference points for one to find one's way. Whether it is during the day or at night the ground looks the same, and anybody running across that vast land stands a very high chance of getting lost for good.

There were a few homesteads of peasant pastoralist nomads who always wandered with no fixed place of abode. Standing on my piece of raised ground I noticed how the expanse of land seemed to merge with the sky, giving me the feeling of being at sea or in a small boat in the middle of Lake Victoria.

By midnight I had gathered a group of about 12 comrades, and being senior among them, I immediately took command. It was when I considered our next move that I reflected on that *lukoola* phenomenon in the bright moonlight. Everybody was looking at me for guidance. Soldiers have that tendency of believing that the officer must always have a solution, and my men were no exception. So I gazed at the *lukoola* and contemplated the next move.

The overall aim was to reunite with our major group. However, to move in unfamiliar territory, where every road could lead into an enemy camp, was my major concern.

Daybreak found us on top of Lwamata hills and the activities began. The Lwamata ranges divide this territory into two distinct economic spheres. When you stand facing the east, you face the Kampala city side. On your right are the Kasejjere hills and the main activity here is cultivation. There are many banana plantations, coffee shambas and a variety of crops grown by the peasants. There are also many iron-roofed houses, trading centres and a market or two. That is also where the main Kampala-Hoima road is located. On your left, as mentioned earlier, is the *lukoola*, where there are no buildings, no plantations and just a vast scrubby belt of nothing but grassland.

Even in the morning, when most people are getting up to prepare for their day-to-day activities, one hardly notices any sign of life in the *lukoola*. Apart from the occasional plume of smoke from a pastoralist homestead, nothing else exists.

Of the two, the populated right and the seemingly deserted left, I chose to use the left. I believed that the more densely populated an areas was, the higher the chances of discovery, since even the government and Tanzanian troops preferred to camp nearer to the population than in the vast wilderness. Many civilian friends I have talked to have wondered how a sane human being would prefer wilderness to the company of other human beings, but for us the wild bush presented the best option for security, while the comfortable houses presented vulnerability.

I recalled the 1972 incident when guerrillas from Tanzania invaded Uganda. I remembered how all of us, civilians, had risen up and hunted for them. I was then in my second year at Masaka Senior Secondary School. I vividly remembered how the schools had closed for two weeks and even the school boys had got involved in the hunt for the guerrillas. We would get up in the morning and move around, chasing anybody in rags or a torn uniform. The guerrillas had come up to Kumbu forest on the southern fringe of Masaka town and started firing. Even now I can recall the sound of heavy machine guns as Uganda Army soldiers fired indiscriminately into that forest. I was staying in Kimanya, a suburb of Masaka, with an old lady.

The firing started at around midnight and we all ran out of the houses to find out the cause. An old man, a brother of my host, immediately developed a running stomach and asked his sister to escort him outside since most rural houses do not have toilets inside. This involved a bit of drama. Whenever the old man squatted in the plantation to relieve himself, the old lady would withdraw a bit to give him some privacy. Then the machine gun fire would start up again and the old man would come running towards his sister with his pants down. After a few minutes the old man would ask to be escorted outside again. This went on for some time, until the sister advised the old man to use a corner of the room he was occupying.

While such incidents seem funny when remembered later, what confronted me now were the eyes of the captured guerrillas. They were routed humiliatingly. The guerrillas had not been prepared. After the initial burst of gunfire they were dispersed, just as we had been. There were many factors that militated against the success of the 1972 Tanzania-based guerrillas; the most important being operating among a hostile population. In 1972 the political situation was not conducive to any struggle against Amin. Amin had overthrown the Obote government, and Amin's popularity was still high. To make matters worse, the guerrillas were from northern Uganda, therefore the ethnic and language factor was against them. After the guerillas had wandered around aimlessly for one week, the civilian population started picking them up one by one and lynching them or handing them over to the government soldiers, who would hack them to death to the cheering of civilians. I had witnessed many such incidents, one of which was the killing of the mayor of Masaka town, Alderman Walugembe. This gentleman, who was a UPC supporter, was killed while all of us looked on. The killers are well known. However, the most memorable incident to me was when three young men, dressed only in trousers, with their hands tied at their backs, were dragged from a military vehicle at the Masaka Hospital mortuary, lined up and knifed to death for all to see. I was 14 years old, but I can still recall the haunted look on the faces of those three people. Looking at my group now, I did not want to imagine such a thing happening to any of them.

Mao Tse-Tung once said, "A guerrilla must move amongst the people as a fish swims in the sea." Now what Mao did not say is that when the water becomes hostile, the fish has to die. In 1972 I had witnessed young, able-bodied men being led to their deaths by old women, just because the young men were starving. That was when the reality of being a guerrilla and a hunted animal started sinking in.

The Baganda have a way of raising the alarm. They beat a certain tune on the drum known as *Gwangamujje,* which is a call to arms. A drumbeat starts in one homestead and is picked up on the next hill, and soon the valleys and all hills are resounding with drumbeats. If you are on the run, you feel surrounded on all sides. Anyone who has ever heard that drumbeat and knows its meaning must have a healthy fear of that sound. I was no exception. If anything helped me to choose the deserted *lukoola* instead of the populated area it was the fear of that drum.

The next task was to look for a guide to help us find directions in that featureless expanse of plain. In my group we were lucky to have a young recruit who was born in the area. This young man, Rwakampala, who is now a major, turned out to be useful, not only to my little group but also to the whole guerrilla force throughout its formative stage.

It was the likes of Rwakampala who later became indispensable for guiding us through this terrain and many other places in the country. We did not have maps. In any case, maps were particularly not useful to us as we were basically infantry soldiers who were using the local population as our guides and cover. These guides became the oars propelling us in our water, "the population".

News of our skirmish in Katera had travelled far and wide and all the surrounding villages were discussing nothing else but what had transpired. Peasants all over the world like to exaggerate things and the Ugandan peasants love a good story. Our worry was that any human being we met would spread the news of our presence. Apart from the peasant talk, the UPC youth wingers were on full alert and the hunt for dispersed guerrillas was on. However, unlike in the 1972 case, this time the majority of the population was on the side of the guerrillas: the people wanted change.

The only hostility we expected was from the UPC youth wingers, the UPC chairmen and the army itself. A small group of 10-20 people, if careful, can easily conceal themselves, especially if the population is friendly.

After I had assembled and briefed my people, we decided that Rwakampala and I should go and try to trace the main group, then the guides would come for the rest. I left one of the senior privates in charge and we set off to try and retrace our footsteps to the bigger group. This was on 20 April. We decided to travel during the day in order to save time. We would not travel armed, so I reverted to my pistol and a grenade. Rwakampala was armed only with the walking stick known as *enkoni* in the local language, that is favoured by the local pastoralists. None of us was in uniform and we easily passed ourselves off as local people. The going was smooth except for a single incident at Makulubita county headquarters. The local UPC chairman had called a meeting and the youth were rounding up people and forcing them to attend. The population in this area was generally anti-UPC so the party chairman had to use force to assemble people in order to address them. We were just coming round a corner when we bumped into a red-eyed young man who asked us harshly why we were not going to the "big man's" rally.

I looked at the man and debated within myself whether to draw my pistol and shoot him or not. What finally decided me was the fact that the group of people gathered for the rally was big and I was not sure what their reactions would be. It would be easy to kill this youth and run but what if the group turned riotous? We were among strangers in the area so the odds were stacked against us. Luckily enough, I had a UPC party card that I had used in Kampala for purposes of disguise. I pulled it out and asked the youth to show me his party card if he was such a good UPC person. The youth fell over himself apologising to this party cadre who even travelled with the party card on himself everywhere he went. We exchanged pleasantries and then we continued on our way. That young man did not know how close to death he had come.

We reached the main camp on the evening of 21 April and found everybody anxious to know what had happened. Incidentally, our leader, Commander Tumwine, had arrived at the base on the night of 18 April. How he had managed to cover those thirty or more miles is his own story. We were welcomed and a guide was immediately dispatched to search for those we had left behind.

At the end of the day, when everybody had reported, we found that we had lost 13 guns, including the mortar, the GPMG and, most importantly, a comrade, Kazahura. Kazahura was probably the first casualty we suffered since we had joined the war. Nobody else had been killed in combat.

Reorganisation and preparation for Nairobi

The total force of the PRA was now about 200 people. We had recruited many willing youth and some soldiers who had deserted the national army (UNLA) to join the struggle. It is very difficult to conceal 200 people, so we rearranged ourselves into six units. We had a total of 90 guns, all rifles, and some anti-tank rifle grenades. We did not have any reasonable artillery or any heavy support weapons. However, we were still confident that we would be able to defeat and overthrow the government forces with or without the presence of Tanzanian troops. The six units we created were named Kabalega, Mwanga, Abdel Gamal Nasser, Mondlane, Nkrumah and Lutta. The first five were named after historical African heroes, and Lutta was named after one of our supporters, Onesimo Luttamaguzi, who was brutally murdered by UNLA soldiers under the command of Lt. Col. Bazilio Olara Okello, then the central brigade commander and later the number two in the Tito Okello military junta which overthrew the Obote II government.

The leaders of these units were mostly officers trained in Tanzania. Kabalega, named after the former King of Bunyoro who had resisted British colonial rule till he was captured in April 1899, was under Commander Tumwine. Mwanga, named after Kabaka Mwanga of Buganda, who first collaborated with the British but later opposed them and died in exile in the Seychelles, was under Brig. (retired) Matayo Kyaligonza, now NRM vice-chairman for Western Region. Lutta was under Hannington Magabi, who died in a pistol accident in 1982, and so he never saw the liberation of the country that he had fought for. Abdel Nasser, named after the former president of Egypt, was under Jack Muchunguzi, now heading a private security company. Nkrumah, named after the founder president of Ghana, was under Fred Mwesigye, Lt. Col. (retired), in charge of the National Enterprise Corporation (NEC) at the time of writing this account. The army's production unit, Mondlane, named after the founding president of Frelimo, the then ruling party in Mozambique, was under Fred Rwigyema, the Rwanda hero who, in 1991, died on the first day the Rwanda Patriotic Front (RPF) invaded Rwanda to overthrow President Habyarimana.

I was appointed aide de camp (ADC) to the leader, Yoweri Museveni, who also acquired three bodyguards. It is very sad that all the other three have since died. My group included comrades Arthur Kasasira, Marius Katungi (Suicide), and later this group was joined by Andrew Lutaya and the two "navy guys", Busagwa and Paddy, thus together constituting five men. The above-mentioned units were now deployed in various sectors of what later came to be known as the Luweero Triangle. This triangle, which covers five districts, is the area through which three major roads pass. The Kampala-Gulu highway, the Kampala-Hoima road and the Kampala-Mubende road all leave Kampala and fork out like three fingers pointing north and northwest. River Kafu, a tributary of the Victoria Nile, which forms the third line of the triangle, is crossed by these three roads. Our six units were detailed to operate along these three major roads by laying ambushes and, at times, attacking police posts and administrative centres. However, once in a while we would operate as far away as Mukono on the Kampala-Mombasa highway, which was outside the triangle. Most of the units left for their respective operational areas, and only Abdel Nasser remained near Matugga, which is just 12 km from Kampala on the Kampala-Gulu road. Our leader was still establishing contact with the outside world.

Luweero Triangle and river crossing

It was in the Matugga area, to the home of a supporter called Kyobe, that most of our people from Kampala came to report and be briefed about the war. Many important and some not-so-important personalities supported the war and they came up with all sorts of advice on how to win it. One of the bizarre ideas we received was from Prince Jjuuko, a Muganda monarchist, who came to see us, bringing with him a Tanzanian witch-doctor, who advised us that on a certain day the sun would stop in its tracks and go back to the east. On that day all enemy troops would be overpowered by his magic and we would march into Lubiri barracks, the headquarters of the Central Brigade, grab the guns of the sleeping soldiers and overthrow the government.

Our leader did not laugh at him. He just listened with a blank face. In order not to discourage his enthusiasm, he told the prince and his "doctor" to continue supporting us but to leave military planning to us, the fighters who were trained in that field. While the prince and his "doctor" were offering their own peculiar means of ending the war, they were roasting a black goat and a black cock. After they had slaughtered the animals, they had put crosses on our foreheads using the animals' blood. My interest was in the meat, so I was looking forward to eating. The Tanzanian "doctor" let us down when he proclaimed that the meat was not to be eaten but to be burnt to ashes. My comrades were a bit sharper than the "doctor". While he was defending his military strategy, they managed to hide some pieces of meat, so when the visitors left we had a feast. Still, the biggest part of the feast was wasted in the ritual.

We spent the whole of March, April and May in total concealment. Our units were establishing themselves in he zones under their jurisdiction while recruitment went on. More and more government soldiers were also trekking in, so we did not want to expose our presence. Among the people who came to meet us was a Libyan diplomat called Mohammed Alfaghee, who came with an invitation from President Ghadafi of Libya to our leader. All this time, we were receiving more recruits. However, our arms were still very few. We were made to believe that people who were outside the country would somehow smuggle guns to us. When the guns did not materialise, Museveni called a meeting of all the commanders and explained that he had to leave the country to follow up on the promised weapons. He left immediately, since any delay would make people forget that we were still in the bush. It is very easy for people to pledge something off the cuff. However, if there is no follow-up, people tend to forget. So preparation for the journey started.

6

The Nairobi Journey (Seven Men in a Boat)

I was not privy to the planning of the journey because we were adhering to the principle of "need to know". However, on 6 June 1981, I found myself among the people who were chosen to travel outside Uganda to look for guns. The journey from Luweero, which is in the middle of the country, to any border was very dramatic, intriguing and dangerous.

Uganda is a landlocked country sharing borders with Kenya to the east, Tanzania to the south, Rwanda to the southwest, Sudan to the north and the Democratic Republic of Congo to the west. Access to Uganda is through the major Kenya-Uganda highway, which traverses the country from the port of Mombasa on the India Ocean to Rwanda; by the East African Railway from Kenya to Kasese and by air via Entebbe International Airport. None of these access routes were viable options for us to use. There were so many checkpoints and the governments of the neighbouring countries had an ambiguous and negative view of any group trying to overthrow the *democratically* elected government of Uganda. The OAU Charter specifically states that no sovereign state should get involved in the internal affairs of its neighbour. Tanzania would not look at us favourably since it was sustaining Obote's regime; Rwanda has no easy access to the outside world, since it is also landlocked, like Uganda, and depends on Uganda for outside access. Sudan was a no-go area. In those days, Sudan was a semi-pariah state. Therefore, access to the outside world through Sudan was not possible. Zaire was a very different country, a francophone country, so it had no real relationship with the Ugandan community. That left Kenya as the only option. Kenya has always been safe for Ugandan political and economic dissidents. We have always had contacts with Kenya and there have always been close civil links between Kenya and Uganda. However, since the Uganda Railways and the Kampala-Mombasa highway were not practical options, the only route open to us was via Lake Victoria. This lake, which straddles Kenya, Uganda and Tanzania, has always been one of Uganda's gateways to the outside world. The fishermen on Lake Victoria, having little regard for the so-called international boundaries, have always traded among these three states both legally and informally since time immemorial, and even now there is little chance that this trade will stop.

Our predicament was how to reach the shores of Lake Victoria from the very centre of the country, where we were. I did not know where we were going to pass. All I saw was a vehicle being driven by one of our supporters, Mr Sam Male, who was working at the Libyan Arab Bank, and another person whom I later learnt was a police officer with the Police Fire Brigade. The vehicle was parked near Mr Kyobe's plantation and four of us boarded the vehicle — that is Yoweri Museveni, Private Kasasira, Captain Katungi (Suicide) and myself. We were dressed in our by now torn and ragged civilian clothes and carrying our guns. Any security personnel who stopped that vehicle would not have doubted that we were up to no good. The words bandits, guerrillas, even thugs were written all over our faces and our attire. It is funny how four months of hiding, and having only scanty meals and rare baths, transforms a self-assured gentleman into a ragtag thug. Gone were all the scents associated with civilisation. The patched and dirty clothes, plus our unwashed bodies, would make even a garbage collector turn up his nose, which our driver, Mr Male, may have wanted to do but, perhaps because of the respect he had for us, he pretended not to be aware of the stench. All of us had lost weight but we were very fit. Our skins had lost their lustre and we appeared to be darker than we actually were. Body lice, now a constant feature inside our attire, were at work, and we were scratching ourselves everywhere. I sat in the front seat next to the driver of the four-door Datsun estate car. Museveni and the policeman sat in the middle seat while Kasasira and Suicide sat in the rear. They would have preferred to leave the rear door open for easy getaway or response in case of an ambush. However, they were restrained as such a move would have exposed us.

We drove from Matugga using motorable shortcuts till we reached the shores of Lake Victoria at the Katebo beach, after crossing the Masaka-Kampala road, which was a very big achievement to us. When one is in the bush hiding from authority, one fears any areas where people exist, places such as roads, and especially highways like the Masaka-Kampala highway. Crossing these places always elicited fear among us. Roads were where the enemy could be found and they were useful only for ambushes — that is they were useful only early in the morning or in the evening but not for regular use in broad daylight.

We arrived at the Katebo beach in the evening and boarded a boat at 6.00 p.m. It was the second time I travelled on water. The first time was when we had crossed Lake Albert by ferry from Fort Portal to West Nile. Compared to the ferry, this puny boat looked rather scary. It was a 12 hp motorboat with a seating capacity of two or three fishermen with their nets and fish. So, as we watched the expanse of water, we tried to imagine how the tiny thing could carry the seven of us across the lake. Our "navy boys", Paddy and Busagwa, just laughed at our fear and told us that there was no safer way to travel than by water in a small boat. We could not argue since it was our first experience. We set off for the Ssese islands on Lake Victoria. It was a nice feeling, with the breeze from the lake adding to our excitement. In four hours, at around 10.00 p.m., we landed on Bukeke island. The Ssese islands are on the Ugandan side of the lake. The islanders, like most people living along African boundaries, have no respect for border authorities. Few, if any, pay taxes and in those days, the early 1980s, there was very limited authority over them. People just fished and smuggled among the three countries without any fear of being caught.

At Butebo island, a man known to Brigadier Andrew Lutaya received us. This man, a distant cousin of Lutaya's, was a supporter of the anti-Obote forces and so automatically became a useful contact. Moreover, Lutaya was now the chief transport officer, since, being a native of Ssese, he knew the lake well. There is the kind of fraternity which comes from staying on water. Because of the constant danger, people tend to know one another, and they take a keen interest in what is happening to any member of their closed society. So when Lutaya told this peasant our mission he was very enthusiastic and he prepared a meal of fish and cassava. Our group of seven now comprised the original four plus Andrew Lutaya and our two "boat boys", Paddy and Busagwa.

We descended upon the food with gusto, except for two in our group, our leader Museveni and Private Kasasira. These two did not find fish palatable because of their Hima background. The Bahima cattle keepers have taboos forbidding them from eating fish, among other foods.However, although I am a Muhima, I had been introduced to fish during my childhood because our deeply religious parents did not adhere to many cultural taboos. So while I was getting my second and third helping, Museveni could not help grimacing when, according to him, he saw me shoving whole fish into my mouth and spitting out bones. We slept out in the open like our host. The people of the island lived a life not dissimilar from ours in the bush. They have a high resistance to the hardships of nature, so to them falling asleep aboard their boats or any island is not a problem.

On the morning of 7 June we boarded a bigger boat, which had a 48 hp outboard engine, and set off for Kenya. The journey was comfortable, till around midday when the scorching sun made us uncomfortable. However all this time we were feeling secure since the islands appeared near, so we did not have any fear. Soon we lost sight of the land. The lake and the sky merged in all four compass directions. We were at the mercy of nature now, but our "navy boys" showed no fear and they assured us that we would see land soon. It seemed like many hours had passed before we started seeing birds. Paddy and Busagwa told us that sighting birds signified proximity to land since, according to them, birds do no make nests to settle on in the middle of the lake. The distance between the easternmost Ssese island called Seguku and the Kenyan island of Ntagamo in the Kavirondo gulf, where we were heading, is over one hundred land miles, but when in a boat with no landmark at all it feels like an eternity. Time seems to stop. We were thirsty but the lake water did not look good enough to drink, for even as we travelled, the lake was being used as an open toilet. It was the boat crew who showed us how to relieve ourselves in the strong wind. We were advised to face downwind so that urine would not splash on the person urinating or the other members of the crew. We also learnt how to light cigarettes in the wind. During the eleven hours we spent on the open lake we had mastered some of the tricks sailors use to stay comfortable on open expanses of water.

Towards evening we saw land in the far east, but soon darkness closed in. However, not long afterwards the stars gave us a clear vision. If we had not been tired, hungry and thirsty it would have been a nice ride. The lake was calm, and the moon had started emerging. It was such a romantic sight, but none of us was interested in the wonders of nature at that point in time. Around 10.00 p.m. we started seeing lights. At night, ahead of us in the lake, all the land looked the same and our comrades became confused. We wanted to enter Kenya from Kisumu, where we had contacts. All the harbours on the Kenyan side, unlike the Ugandan ones, are well lit, so the whole shoreline looked the same, especially to someone in a boat at night, and our people had spent some time outside to Kenya. Although fishermen travelled on that lake with no hindrance, it was still difficult to enter a foreign country.

At 10.00 a.m. we saw what looked like a reasonable port, very reasonable, of course, compared to Ugandan ports, and assumed that it was Kisumu. We set off towards it and landed. The boat crew left us in the boat, went ashore and started talking to their Kenyan counterparts, only for them to be told that we were in Homa Bay, some sixty or so miles from Kisumu. They came back and we resumed our journey.

Kisumu

It was at dawn that we landed at Kisumu Port. A boat coming from the Ugandan side and landing at Kisumu in the morning is common; so there was no cause for alarm among the Kenyan people. All they wanted to know was what *mali* – smuggled goods – we had brought with us and what we wanted in exchange. Nobody looking at us would differentiate us from common smugglers, so that Museveni had a hard time convincing the smugglers that we had no merchandise but we were simply in transit and would soon continue our journey. I disembarked with Suicide to see what was going on ashore. When one is a fugitive from the law, any kind of uniform which signifies authority poses a threat. The first people we saw in uniform were ordinary security guards but we thought it was an enemy ambush. It seemed to us that the whole Kenyan shoreline was being patrolled by soldiers who, by some miracle, were aware that we would be coming to Kisumu.

We returned to the boat and reported our findings. However, Andrew Lutaya, who was more knowledgeable about such things, just laughed at us, and soon he set off to try and contact our people in the town. In the meantime, it was becoming embarrassing just loitering around the fish-landing site with nothing to do. Everybody else was busy offloading fish and loading merchandise, most of which was destined for Uganda. We had come with two rifles and some grenades, which we immediately hid in the boat. We were just standing around on Kenyan soil without any identification. We did not have any Kenyan money. We looked suspicious anyway, but we did not attract undue attention since we looked just like almost everybody else.

Around 9.00 a.m. Lutaya came back and reported that he was still trying to locate our people. However, he had managed to book us into a certain dingy lodge where we could wait. Sneaking into the lodge through a busy town was not easy. However, since nobody knew us, we just marched up majestically and entered the rooms. It is easier to appear at your worst in a place where nobody knows you. Maybe that is why our people say that "you are behaving like a stranger" when they see someone acting in an unbecoming manner in public. Now our being strangers reduced our embarrassment as we sneaked into that drab lodge. We were dressed very shabbily; even Museveni wore smudged jeans and a not-so-clean T-shirt. Around 10.00 a.m. Lutaya managed to locate our people, Amama Mbabazi, now the Minister of Defence, and Sam Katabarwa (deceased). Those two and others were our people in the external wing. They stayed outside the country most of the time we were in the bush. Mbabazi and Katabarwa were well-dressed and driving two posh cars. We were made to understand that the cars were the best camouflage for the type of work they were doing.

Nairobi and its glamour

Without further delay we got into the cars and set off for Nairobi. It was a big transition from being shabby fishermen to be sitting in a posh Audi. We, the bush people, were mesmerised by the grandeur of the streets. The well-paved roads, the sleek cars, the neon lights, the smart sidewalks, the flower gardens, but mostly how our people, Katabarwa and Mbabazi, fitted into the picture. I started wondering if we were in the same war as the External Committee people. The journey from Kisumu to Nairobi took about two hours, and at around 12.30 p.m. we entered Nairobi city.

I have talked about my first time in Arusha while I was an officer cadet in Tanzania. What I saw in Nairobi the first time seemed to me like a picture from a book of fairy tales. While President Idi Amin was wreaking havoc in Uganda, Kenya was progressing, either in spite of or because of the sad state of affairs in Uganda. Kenya's Nairobi was very different from Uganda's capital city, Kampala, that I knew quite well. It was as if the two did not belong on the same planet, let alone the same continent, and had been members of the same (defunct) East African Community.

I was later to see the other side of Nairobi when I visited Eastleigh, Kibera, Mathare and other slums, but the first glimpse of the affluent part of Nairobi was breathtaking. We travelled along good roads and past some impressive shopping malls till we stopped at the steps of a single-storeyed building. This was where Mrs Janet Museveni, wife of our leader and now First Lady, stayed. Even now I can remember the feeling that I was a town urchin who had wandered into a respected person's residence.

Madam Janet stood on the steps watching as we got out of the cars. Her first words were, "Yoweri, where are our people coming from?" She could not control the tears of relief. From behind her the kids were peering at us with open-eyed curiosity. We were afraid we would soil the well-polished floor and nice carpets, but she ushered us in. We gingerly sat on the edge of the sofas. We were very conscious of our dirty clothing. However, Madam Janet and the whole household were just gazing at us in awe. The first thing I had asked Katabarwa was to get us some clothes. I need not have bothered, as it seemed all our needs had already been anticipated and the necessary arrangements made. After being given glasses of juice, we were shown the bathrooms. We bathed, or rather scoured the dirt and grime from our bodies. We took off all the clothes we had been wearing and threw them into the garbage bin. We started feeling like human beings again. After eating a heavy, delicious welcome meal, the next step was for us to go to the barber's. Our hair was full of lice. We thought the barbers in Nairobi might wonder what type of people we were since now we were decently dressed and being driven around in posh cars. How come we had lice in our hair? Each one went to a different barber and solved the problem of being identified as a group in this way.

By evening we were clean-shaven, spick and span, and ready to admire the wonders of Nairobi. We did not have a chance to do so since the city was preparing for the OAU summit, which was about to take place there. City security was on the alert and anybody without proper identification could easily end up in prison and stay there till the conference was over. We were immediately driven to a different house where we spent the night. Almost all the Ugandan people in Nairobi were anxious to meet us. They were eager to know what was happening back home as most of them had fled into exile, running away from the Obote regime, and saw in us a chance to go back home. For security reasons, our whereabouts were kept secret since our presence could easily be leaked back to Kampala, either through Obote's intelligence network or just civilians' loose talk. So, right from the beginning, as fugitives from the Luweero bush, we were forced to stay underground in Nairobi, but the Nairobi underground was heaven compared to Buwambo forest which we had come from.

7

ADC to Two Different Personalities (Yusuf Lule and Yoweri Museveni)

In Nairobi we were underground, therefore we changed residences frequently. We also had to be separated because we feared that a group of young men with foreign appearance could easily attract unnecessary attention. I moved into a house which I shared with Museveni. I was working both as his ADC and batman. It was not a difficult task since we were living a frugal life. During the next week we met very important people every evening, both Kenyan officials and prominent Ugandans in exile.

Among the prominent Ugandans we met were people like the late Chris Mboijana, an affluent lawyer who had connections with the Kenyan Attorney General of the time, Charles Njonjo. Chris Mboijana lived and behaved like a British lord in character, mannerisms and speech. The tastes reflected in his house and his choice of vehicles were clear testimony to his being a person of substantial means. He was wealthy and he flaunted his wealth. Among his many cars was a state-of-the-art Jaguar that he used only on weekends to go to his club, the African Safari.

Formation of NRM/NRA

It was in Mboijana's house that we met Njonjo who, according to Mboijana, was a linchpin in the Kenyan government hierarchy. However, Museveni had his reservations about that description, as he later told us that to African dictators, nobody is indispensable. It was also in the same house that we met Yusuf Lule and formally set up the NRM/NRA. We had been meeting many people, including some former army officers and ministers from past regimes. We had met Lieutenant General Moses Ali and even former President Godfrey Lukongwa Binaisa. With Moses Ali it was agreed that he should continue with his side of the war in West Nile but that we should coordinate. Binaisa gave us moral support and he gave me two hundred Kenyan shillings, which at that time was a lot of money. Binaisa's reason was that since Museveni was a tea drinker, he did not appreciate the fact that the soldiers need a relaxant after a heavy schedule. Up to now I remember Binaisa for his consideration.

Back to Lule. The old man who ruled for 68 days while he was 68 years old, according to Milton Obote, had the feeling that he was of great importance to the war. His overthrow had caused a very violent reaction from civilians, especially around Kampala. Many anti-Obote groups were using Lule's name to win credibility. A few shrewd young men started telling him lies, that they had fighting forces in Uganda. It was fashionable those days to have a force fighting Obote. Many briefcase and desk guerrilla commanders were flocking to Nairobi. It seemed Kenya would be the staging ground for the anti-Obote struggle, just as Tanzania had been for the anti-Amin struggle.

The Kenyan government was a bit more mature. While it did not disapprove of the dissidents, it did not want to get involved in our wars. Lule said he had a force called Uganda Freedom Fighters (UFF). This was under the command of a young man who claimed his name was "Mucuba". Since the Cuban mercenary days in Congo in the 1960s, Ugandans tended to name anyone who does menial work for hire a Cuban. Hence they concocted term the *Mucuba*. A *Mucuba* can be anything, from a hired fighter, a hired load carrier in the local market, to a taxi tout instructed to drive in place of a qualified driver. During those days of people's resistance to the established rule in Uganda, many acronyms were concocted to tell people what each group represented. Ours was Popular Resistance Army (PRA), Lule had UFF, Kayira had Uganda Freedom Movement (UFM), there was Former Uganda National Army (FUNA) composed largely of soldiers of Amin's defeated army, etc. Each group was claiming to have the best combatants and means of acquiring weapons to overthrow the Obote government.

Our strategy was to work with anybody who was against the Obote regime, and we appreciated the support Lule enjoyed, especially in Buganda, which is in the centre of the country and which has a very dynamic, vocal and big population. When we asked about his troops and their positions in Uganda, he told us to ask his Commander, Mucuba. Museveni asked me if I had trained with the young man or if he belonged to any former army. The young man, without blinking an eye, told us that he had done his training on the northern island of Mozambique. We all knew that Mozambique was not an island, much less a "northern island". We all cocked our ears, and went on to tell the young man that this was a serious political discussion and we were not in the mood for jokes. Mucuba insisted with a straight face that he had done his military training on the northern island of Mozambique. Museveni could stomach him no more, so he ordered me to take the young man out and let him cool down.

I took Mucuba to the gardens and asked him why he was turning such a historical event into a circus! "Friend," confided Mucuba, "you are also a young man like me. This is my deal, why do you want to sabotage it?" I could not find the words to say to Mucuba. How on earth could someone term what we were going through as a deal? I gave him a cigarette and told him that the time for deals in Uganda's history was long over. I told him that if he wanted he could join us, he could undergo training like everybody else and become useful to his country, but telling lies to the old man, Professor Lule, and making him look a fool, was unacceptable to us. The young man continued sulking till the formality of signing the merger of UFF and PRA to form NRM/NRA was over. I do not know where that young man ended up. However, his revolutionary ideas ended the day the merger protocol was signed and he must have gone to look for other deals.

The next day a new house was found for Professor Lule and I was asked to be his ADC. I had an uphill task conforming to the old man's way. He was an aloof and sometimes arrogant and genteel conservative Muganda. I had a hard time adapting to his polite but arrogant comportment, but he had his own peculiar sense of humour and taught me a few facts of life. One of the things I remember him for that he admonished me for being extravagant. If Museveni was leading a frugal life, Professor Lule was the epitome of economical living! Two examples illustrate my observation. While we were in the middle of the negotiation about the merger of our two groups, he remembered something, then called his driver and sent him to buy that thing. To Museveni, with his socialist leanings, this was an abomination. How could a leader, in the middle of such an important meeting, remember to send for something which was not part of the agenda? Worse still, how can a leader handle cash? Museveni felt that this showed lack of seriousness and he told me so. He told me that to a leader something like counting coins is a cause of diversion. A leader should concentrate on his work and leave other people to handle all other mundane things or activities. The next example was when Lule found me sweeping away a small piece of laundry soap. He asked me why I did not preserve that piece of soap for washing my hands and the dishes. He told me that the poor are the most extravagant because they can never appreciate the value of wealth. He quoted an old English saying which goes something like: "Take care of the pennies and the pounds will take care of themselves."

Museveni left for Libya after one week in Nairobi and I stayed with the Lules. My comrades were in another part of Nairobi. Lule was taciturn in character, a frugal eater and extremely clean, a trait he shared with Museveni. I had to restrict my smoking, could not play loud music and had to keep sober and alert all the time. I used my stay with the Lules to read extensively and somehow I managed to acquire some books. Apart from thrillers, I started reading serious books such as Sun Tzu's *Art of War, The Red Star over China* by Edgar Snow, *Selous Scouts* by a South African colonel and many other bush war-related books. I also read *Your Erroneous Zones*. I gained a lot in the course of my stay with the professor.

When Museveni returned from Libya, he went to stay with his family. I joined my comrades, Kasasira and Suicide. We were booked into a hotel so we had time to tour Nairobi. Unlike Uganda, Kenya has always had a national identity card system and security personnel could round up people at any time and demand *kitambulisho*, that is travel documents. There were many discarded identity cards, especially near shopping malls. Either the real Kenyans did not find them useful or they were just careless, but discarded identity cards littered the streets. Some were even pinned on trees. I had my UNLA identity card certifying that I was a second lieutenant of the Ugandan army, which was very dangerous for me then, so I found a lost identity card in the name of one William Majwara, a resident of Kakamega. What I did was to carefully rub off the pips on my UNLA card and fix my picture on Majwara's card. From then on I was Mr William Majwara from Kakamega to the Kenyan Police and other authorities. I used to travel on buses or *matatu* (minibuses) that serve as taxis in Nairobi, and whenever the police or General Service Unit (GSU) stopped the vehicle I was travelling in to demand: *Wananchi vitambulisho!* (Citizens' travel documents please!") I was always among the first people to show mine. This trick worked well, and, whenever some security personnel talked to me in the local language, I answered in Kiswahili, which is the official language of all the East African armed forces. If the person insisted on speaking Kikuyu I would remind him that Baba Moi, the Kenyan president, had called on *wanainchi* (citizens) to avoid *majimbo* (tribalism) or sectarianism and pleaded with Kenyans to speak the national language, Kiswahili. That would dispel any doubt about my nationality. That is how I avoided ending up in the detention centres where undesirable aliens in Nairobi were held.

It was during those escapades that we made contact with the Ugandan community in exile. We met many of the current leaders and prominent people. They all welcomed and pampered us. To them we symbolised a chance to go back home. These people were refugees even though they were not in refugee camps. Their movements were restricted, they were not earning much but they were willing to contribute to the struggle to the best of their abilities. Although they were not at home, they maintained a fraternity created by shared problems. Whatever differences they may have had at home were now forgotten. They were Ugandans who wanted to go home, given the chance. Some had well-paying jobs but they could not invest their money. There was that feeling of being aliens. They patronised certain places and avoided most of the big hotels and restaurants where the indigenous Kenyans converged. These foreigners were resented by indigenous Kenyans for one reason or another.

Ugandans are an ingenious and hardworking people when they are not at home. It is interesting to note that the same Ugandans who used to work hard towards a common goal are now lazy and spend a lot of their time idling around in drinking places and engaging in cheap political talk. An exiled Ugandan could put in more work than an indigenous Kenyan, but now immigrant Kenyan workers put in more work than indigenous Ugandans when in Uganda. This phenomenon needs studying.

Life in exile went on normally for the Ugandan population. There were weddings, baptisms, births, and other events that characterise ordinary life. One of the weddings that my comrades Kasasira, Suicide and I attended was that of Mr James Tumusiime, who was a member of our external wing and is now the Managing Director of Fountain Publishers, but who was at that time a journalist with Kenyan newspapers. He also penned a popular cartoon, *Bogi Benda*, an offshoot of *Ekanya*, a popular cartoon in Uganda done by Dr Tumusiime Rushegye. We attended James Tumusiime's wedding incognito, and we enjoyed everything from behind closed doors. We enjoyed the food, drinks and music and listened to the speeches. Of course, we flirted with the maids serving the drinks and had a hell of a time. This is one of the best weddings I have ever attended.

Some people went out of their way to make our stay in Nairobi comfortable. One of them is a lady of Rwandan origin called Tereza Karuretwa, wife of Mr Gregoire Karuretwa, a rich man who is now in Rwanda. This family was well-to-do and contributed generously both to the NRA war and the subsequent RPF war. The old lady, Tereza, made a point of feeding us well. While other well-wishers and sympathisers wanted to take us out for drinks and political talk, she would insist that we had a full tummy first before leaving and she earned the name of *mama* from us bushmen. Of course, there were Ugandan exiles, especially from our very own group who, for reasons of cheap popularity, wanted to downplay our significance. They had been in the limelight as the liberators and here we were overshadowing them.

The Ugandan exiles in Kenya started identifying with us and thinking of us as the real liberators, so there was an undercurrent of resentment from the armchair fighters. Once one of these people asked me to wash his car so that he could give me money to buy cigarettes. If I were a civilian I would have lost my cool and told him that, after all, the car he was driving and the money he wanted to give me was from the civilian sympathisers. Even my comrade Privates Kasasira and Suicide felt bad when they saw their commander being humiliated. However, I checked my temper and laughingly told the gentleman that since I was from the bush I could not trust myself to wash his car to his expectation. We laughed about it and the episode ended there.

All the time I was in Nairobi, I used to telephone my darling (future) wife Dora. The East African telecommunication system was still working. However, phone calls from Nairobi to Kampala were more expensive than those from Kampala to Nairobi. Dora was staying with her cousin, Mr John Kakamba, who was working in the Ministry of Foreign Affairs and who had also been Uganda's First Secretary to India. Kakamba's wife, Nora, was the secretary to the Managing Director, Uganda Blankets. Dora used to talk to me on the phone of Kakamba's wife, Nora. Since I did not have enough money I would "beep" her (to use the parlance of the cellphone age) from a call box. She would phone back and then we would talk for about thirty minutes, to the chagrin of other potential call box users.

One important lesson I learned in Nairobi was how, unlike Ugandans, Kenyans were averse to war. Almost everybody was talking ill of the Moi government but any hint of war or violent overthrow of his regime was met by actual hostility. The Ugandan upheavals had taught Kenyans the value of stability and continuity. Having received Ugandan political dissidents right from the mid-sixties, Kenyans had come to the logical conclusion that nothing good comes from violent and abrupt change in a country's government. I think their experience during their Mau Mau war for independence had taught them the futility of violence. The Mau Mau experience had shown them how destructive and devastating wars can be.

Uganda has seen eight governments since independence in 1962, while Kenya and Tanzania have had only three each. Kenyans were opposed to what was going on in Uganda and they did not relish it. It is gratifying to note that Ugandans too are beginning to appreciate the value of stability. Later, after our bush war, I asked some former rebel Uganda People's Democratic Army (UPDA) soldiers who had returned to civilian life following the peace agreement with them in 1988, what they thought of abrupt changes in government, and they said that making money and rebuilding their lives depended on government stability and continuity. At the time they had just completed a contract for building roads and were waiting for payment from the Ministry of Works and looking forward to taking up more jobs.

8

Return Journey from Nairobi

When Museveni finished his duties in Nairobi, it was time to return to Uganda. One would have expected us to be unwilling to leave the good life in Nairobi for the harsh bush life we were sure to face. On the contrary, we were very eager to go back to Uganda. All our comrades were in the bush, fighting, while we were playing darts in Nairobi hotels and it seemed unfair. Furthermore, in a protracted people's war, any moment can bring a disastrous or victorious change and we were anxious to be part and parcel of all these events. I was not happy being an ADC. I had been trained to be a commander of troops and I felt my skills were being wasted. Each of us may have had his own reasons, but above all, Nairobi life was not easy for someone who was not working. The feeling of euphoria and the hospitality of our compatriots in exile towards their liberators were wearing thin, and their handouts were dwindling too. It was time to go back home and do what we had set ourselves to do.

We did not say farewell to all our friends in Nairobi, we had to leave as clandestinely as we had come. The reason was that our overenthusiastic supporters would leak information about our movements intentionally or out of ignorance. So it happened that on 6 December 1981 we sneaked out of Nairobi and by evening we were in Kisumu embarking on a boat back to Uganda. This time around we had a bigger boat and we were dressed decently compared to when we arrived. I had some cigarettes, a bottle of whisky and a few bottles of beer in my pack. Each one of us had equipped himself as he thought best. We were dressed in hard-wearing jeans and jackets, beautiful T-shirts and pullovers, plus tourist jungle boots with packs. We looked like young campers. With Suicide donning dark sunglasses, we could have been mistaken for rich young men out on an adventure hike.

We boarded the boat with all the bravado of European explorers coming to Africa. After exchanging pleasantries with the authorities in Kenya and being wished well, we set off.

For starters, we lacked life jackets and a compass but our "navy boys" assured us that it was the norm among sailors on Lake Victoria. This new boat could fly; it had a bigger engine and was well-maintained. Soon it was dark. One thing that impresses me about the people who ply the seas and oceans is that they have an uncanny harmony with the universe. For instance, Busagwa and Paddy could just look at the sky and plot our exact position vis-à-vis the islands of Kenya, Uganda and Tanzania. They could also tell the time without the use of watches. To them the stars and the positions of the sun or the moon are an open book and compass, which they could interpret without problems. They never showed any signs of uncertainty as to where we were at any given time in the middle of the lake, even at midnight when the darkness was total.

Our intention was to land on Ugandan shores by morning. However around 7.00 a.m. our luck ran out. Apparently, the smiling Kenyans had sold the crew of our boat diesel mixed with water. Now, the boat, which had set out with a full tank, started getting seizures, and where it had been flying, it was now only drifting. It is difficult to pilot a boat with a non-operational engine. One would rather have a canoe with oars. One cannot pilot an engine-laden watercraft easily since the engine that is supposed to provide propulsion now becomes part of the burden. Heavy things have a tendency to either sink or drag in water — that is what we were experiencing.

Anybody who has ever taken a car for an engine check knows how many tools a mechanic needs to open up a carburettor and how many spanners, nuts and needles he tinkers with. Paddy and Busagwa had only one toolbox and they were working, not in a mechanic's toolshed, but on top of water. Any tool lost would not be found and, on top of that, they were working by the light of one electric torch. These two opened up the carburettor, blew off the dust, poured the water away, thus reserving the little diesel there was, and started the boat engine again. These boys, who could not even write their names, let alone read instructions about the engine make-up, which was given in German, could put two and two together and thus shape the destiny of Uganda.

All floating objects tend to drift towards land. Our main worry while Paddy and Busagwa were working on the boat engine was that we would drift into a Tanzanian port, which was, at that time, hostile territory to us, or worse still, onto the beaches around Entebbe or Kampala.

The boat engine kept stalling, every now and then roaring back to life, till it was almost daylight. The most unnerving experience was when we drifted towards Entebbe and the control tower lights shone down on us. Mzee Museveni asked me in vernacular whether the myth that Obote had magic was correct. I had never believed in myths and the possibility of being bewitched has never crossed my mind. I laughed it off, though I felt very vulnerable. I could not get off the boat, take cover and fire back if I was accosted by any enemy at that time. I was feeling helpless and not in charge of the situation at all. I just said my old prayer silently: "God, help me overcome this problem as you have always helped me overcome others." That was all. God answered my prayers. Instead of drifting towards Entebbe we drifted towards an island which is too small to have a name. We had been on water for 24 hours and the main problem was thirst — we had some beef and biscuits but we had no water. We, apart from Museveni, had shared our whiskies and beef, but he, being a teetotaller, had a particularly parched throat. Being a particularly health-conscious person, he had resisted the water given to us by the people we found on the island as being unboiled and therefore unhygienic and he was in bad shape. He could not even brush his teeth using lake water, so when he saw me with my bottle of White Cap beer he asked for it, gurgled it and cleansed his mouth. It was the first time I saw Mzee "drink" beer, if it could be called drinking.

Andrew Lutaya left us in a canoe to go to Kampala for some clean fuel since what we had in the boat was contaminated. Lutaya was delayed and we became apprehensive. It is very risky for a member of any clandestine group to fail to keep an appointment since anything could have happened to him. If Lutaya had been arrested and was tortured it would be difficult for us to make our way back to the bush. There are times when the struggle hinges on just one individual. In our situation everything depended on Lutaya's survival instincts and ingenuity. In the afternoon, at around 4.00 p.m., we hired a canoe from some fishermen, they were willing to row us to the Ugandan shore. We had intended to land at the Kajjansi landing site. However, for security reasons we landed at Kitubbulu, near the Entebbe-Kampala highway. Just 400 metres from where we landed was the famous permanent Katabi roadblock. This roadblock, which effectively cuts off Entebbe International Airport from Kampala, was notorious. A female UPC chairperson had turned it into an open-air torture centre. Stories are still told of how she used to force men to wash her panties and drink the water. She had designed a torture method involving hanging a person upside down from a tree branch and lighting a fire below. This woman, who was at that stage a girlfriend of the late Paulo Muwanga, the then de facto number two in Obote's regime, had turned Entebbe Road into a no-go area. It is said that if someone ventured to Entebbe from Kampala, he had first to write a will and make peace with his Maker before the journey. Today this woman is alive and kicking and shows no remorse for her acts, and today she still boasts that she was doing her duty as a good citizen to rid Uganda of undesirable elements who were anti-government.

We landed just 400 metres from this woman's workplace at around 8.00 p.m. Trust people to be reliable, particularly when they want to protect their own, especially from an unpopular regime. The peasants at the shore whisked us away and soon we were inside an old house where the owner prepared us a meal. We remained inside throughout the night and for part of the following day. We had not yet determined what had happened to Andrew and we were worried. There was no means of direct communication. At that time mobile phones had not yet arrived in Uganda and the only means of communication was the age-old face-to-face method. We heaved a collective sigh of relief when Alhaji Moses Kigongo, now vice-chairman of the NRM, and the same Male who had brought the Libyan delegates to the bush, showed up. They had two light-blue BMWs which had become one of the status symbols of UPC chairmen. So, in a way, they could offer cover to any anti-UPC element. All one needed to do was to dress smartly in UPC colours and drive a light-blue BMW and the host of roadblocks would open up automatically to drive through. So here we were, driving unconcernedly from Kitubbulu to Kampala. In the front car were Andrew Lutaya, Male as the driver, and myself. In the following car was Museveni, Suicide and Kasasira, with Alhaji Kigongo driving. Our aim was to drive through Kampala city, follow the Gulu road up to Matugga, our forward edge of the battle area (FEBA), if such things as FEBAs exist in guerrilla warfare. Unknown to us, our presence had been detected by the enemy.

Somehow information about our movements had leaked to government intelligence. Someone had even described the clothing we wore. It might have been any government informers, who were quite numerous both on the Kenyan coast and on the islands, but most likely it was one of our supporters who had rung Kampala excitedly to tell someone that the boys were coming back. Information in the hands of civilians is very dangerous for a clandestine operative. Those days we were hot news and every civilian tried to outdo the others about knowledge concerning the "boys" movements. Whatever the source of the leakage, information about our wherabouts reached the National Security Agency (NASA), and UPC youth wingers and roadblocks were thrown up at all the entry and exit points around Kampala. These were not the usual random roadblocks. This time the enemy had a specific group of people in their sights, a few youthful men who should be rounded up.

I should digress here and express my respect for people such as Male and Hajji Kigongo, who seemed to know Kampala city better than the backs of their hands. On the way from Entebbe we did not meet with any hostility. The only person we met was Edward Rurangaranga, an old UPC diehard christened "major" by Obote because of his activities in advancing the UPC cause. The old man was in his Land Rover driving to Entebbe. He must have had a hangover since he never paid any attention at all, being too busy trying to steer his vehicle, which was wobbling all over the road. As we climbed Kibuye Hill we noticed soldiers setting up a hasty roadblock at the Kibuye roundabout. It is the junction where Entebbe Road, Kampala Road and Masaka Road converge. It is a very strategic intersection if one were dealing with amateurs. However, when one has to contend with the likes of Male and Hajji Kigongo, whom I suspect must have had some experience as taxi drivers in Kampala, even at the point where the roadblock was located the ground loses its tactical importance. We simply turned right and entered the Kibuye market. The market was in full swing, and touts were shouting and the customers bargaining. Nobody paid any attention to the two vehicles which were snaking their way around the market stalls. We edged forward at a snail's pace, dodging stalls and pedestrians and men carrying sacks of charcoal, best known in Uganda as *fasi fasi*, meaning "Space! Space!" or "Open the way! Open the way!" Soon we were through the market and had crossed Masaka Road and reached the old wall fence of the Kabaka's palace, which then was the headquarters of the famous Central Brigade of Bazilio Okello and Caption Ageta. Talk of putting one's hand in the tiger's mouth! We were literally sitting on the cat's belly. We drove along the wall till we reached Kabakanjagala Avenue. That is the hell's gate road between the Kabaka's palace, then the headquarters of the Central Brigade, and Republic House, at that time the army headquarters. This place is Bulange — "the Buganda Parliament". This is the road where Captain Ageta had murdered my friend, G.G. Kalenzi, some time back. This was the headquarters of hell, if there has ever been one.

Confidently, we drove up to the quarter guard of Republic House. I have read many thrillers and watched James Bond films in which the main actor enters the enemy's bedroom. This was more like it. Only, this was in real life and not fiction. We turned right, circumventing the Republic House wall, and that is where I lost track. Our vehicles made many unpredictable turns and soon I did not know whether we were heading east or west. Eventually we found ourselves in Buwambo, that is southeast of Bombo barracks. The question now was how to cross the Kampala-Gulu highway in order to go back to our areas of operation. After crossing many footpaths passing through people's compounds, we ended up in Kigogwa, the very place where I had joined the bush. Kigogwa is situated 14 miles from Kampala on the Gulu road.

The warm UNLA welcome

We met our people under Commander Sam Magara, who was now the acting army commander. He had brought two sections of soldiers as the reception committee. We slept soundly but at around 10.00 a.m. on the morning of 10 December 1981, the enemy attacked. Somehow our tracks had remained visible, so the enemy followed us to our resting place. They started firing while they were still far away, and at the same time, they tried to surround us in the thicket where we had camped. There was a stampede when we tried to withdraw. It was our doctrine, reminiscent of Tsan Tzu's *Art of War* teaching, that when the enemy attacks, you withdraw; when he follows, you ambush; when he camps, you harass. Withdrawing from a thick forest criss-crossed by river tributaries was not very easy. We plunged into the middle of the forest with the aim of getting out on the opposite side.

As we emerged we bumped into an enemy group that was trying to encircle the forest. They fired at us and we rushed back into the forest. That was when Museveni fell into a ditch and our comrades used him as a stepping board as they flew across a rivulet. I, with the help of Commander Joram Mugume, now a retired major general and former deputy army commander of UPDF, pulled Museveni up. Museveni became quite stubborn. He wanted to turn back and fight, instead of just fleeing. His reason was that it was unbecoming for a man to be shot in the back. To him that was a sign of cowardice and did not suit for a leader. We persuaded him, arguing that we were too few to put up any meaningful resistance. Eventually he agreed and we continued running. After some time, we came out of the forest and climbed a hill. Our comrades were making good speed while we, the Nairobi group, were finding the going tough. The bush boys really had stamina and were overtaking us as if they possessed engines in their chests, while we, the Nairobi group, climbed the hill ponderously. To lighthen the moment I told my comrades, Mzee inclusive, that the UNLA was generously helping us get rid of the sausages and bacon of Nairobi.

After a brief rest we continued until we reached a place called Bubale, where a bigger force of ours was stationed. This force had commanders like Salim Saleh, Kyaligonza, Mugabi and others. We had instructed our rear guard to plant anti-personnel mines (APMs) in our wake to discourage the pursuing enemy troops. I highly doubt whether the APMs were well laid; most likely they were just thrown on the route because of the pace at which we were withdrawing. Despite the undignified way in which we arrived, our comrades welcomed us heartily. It was good to be back where we felt we belonged. To some of us coming back to the bush was much more heart-warming than our sojourn in Nairobi had been. To us this was home, nay, much more than home because we were among real friends, people who were willing to lay down their lives for us, as we were ready to lay down our own lives for them. It was a grand reunion. Some comrades had joined from the enemy ranks while we were still in Nairobi. The main topic was who was where and who had not yet come, who had fallen to the enemy and who was still alive but unable to join. There was a lot of news. A number of operations had been carried out while we were away. Our ranks had swollen tremendously. We were now a formidable force and no longer a bunch of fugitive soldiers. The civilians' support was really touching, everybody wanted to contribute in any way possible. Stories of the heroic deeds of our comrades were many. The most captivating was the introduction of landmine warfare into the PRA, now NRA.

The weapons promised by the Libyan leader had arrived but most of our people, the former UNLA, were at first disappointed when they received a few guns and some ammunition with some boxes which they did not know how to use. However, one of our new comrades was a former Uganda Army ordinance/demolition expert. He told our people that those boxes contained both anti-vehicle and anti-personnel mines. Of course our people were skeptical about the effectiveness of these new devices. The former UA comrade whom we soon baptised *Mutalamu*, a Kiswahili word for "expert", took our boys to demonstrate to them the power of mines.

After we had successfully overrun Buwambo Police Post, Mutalamu laid four anti-vehicle mines (AVM) on the corners of the police building after everyone had withdrawn. He then detonated the mines using a vehicle battery. According to our comrades, even as they were narrating the story three months later, the debris of the police post was still wafting down from the air. From that day on, and especially after a few practical demonstrations involving enemy vehicles being blown up, the NRA started respecting mine warfare. Many skirmishes had taken place, mostly ambushes and shots during raids. In one of these raids Commander Elly Tumwine lost an eye. This was during the operation in Bukomero on 1 November 1981.

So while we were entering the bush, Tumwine was being stealthily evacuated from the frontline to our rear, which was, ironically, Kampala, the capital city. The overwhelming civilian support was at work. Tumwine, a wounded guerrilla commander, was operated upon by government doctors at Mulago Hospital, just as the body of Comrade Seguya, the first PRA army commander, was treated and preserved at the same hospital. In fact, instead of the guerrillas being surrounded, it was the UNLA which was surrounded by angry civilians.

One of the victorious battles we were told about was the destruction of a World War II vintage Sherman tank. This tank, which ought to have belonged to a war museum, was assembled and driven from Kampala to Bombo. The idea, according to the enemy, was that the mere noise of the tank engine would throw the guerrillas into disarray. This was good reasoning on the part of the enemy because throughout my stay in the army, I found that African soldiers, perhaps because of lack of exposure, fear the sound of the guns more than their actual effect. Africans have a deep fear of the unknown, and field guns can easily disorganise a well-established African army. A good example is the Uganda Army, which was routed by the so-called *Saba Saba* (BM21s, 122 mm howitzers and sometimes tracer mortar bombs fired by the TPDF). The Uganda Army soldiers believed that the bombs would hunt them down like guided missiles and so they fled. The Tanzanians had taken eight months to march from the Tanzanian border to the Sudanese border, and it is a proven fact that less than 10% of the 20,000 Ugandan Army personnel (of Idi Amin) died. Because of the noise of the guns, however, that psychological fear of noise is still embedded in the African soldier's psyche.

The UNLA, in their wisdom, thought that with a tank paving the way, the guerrillas' ambushes would just disintegrate. In fact, when the civilian lookouts came to report that a tank was advancing, they showed signs of resignation. To them the war was over, since a tank was a machine, which, unlike enemy soldiers, could not be defeated. There was near-panic among both the guerrillas and their civilian supporters. Then three comrades, Julius Aine, Enock Mondo and Dampa (Benjamin Muhanguzi) volunteered to go and investigate this new threat. Armed only with one RPG which had one shell, one anti-tank grenade rifle and one AK-47, they went out on the first tank-hunting mission in the history of the Ugandan armed forces. The old tank had broken down at 21 km on the Kampala-Bombo road and the operators were trying to repair it. Our comrades hit the tank with only one RPG shell and it burst into flames. The tank hunters flew back to the bush, chased by the blasts of the tank bombs. They did not know that the bombs were going off at random since nobody was firing at them, so they continued running till they reached their camp.

It is sad that the only surviving testimony to that heroic feat is the desolate tank shell, which, until 2003 still lay 21 km from Kampala on Bombo road. The three heroes are all dead. However, their feat marked the end of tank warfare in the history of the struggle. Incidentally, most of that tank's crew members soon deserted the UNLA and joined the bush fighters, their reasoning being that if the guerillas could disable a piece of hardware such as a tank then they must be winning the war. If, as the old saying goes, you cannot beat them, then join them, they reasoned. Some of those former tank crew members became very good fighters, such as my friends Medi, Kawuma and Magezi. Such and many other interesting stories were what we had missed while in Nairobi. On our part, we had few exciting stories to tell and so we did more of the listening.

After reorganisation, the Chairman of the High Command (CHC), Yoweri Museveni, started to tour the units, since now we had units to tour and no longer only the one camp we had previously set out from. As soon as we joined our people, I requested the CHC to excuse me from the duties of ADC. My reason was that my training was in combat duties and not political leadership, so I felt that my skills were needed elsewhere. I requested an independent command. The truth of the matter was that I would be missing most of the action, the thrill, the surge of adrenaline while in combat and the subsequent euphoria of having achieved a mission, if I remained an ADC. The other underlying factor was that I was not good at what is known as palace politics. I have always been poor at protocol and office duties. I was trained and I enjoyed being a field person. The CHC acknowledged my wish and promised me a unit. I felt as exhilarated as when, two and a half years before, Commander Fred Rwigyema had released me from acting as military police personnel and given me command of my company during the Kakoba days. In the meantime, however, I still acted as the CHC's ADC as we toured and reorganised the units.

While the first stories were about the success of our comrades, we soon started getting negative stories. In any new organisation, especially during a new guerilla war, it is not advisable for the leader to be away for long. While we were in Nairobi, some problems had cropped up among our comrades. The main one was the question of leadership. Who was senior to whom? The trained members of our group were soldiers who had deserted a formal army and so felt the temptation to rebel. The civilian recruits had never known the unquestioning acceptance of orders expected of any soldier, but the most disturbing group was the university students who had deserted the campus to join the bush fighters. Some former student guild leaders assumed that because of their academic superiority, they would automatically be the leaders of the rebel group. The intellectuals, as they were called, could not imagine how a peasant who did not even have shoes on his feet could order them to fall in line. "We have led hundreds of university students," they reasoned. "How can we take orders from people who cannot even write their own names?" they wondered. The bush corporals and sergeants just told them off: "You have been leading people armed with plates and cups and at the worst books! But here we are armed with guns and bullets and bombs, so your qualifications are immaterial."

This may appear to the simple quibbling among young men. However, it had a long-lasting and dangerous impact, especially in an army still in its infancy, more so if that army comprises rebels and lacks mechanisms for imposing law and order. There were no prisons and even the types of punishment to be given to wrongdoers had not been agreed upon. To make matters worse, Commander Magara, who was now acting army commander, wanted to impose his authority by using harsh methods. Soon divisions surfaced among this group, which was less than a year old. There were the former government soldiers who demanded unquestioning military discipline, the intellectuals who advocated explanation and consensus and the civilian recruits who felt that since they had run away from government tyranny, they could not be reprimanded by anybody.

The most damaging act by Commander Magara was the killing, by firing squad, of one of the oldest combatants, Shaban Kashanku. Shaban had been to Mozambique and had trained in urban warfare, so he acted as a courier between the people in the bush and the supporters in Kampala. In order to avoid attracting attention, Shaban had to dress and behave like a town person. Also, to establish contact, he had to stay in town for long periods of time but this did not go down well with the people in the bush. Soon he was being accused of being a "soft fist" and a malingerer. When the enemy offensives intensified, he was cut off from the people in the bush. When he surfaced later on, he was accused of being an enemy agent, he was tried and condemned to death by firing squad. All this happened the span of a few days, like all field courts martial. The execution of Shaban did not go down well with the comrades; not everyone supported it.

It was in the heat of that internal disgruntlement that I accompanied the CHC on his tour of our units, Nkrumah in Singo, Mondlane, Lutta and Kabalega in the Luweero areas. In each unit we carried out joint meetings with both officers and men. The CHC allowed the combatants to freely air their grievances. Many officers were found to be at fault and that is when our methods of work were spelt out to us. The situation would have been disastrous but I think two factors held our people together and stopped the group from disintegrating. The first one was that the government wanted all of us dead, and the treatment of captured rebels by the government forces was something nobody wished to undergo. The NASA operatives and the UNLA soldiers had earned themselves the reputation of being the most heinous group in Uganda's history so that no sane person could even imagine surrendering to them. The next and most important factor was the return of Mzee Museveni who had gone abroad to acquire weapons for the guerrillas. There was the belief that when Mzee, as the CHC was fondly known, returned, everything would be all right. Hope is a wonderful glue that keeps people from degenerating into senseless anarchical beings. People live through hell on earth because they hope there will be a heaven after death.

Our comrades' hope in their leader kept them from disintegrating into armed bandits like most of the other groups that were fighting Obote's regime. As I stated earlier, there were more than twenty groups fighting Obote's regime. However, it is the NRM/NRA which survived until it captured power after five years. Our main secret was the right method of work. We held meetings with the units whose population now numbered around 900 people, most of whom were unarmed but ready to take up arms when arms became available. The CHC had a hard time explaining to these angry civilians the intricacies of obtaining weapons from beyond Uganda.

At one time one, civilian comrade Rwamulago asked the CHC to be specific. He used an old native analogy of the legendary *Ishe Katabazi*. Ishe Katabazi is a folklore character who used to ask and do funny but educative things. Rwamulago asked the CHC "Sir, you have left us in suspense! You know, sir, as Ishe Katabazi once said, when someone beckons me with his hand I know that that person is calling me, when a person shoos away with his hand, I understand the person is chasing me away. However, if someone just waves his hand from left to right I do not understand. Now, sir, we have heard all the talks you have given, are the weapons coming or not?" We all stifled nervous fits of laughter as the CHC laboured to explain how far the weapons negotiations had gone. This was one of the many tactics the CHC used to mould a group of rebel soldiers, undisciplined civilians and arrogant intellectuals into a formidable, highly disciplined (by Ugandan standards anyway) and focused force, which has transformed Uganda's political history irreversibly, the capacity to listen to anybody regardless of rank and then explain.

It was through explanation and understanding of what was at stake that consensus was built right from the raw recruit up to the high command. Everyone knew what we were fighting for and why and how we were going to win the war. Up to today, more than two decades after we left the bush, most Ugandans still wonder how we were able to view Uganda's problems in such an analytical and uniform way. People think we were brainwashed. It was not brainwashing, it was a systematic analysis of the situation and coming up with a logical conclusion, given the circumstances. The first lesson was to identify and isolate the enemy. The next was to try and persuade as many Ugandans as possible to join our cause. That is after asking yourself, is the cause I am fighting for right, not only in my eyes but also in the eyes of most Ugandans? Were we for the people or were we against the people? The most crucial question was whether the war was winnable. It was through this analysis that we adopted the code of operation and the code of conduct of the NRA. The codes have stood the test of time and have even been integrated into the Uganda constitution. Our belief has always been that, when you are fighting for what is right even against the biggest odds, you will win, provided you use the right, strategy and tactics, bearing in mind the people's views.

After meeting at Kanyanda in Segirinnya forest, which had become the de facto headquarters, I was given command of the C coy sector. C coy was part of the mobile brigade which was always on call, while the other units such as Lutta, Kabalega and Mondlane were zonal forces. The mobile brigade always went where it was most needed. It was a sort of rapid deployment force under the command of Commander Salim Saleh and Fred Rwigyema. Whenever there was a lull in the enemy offensive, this brigade split into companies and guarded our operational areas. Owing to the use of mines and many successful ambushes, the enemy was now besieged in Kampala and Bombo while the whole swathe of territory comprising Semuto, Kapeka and 'Masulita' — that is Wakiso up to Kyamusisi in Singo — the so-called Luweero Triangle, was effectively under the NRA.

We had created a nation within a nation. We went about establishing our own administration known as the Resistance Council (RC) system. Owing to the size of the area under our control, the civilian population was big and we could not be everywhere to police them. We asked them to elect from among themselves people whom they trusted as their leaders. The first RC to be established was in Kannyanda and I am happy to have been there to witness its establishment.

For the first time, people were creating their own administration without waiting for orders from above. The RC system became so popular in Uganda that even today is viewed by many Ugandans as the best system to govern this country. To some of us, all this fuss about people's governance seemed of no importance. What we were more interested in was how to fight and win the war. The CHC saw the fallacy in our thinking and introduced political education in the army. Since we had little historical knowledge of the military, we believed that politics and the army could never go hand in hand. In most army establishments there is an unwritten law that politics and religion should never be discussed in the mess. As soldiers, we believed that politics belonged to civilians and intellectuals who, in any case, were unfit for military service or, as a Tanzanian instructor believed, could only be lazy cadets.

My interest in the formation of the first RC in Uganda was only for the safety of the CHC and the many civilians who had rallied around him. In those days, any gathering of people in the Luweero Triangle was a legitimate target for the UNLA's massacres. So while people were jubilating about who had become RC I secretary for youth, I was on the lookout for any enemy agent. The good thing about dealing with peasants at the grassroots is that each person is known to, and knows, the other person, so it is not easy for a hostile foreigner to infiltrate them.

In order to introduce effective political education in the army, the CHC introduced the rank of cadre. A cadre was a person who understood what the war was all about, why it was being fought, how it would be won, and was able to explain all this to someone else. A cadre was someone who understood the war strategy and tactics and was able to defend the cause with his own life. Hence, ideally a cadre had to be a good combatant with leadership potential. The group best suited for this rank, according to the CHC, were the intellectuals. The university students and graduates could easily articulate the cause to the masses. Most of the elite civilians were made cadres.

It is unfortunate that this decision rekindled the old division between the trained peasants and the arrogant intellectuals who had never fired a bullet in anger or been fired upon with the aim of being killed by the enemy. Resentment towards cadreship cropped up. The fighters, as they called themselves, found it hard to respect these untrained fellows from Makerere University. On their part, the intellectuals resented the peasant sergeants and corporals who were called upon to drill them into soldiers. A cold war ensued between the instructors, who could not even write their names but understood military science, and the educated elite who could not dismantle and assemble a rifle in the given training time or even understood basic military science.

The group selected for cadreship were sent to a training wing in Kasejjere, in the Singo area. In their misconception, the instructors tried to make soldiers out of this bunch of civilian intellectuals, so they were a bit harsh. The intellectuals were not any better. Instead of "committing intellectual suicide", as the late Samora Machel of Mozambique called it, they maintained their arrogance and only a few managed to become real soldiers.

Of the few who agreed to become soldiers, some became really good fighters and commanders, people such as the late Jet Mwebaze, the late Kagumire and a few others. The rest remained desk-bound officers and they are still more into politics and intelligence than in the fighting forces.

Political education proved very valuable to us in the long run although some of us initially rejected it. It was during those political lessons that we learned of a new phenomenon called the people's protracted war. This was very different from what we had been introduced to in our recruitment and the military academies we had attended. This was a war with no beginning and no end. It was a war which did not have communication lines and a logistical chain — It was war with no defined duration. This was a war which could end any day — this week, or in ten years. There were no medical supplies, no casualty evacuation procedure (CASEVAC). On the front, one rarely expected re-enforcement since everyone would be involved. Each individual guerrilla was a military formation of his own.

Most important, we learned that we were a people's army and not government soldiers who expected salaries at the end of the month. We were freedom fighters and our pay would be the freedom of Uganda. We learned the differences between career professional soldiers, warriors and liberators. We belonged to the last category. In order to be equal to the task, we had to identify more with the civilian population. We started shunning high-sounding military ranks, such as general, brigadier or colonel, which we associated with the oppressive government we were fighting. When assessing a new entrant, the question was not how well-trained the person was, but if the person was angry enough with the government to want to fight it.

It was a totally different approach from the standard military discipline and ethics that is taught in military institutions, though we maintained military tactics and formations. Those we viewed as just a means and not ends in themselves. Concepts like ground of tactical importance lost meaning. Sayings like one would rather lose a battle and not time were laughed at. Who cared about time in a protracted struggle anyway? We valued the number of soldiers and the amount of ammunition we used more than capturing a tactical hill or a bridge. It was better to run away and fight another day than die in an attempt to capture a town. As a people's army, our allegiance was to the civilian population who were our fathers, mothers and siblings. They were the source of our food and recruits and the mighty shield that protected us from the enemy. The civilians gave us information and denied the same to the enemy. Any commander who has ever been to war knows the value of information.

It is information that dictates a commander's plans, his deployment and assessment of the situation. The civilian population was providing us with information while the enemy would be led off course while chasing us. The civilians afforded us the most accurate information about the enemy's whereabouts. Therefore, the critical thing was to be friendly to the people. As Mao Tse-Tung stated about a people's war, the population was the water and a guerrilla is a mere fish, which has to swim and live in that water, so he should never antagonise the water.

For effective control of our operational zone, we staged ambushes at all the inlets. The triangle is bordered by the big rivers Kafu, Katonga and Mayanja, whose many tributaries criss-cross the triangle. All the roads into the triangle have to cross one river tributary or another and it is at those river crossings that we set up obstacles to any enemy movement. Apart from landmines, which had paralysed the enemy's motor movement, the river crossings also constituted good killing ground for any advancing enemy.

My sector of command was C coy, on the Kalongero bridge facing the Masuulita-Kakiri access and Danze bridge on the Matugga-Bombo access through Kalasa. We dug good trenches and cleared the killing fields at all the river crossings and for some time we concentrated on training and mobilising of the masses.

It was after appreciating that our war was a protracted war that we set about acclimatising ourselves to the local, peasant way of life. In about two months we had become like the peasants. Soon we were on first name terms with all the elders, most of the young men joined and were recruits in training, and the young girls started eyeing us. One of the rules in the code of conduct was that a guerrilla should never get involved with the local girls since, according to our leadership, each woman must have a father and a mother and also a suitor or a husband so there were no free women for soldiers. This matter and the issue of telling soldiers to abstain from indulging in alcohol were supposed to become the norm but this never came to pass. At one point, in a meeting of senior officers, when the CHC was telling us to stop drinking, one comrade, former Uganda Army Captain Matovu, suggested that, since there was no whisky which was usually drunk at the officers' mess while preparing for a briefing, we as guerrillas could do with *waragi*, a local Ugandan spirit which was readily available. Of course, those of us who knew the CHC's distaste for alcohol just looked on, expecting the big man to explode in anger. However, being the person he is, the CHC calmly explained the danger of being caught off guard by the enemy when drunk.

9

UFM Attack on Lubiri

When Prince Jjuuko and his Tanzanian witchdoctor failed to convince us to attack Kampala in April 1981, the prince did not give up hope. He looked for the next group fighting the Obote regime and discovered that there was no group better positioned than the Uganda Freedom Movement (UFM), led by Dr Andrew Lutakome Kayira, a former prison officer and criminologist by profession and born in the area. The UFM, like Fedemu, Vuumbula, Buruli Fighters and other groups opposed to the government, was fighting on the periphery of Kampala city. The UFM was a much more serious group than the others. We had met the UFM in Nairobi, agreed to work together but not merge, the same agreement we made with the UFF of Yusuf Lule.

The UFM had highly placed people in all walks of life, and in their diplomatic work they were better placed than the NRA/NRM. Their propaganda machinery was very active and to some extent effective. When the Libyan leader, Col. Muamar Gadaffi, was sending overtures to the PRA, the UFM also got an invitation. Therefore, when the CHC went to Libya, he also met a UFM delegation there. The Libyan leader could not understand why the two groups were not working together. Col. Gadaffi's view was that if all opposition groups could merge, he would facilitate the removal of Obote. This was the view held by all foreign powers and even donors when they met groups of dissidents fighting a common enemy. Their advice is always to merge the dissident forces into one big opposition force. The Tanzanians had done it through the formation of UNLF when they brought together all the groups opposing Idi Amin. Even recently, when a non-Congolese saw the factions fighting to overthrow President Joseph Kabila, he would wonder why they did not unite since they controlled a bigger part of the Democratic Republic of Congo (DRC) than the DRC government at that time.

These issues are more complicated than they sound. In other words, the intrinsic necessity of forming a union or a nation is best understood by the main stakeholders of that nation, who are the natives. It is an established fact that a revolution is never imported, neither can it be exported, so while Mwalimu Nyerere of Tanzania and Muamar Gadaffi of Libya wanted to export their own version of Uganda's revolution, they were both unsuccessful.

At the end of the meeting between the Libyan leader, the CHC of the NRA, the UFM delegation and Brigadier Moses Ali's Uganda National Rescue Front (UNRF), it was agreed that each group would be assisted separately. However, it was also agreed that the fighting groups should co-ordinate their operations.

The UFM had established a base around Kampala where they carried out high propaganda-oriented operations like urban terrorism. They received a bigger part of the Libyan consignment of arms, which was supposed to have been shared equally with the NRM. However, owing to the streetwise methods of Kayira's group, the biggest chunk went to them. Now UFM, with this consignment of arms and relying on Prince Jjuuko and his Tanzanian juju man's counsel, decided to attack Kampala and overthrow Obote's government in one blistering operation. For some time, the UFM had been provoking the UNLA and running away to find refuge in our operational zone, leaving the civilians to face the wrath of the enraged soldiers. This time they decided to attack the queen bee of a very active beehive.

The attack on Lubiri barracks, which was the headquarters of the UNLA's Central Brigade of Brigadier Bazilio Olara Okello and the nerve centre of the regime, was carried out in May 1982. It should be remembered that Prince Jjuuko had told us to attack in April 1981. Now Kayira's group, in their military judgement, thought that after one year and with guns from Libya, the capture of Kampala would be a mere walkover. When we later talked to the young men who had participated in the attack on Lubiri barracks, some of us felt not only sympathetic but were ashamed to see how backward and easily deceived an African youth can be. The preparation for the attack on Lubiri not only lacked any military science but even an idea about the fundamental effect of the weapons. At least, they should have known the difference between a rocket-propelled grenade (RPG), a shoulder-fired missile and a mortar bomb.

Here again the African misconception of machines was at play. There was the belief that mere noise can cause harm to one's enemy, just like the noise from *Saba Saba* had scared the Uganda Army into panicky disarray. The UFM combatants crawled near the fence of the Lubiri barracks and fired RPG shells in the air. Somehow they thought the RPG mid-air bursts would affect the enemy. To add to the fracas, the UFM combatants had come with three motorised lawn mowers which they had placed at the four corners of the palace wall. They imagined that somehow a lawn mower sounds like the firing of a medium machine gun. The UFM combatants expected the UNLA soldiers simply to come out of their trenches with their hands up and surrender to the conquering UFM.

The attack was the kind of fiasco worth noting in the annals of Uganda's military history. It was a huge victory on the UNLA's part and a real disaster on the part of the UFM. The UFM was dispersed in such a manner that their commander-in-chief, Kayira, made one of the most famous withdrawals in history, since he only managed to reorganise himself in Washington, DC, in the USA. According to the participants in that infamous attack, the withdrawal signal was *Buliomu kululwe*, a Luganda expression for "everyone on his own". After being abandoned by their commanders, the UFM scattered in all directions. Not only did the UFM commanders and their soldiers abandon their mission altogether but they also abandoned the civilian population. When the UNLA stormed out of the confines of their barracks, they were like lions that had escaped from a cage. They were really hungry and angry.

The UNLA unleashed hitherto unheard-of terror on anything they came across on their way from the moment they left the gates. They panned out, shooting, killing and looting anything in their way. Lubiri hill, where their headquarters was located, is the centre of the Buganda kingdom and directly overlooks Kampala city centre. The indigenous population around were the enemy, so the soldiers did what they thought had to be done. Goats, cows, chickens, ducks were all looted. The looting and raping spree took about three days before it calmed down. By then, the looters had advanced from Lubiri barracks in a radius of 10 kilometres on all sides. The Baganda as a people easily get excited, so when the civilians started running away from the rampaging soldiers, even those who were five kilometres away did not wait. Soon the whole town was deserted. All a person needed was to hear that there was fire in Lubiri. Whether one was in Bwaise, on Bombo Road or Nakawa on Jinja Road, nobody hesistated. Household property was abandoned; at worst babies and toddlers were also abandoned.

Stories are told of a soldier from the Makindye military police barracks (it was not only Lubiri on the rampage, even Makindye, Bombo and Bugolibi barracks had joined in the free-for-all looting) who looted a mattress but on reaching his *uniport* found that he had carried a two-day-old baby rolled in the mattress. Nobody bothered to find out the fate of that baby.

After the attack, each of the combatants was left to his own devices as their withdrawing command had directed. Quite a few were caught quite easily like grasshoppers, a replication of what had befallen the invaders of Uganda in 1972. Only, this time the civilians were not on the side of the government forces. All the civilians and the UFM fighters were on the run — each person was on his own.

It was in the middle of this pandemonium that one of the UFM fighters had the presence of mind and the courage to jump into a truck which still had some weapons that had not yet been deployed and drive it away from the Lubiri quarter guard. This young fighter, the late Lt. Colonel Ssonko Lutaya, nicknamed *Stamina* because of his weightlifter's physique, drove the vehicle outside Kampala and debated where to proceed with it. The UFM had attacked the enemy and had not prepared any fallback position. They had no rear base; they had attacked with no hope of withdrawing. In their thinking, I deduce, they were saying no retreat, no surrender. Their aim was to capture Lubiri, advance on Makindye, capture Radio Uganda, and the war would be over. It is absurd but most banana republics in Africa are overthrown in that manner and Uganda is unfortunate enough to have had three similar government overthrows.

All the rebel soldiers had to do was capture the national radio and make an announcement of a takeover. Amin had done it in 1971, Oyite Ojok with the help of TPDF had done it in 1979. So why not the UFM in 1982! African governments from the 1960s up to the 80s were prone to being overthrown on radio. The national radio was the only channel of communication between the leader and the led. In fact, in 1990, while I was attending a course in Ghana, it had been arranged for us as candidates of the Ghana Armed Forces Staff College (GAFSC) to visit the Ghana Broadcasting Corporation (GBC). The visit never materialised, as the GBC was considered a very sensitive national security secret which could not be accessed by a senior officer in training. This must have been a valid fear because the then president, Flight Lieutenant JJ Rawlings, had used the same facility to announce his coups, not once but twice. The UFM plan did not lack precedents.

Back to Stamina. After realising that the base from which they had set off, that is Nswanjere forest on Mityana road, was inaccessible because the UNLA had already surrounded the forest, Ssonko decided to do the only logical thing — to drive towards the NRA operational area. After all, the NRA were a friendly force and not as hostile as the UNLA. It was an important decision on his part since he was just a junior man and he knew that the leadership of his organisation had no kind words for the NRA, which was "led by westerners". Lutaya took the initiative as a fighter to save the weapons from falling into the hands of the UNLA and headed towards Masuulita. To date Lt. Colonel Maj. Ssonko Lutaya Stamina is recognised as one of the heroes of the NRA/NRM struggle.

I was at my tactical headquarters, the hill overlooking Kalongero bridge, when three civilians carrying three guns each and riding at breakneck speed reported to me that "our guns had arrived". It was around 10.00 a.m. and I had just had my breakfast and was contemplating what the day would bring. We were engaged in training and mobilising the civilians because of the lull in enemy activities. I had planned a rally in Bugozi in the Semuto area. Our methods were rather reactive and not proactive. We used to wait for the enemy to make a move and we would respond appropriately. So, usually, from 4.00 a.m. we would enter our trenches and wait for the enemy, and if by 8.00 a.m. the enemy had not attacked or if we had received no information from our lookouts about enemy movement, then we would prepare breakfast and go about our daily routines.

These vigilantes came with about nine guns but without bullets and reported that our weapons were in the vehicle, which was stuck in the mud near Dambwe. Immediately, I sent a message to the CHC who was in the camp in Kikunyu, just four miles from my camp, and set off with about a section and some young civilian men. In just a few minutes, starting with a section, I had about a platoon of young men, all eager to go and get "our" guns. The CHC also set off immediately with just one section. This time we travelled in broad daylight, which was against our standard operational procedure.

It is amazing how even peasants can organise themselves when they identify with a task. Almost all the able-bodied members of Kalongero organised themselves into a good formation and the lorry which had been stuck about twenty kilometres from our defence was pushed out of the mud and, with jubilant young men and women accompanying it, it entered our operational area around 10.00 p.m.

It was a big haul of weaponry with more than 200 rifles, some mortars and machine guns. Lutaya, now perceived by all as a hero, had been removed from behind the steering wheel and another person drove the lorry up to Kirema Primary School, which was to be used as the offloading and distribution centre for the weapons.

While everyone was commending comrade Lutaya's initiative and bravery and lauding him as a hero, the poor man had his misgivings. He did not know what reception he would get from these "westerners" whom his leaders in UFM had always talked ill of. There was also a feeling of deserting one's comrades. On top of that, he had a mortar fragment in his buttock and he was tired and hungry. I went and saw him where he was lying down on a mattress and started talking to him. He was happy to be met by someone who could talk to him on the same wavelength and who reasoned like him. We immediately struck up a rapport and he was a faithful soldier and officer until his death due to natural causes in 2002.

The Kikunyu-Kalongero bridge

After distributing the weapons brought by Lutaya among the units, my sector C coy area was augmented with a medium machine gun (MMG), some RPGs, some anti-tank rifles, grenades and a few more rifles. We grew from company strength to about a company and a half. I was now in charge of the main enemy entrances; the Kalongero bridge on River Danze and the Danze bridge on the road from Matugga to Ssemuto. These two sectors were crucial as they were the only main points of access.

If the enemy wanted to dislodge us from Ssemuto, which had now become our de facto capital, they had to use the two bridges. The areas of Kikunyu, Ssemuto and even Masulita across the bridge were under my command. The headquarters was in the Kikunyu area. Mondlane from Nakatagira up to Bugozi Hill was under Colonel Kihanda. The Kyeererezi up to the *lukoola* area was under Late Colonel Stanley Muhangi.

All these units were designed to put a protective cordon around our operational zone, which we had gone ahead to form into a "government" within a government. Our government was very good since there were no taxes to pay. Neither did it have a prison or a police force. It was the civilians' responsibility to police the entire zone and it was hard to find a case of corruption since the leaders were voluntary workers with no pay. The sector commanders were viewed by the population as governors. We were in charge of their security and they saw us as the answer to what they had always missed. They were in touch with the real power in their midst and they held their destiny in their own hands. As sector commanders, we were responsible for the security of all.

However, we found ourselves solving day-to-day problems, even settling small village disputes. Although most of us were young, elderly people used to come to us for counsel! We had to portray a sense of fair play to win the people's confidence. If it were not for the tight control of the CHC it would have been easy for us to turn into warlords. The type of power we had could only be equated with what I saw in 1987 when I visited Zaire (now Democratic Republic of Congo) and interacted with the governor of the province neighbouring Uganda. A Congolese governor was a real governor in those days. Whatever he demanded would be done without question. In my Kikunyu, Kalongero, Kannyanda and Ssemuto empire, whatever I said would be taken as a serious matter.

During that time, the enemy developed deep fear of landmines and ambushes, so they carried out token missions, when they would fire bullets in the air and go back to their barracks. One thing the UNLA never forgot was to shell the forests of Luweero religiously every morning. This shelling was very beneficial to us, as we were able to show our recruits that the noise that bombs make do not kill. Soon everybody was making fun of the UNLA "good morning Africa", as we called those morning shelling sessions.

10

Kalongero: A Bridge Too Far for UNLA

After dispersing the UFM in Lubiri, the UNLA developed the illusion that they could do to us what they had done to our counterparts. In June 1982, the UNLA launched its first major offensive against us. That is when we started showing the people of Bulemezi that we were capable of defending them. It was also when our recruits received their baptism of fire. The UNLA advance towards our operational zone intensified in May but the major thrust was on the Kalongero and Dambwe bridges on River Mayanja, which was my area of command and my men were more than ready to welcome the UNLA forces.

We had strengthened our trenches and prepared good killing grounds. So when information about the enemy advance reached us, we dug in and waited. The UNLA was a regular army and the soldiers did their fighting in a regular, regimented manner. They would come from their base in Bombo early, start fighting at around 8.00 a.m. and withdraw back to their base by 6.00 p.m. They were fighting as if they regarded a battle as a simple trip to their offices. They would start shelling at around 8.00 a.m. and this would go on for about one hour and then they would advance. The first batch we fought against were poorly trained Acholi militiamen known as NYA (not yet allotted army number). These were peasant boys whom Chief of Staff Brigadier Oyite Ojok had armed and brought to Kampala to terrorise the civilians, with the lame excuse of providing security for the 1980 elections. They had the misconception that they were brave warriors who were not subject to fear, unlike the lazy westerners whom they liked to refer to as *Banyarwanda*. High on bhang and *waragi*, they called themselves *wang peding*, *macho kali* (fearless, red-eyed) while singing, and with flutes and horns blaring, after bombing an area, they expected to find us already gone. They had convinced themselves that we who were not from any of the acknowledged warrior communities unlike them, could not withstand the air burst shelling and their bloodcurdling cries. So they marched to battle without taking cover; they called that *kifuwa wazi* (open-chested march).

Poor fellows, they were in for unpleasant surprises. We would just lie still and wait until they were in our killing grounds and then just mow them down. The story of the headless combatants represents one of the many common incidents of those battles on the bridges.

One incident, which will remain implanted in my soul, is a battle at Kalongero Bridge, where I met Marius Suicide Katungi with another combatant, evacuating a fallen comrade. I was taking chains of general purpose machine gun (GPMG) bullets to Enock Mondo, who was our best machine gunner, who waited in a trench under a hail of bullets and bombs, when I met these two carrying a combatant, each holding the soldier under the armpit and balancing him upright. The grisly fact was that the soldier had no head.

The enemy soldiers, after many encounters on the river crossing, had mastered the art of firing RPG shells at ground level. We used to call it *kiasi kayacucha* — at toenail level. The combatant had just lifted his head to observe what was happening in front of him when an RPG shell severed it, leaving only a small part of his neck sticking out and spouting blood like a slaughtered bird. The two combatants with their dead comrade, his body still twitching, were only interested in getting their burden out of reach of the enemy soldiers at the risk of their own lives.

It was part of our code of conduct to prevent the enemy from getting our dead bodies, as that was bound to raise the enemy's morale.

Suicide and his comrade proceeded to the rear and I reinforced Mondo. We continued to hold the enemy down and I observed Mondo's body posture. He was really angry at the enemy, gnashing his teeth as he continued picking enemy soldiers off one by one. One thing that made it easier for Mondo to hit the enemy was that, apparently, one of the enemy officers had been hit and was crying out for help. Whoever crawled near enough to help him, offered a good target for Mondo's GPMG.

Kalongero bridge had become a bridge too far for the UNLA. We started enjoying the game and I teased Mondo about expressing anger at the enemy soldiers. "Why do you lose your temper?" I asked him. "You do not know the man from Adam, he is not your rival over a girl and I do not think his father shares a land boundary with your father either, so why the anger? Just relax and shoot straight," I admonished him. But Mondo just ground his teeth and continued firing.

The battle lasted till evening, when the enemy withdrew. We crawled up to their position and charged the dead soldiers' uniforms and guns, as was the norm. That is when I started realising the phenomenon I was to experience many times in battle. The faces of the dead soldiers expressed surprise, not fear or agony, as one would have expected. It was later, while studying psychology at Makerere University, that I learned that the survival mechanism of a soldier does not allow him or her to accept that it could be he who would bite the bullet. Each person has that feeling of "not me". People go to battle expecting to come out alive, and the dead enemy soldiers and our own comrades were no exception.

It was later, after reorganisation at the camp fire, while we were recounting the battle, that the image of the headless soldier hit me. Otherwise, we were too busy counting our losses and gains to think about such mundane things as the dead.

Suddenly, I developed goose pimples and broke into a shiverish cold sweat. I called Suicide Katungi, who was one of the section commanders under me, to ask what had happened to our dead comrade. He told me that burial preparations were under way. That image of the headless soldier has never left my mind. This and many similar experiences taught us that in the middle of a firefight, soldiers' minds concentrate wonderfully on winning the firefight. Then the mundane things, like hunger, thirst or any other physiological needs, tend to be forgotten.

The action of Suicide and his fellow combatant was prompted by the need to uphold the code of conduct and to deny the enemy the sight of the fallen comrade's body, while the cries of help from the enemy officer drew the enemy soldiers' attention. None of the soldiers did what they did with their full consciousness. All were doing what is usually done under such circumstances.

Every soldier, at one time or another, is bound to act like a robot. The act of lovemaking captures that sensation wonderfully at the stage where the two bodies get caught up in that tender rhythm before the climax. The shuddering and goose pimples are somehow similar to the aftereffects of lovemaking, although it is hard to compare the two. Even on a long march there is a time when one loses oneself and becomes part of the march so that one is no longer aware of what the body is doing. However, the feeling of having survived a battle is extraordinarily exhilarating.

Necessity, they say, is the mother of invention; because we had few bullets to spend, as our supplies were not regular, we learned to conserve our firepower. Whereas the UNLA could spend thousands of bullets and bombs, each bullet fired or bomb released by NRA soldiers had to be accounted for. When the enemy stopped using vehicles we turned mines into booby traps. People under the tutelage of Nsungwa, best known as *Mutalamu*, learned how to lay mines and wires with detonators using vehicle batteries; this could blow up columns of advancing UNLA soldiers. It was a high-risk operation since we lacked the security of numbers. The person concerned would lay down his mines, take cover and wait, ready to connect the wires when he saw that a big number of enemy troops were in the mine killing field. Often, the mine would fail to go off. Other times it would detonate prematurely. The most interesting case, however, was when Karate (a nickname this fellow had earned because he had some martial arts skills) was waiting with his eyes glued to an advancing column of UNLA when an enemy soldier put the barrel of his gun on his head and told him to stand up. Unknown to Karate, the enemy had learnt some anti-ambush drills. So, while the main column of the enemy army advanced along the road as usual, sections of the soldiers could move in the bush adjacent to the road. This would be an effective anti-ambush drill. But the UNLA were undisciplined, so they were usually detected before they could hit our ambushing forces.

On this occasion, Karate had been caught with his pants down, as they say. So he sprang to his feet with his arms up as the arresting soldier smiled with triumph. Karate just dived between the soldiers' legs and took off like a rocket. The shower of bullets that were aimed at Karate would have stopped an advancing company of soldiers. However, luckily for Karate, not even one scratched him. Another such incident took place when Samson Mande, now a retired colonel and a renegade, fell in a UNLA ambush in the same area of Danze bridge. The UNLA had, for the first time, come early, and observing unusual discipline, laid an ambush along the road. Mande had set off on a reconnaissance mission with a view to getting a good ambush location. He recalled that, while he was moving in the early dawn looking for a good ambush site and cover, he saw the barrel of a gun which he thought was an abandoned rifle of the many enemy soldiers who usually abandoned these weapons after falling into our ambushes. When he bent over to pick it up the rifle receded. On closer observation he saw a cap. Now, when you are a guerrilla, one of the identifying marks of a government soldier is a cap. Guerrillas have no fancy articles of dress such as caps, so Mande realised that he had entered an enemy ambush.

The ambush was very carefully laid. The enemy had laid a linear ambush on one side of the road, which had forest cover, while the other side was a steep embankment. This particular location had offered us two good harvests of enemy casualties before. Now the roles were reversed. Mande was in the jaws of death. Like any guerrilla, the first reaction was to flee, which Mande did. He must have grown wings because, by the time he reported back to the camp, half of his greatcoat had been cut away as if by scissors, though it was actually by enemy bullets. The fact that Mande and most of us survived must have been a miracle.

The support of the population increased when they noticed that, day in and day out, we were chalking up victories. Human beings have a sense of knowing what the winning side is in any conflict and, like rats that abandon a sinking ship, they always know which side to run to. More and more people started coming from every corner of the country to join us. Stories of defeated and dejected government troops travelled far and wide. The Ugandan population is prone to exaggerating any story, and stories of the invicibility of the NRA spread. The chief campaign manager of the NRA was a former Ugandan president and his soldiers. The UNLA had vowed to beat the stubborn Baganda and westerners, and the target group had demonstrated that they could hit back. What I observed of the UNLA atrocities in West Nile in 1979 was now multiplied many times over. Any non-Ugandan reading about what Joseph Kony and his Lord's Resistance Army are doing cannot believe that it is humanly possible. However, to some of us who had observed the trend of events, this phenomenon started in West Nile in 1979 after the overthrow of Amin. It matured in the Luweero Triangle and is now winding up in Kigtum, Gulu and Pader districts in Acholi, northern Uganda.

By August 1982, we had thoroughly repulsed the UNLA offensive and we had consolidated our defences. The killings on the periphery of our operational zone went on unabated. Soldiers and officers from the so-called wrong communities were being taken and killed at Katikamu, which had become the regime's Treblinka, only that, instead of the gas chambers and other heinous methods used by the Germans, the UNLA were using machetes and bullets. Of the many people who were killed in Katikamu was 2nd Lt. Steven Mwesigwa, who was husband to Petty Kankunda, my wife Dora's sister. We had persuaded this officer to desert Obote's army earlier on, but he held back for no known reason. Whenever he went on a mission to hunt for us guerrillas he would perform well. His seniors felt he was stealing the limelight from them and decided to kill him. Their reasoning was that he had to be on our side since he used to go into the field and come back safe, while his colleagues used to lose soldiers. Therefore, he was supposedly collaborating with the guerrillas.

Someone else close to me was a civilian named Kali. He was the first born in my wife's family. This young man was captured at the beginning of the struggle, imprisoned in Nile Hotel with two current senior officers of the UPDF, and later butchered in Katikamu.

The civilian population was seeing our operational zone as the only safe area in Uganda. No wonder we had a hard time trying to tell them to escape when the going got tough. Many stories are told of individual battles. However, I intend to concentrate on those where I was present. I am aware of the distortion of second-hand narratives. So I will try to tell the story of the revolution as I saw it.

Kakiri II walkover

While we were consolidating our defences and repulsing enemy attacks, we also carried out some offensives. The best defence, according to military doctrine, is offence. We would carry out reconnaissance on an isolated enemy post and destroy it. That is the way we acquired guns and ammunition. At that time the chief logistics officer of the NRA was the government and the UNLA. If we had not captured bullets and arms we would not have survived. The *modus operandi* was to carry out a thorough recce, then attack the unit at dawn. Information was initially received from civilians. Then trained combatants would confirm the truth of the information after meeting with the commanders involved, and the mission would be carried out. We tried to avoid pitched battles since our bullets would never be enough. In fact, whenever a comrade fell to the enemy, the question was always: "Oh, comrade so and so has died, has the gun been taken?" We could not afford to spend bullets like the UNLA, for they were government troops supported by a national economy.

Much explaining is necessary if one has to keep people fighting for long with no visible end to a war. That is why explanation is important. In fact, Sun Tzu, a Chinese military writer, sums it up well when he says that "war is like an illicit love affair, a lot of talk and explaining before, then a short sharp violent action, then a lot of talk and explaining afterwards."

When introducing new recruits to the baptism of fire, it is necessary to aim at high successes on one's own side, so that your troops start believing that they can win. It would be disastrous if, in the first battle, you lost many people or lost complete control, as happened with the UFM. Veterans can afford casualties and they can always withdraw and regroup later, but raw recruits, when routed, will never develop confidence in the whole enterprise.

To wean peasant recruits from their fear of guns and the noise of bombs, the commander must accompany them and show them that sheer noise does not kill and, most importantly, that the enemy is also vulnerable to bullets. They (the enemy) can be killed and they can run away like any other human being.

Our other major battle with our peasant fighters related to their belief in witchcraft. Even the elite believe in it. The peasants from northern Uganda, who were the majority in the UNLA, believed there was some talisman that would make them bulletproof. Our peasant recruits were not any different. It may sound unbelievable but whenever an enemy soldier died in our ambushes, our people, instead of running to take his gun and other military hardware, would first look for the talisman that the enemy soldiers usually wore around their waists or donned as amulets. When asked, the poor recruit would explain to you thus: "You know these people from the North have magic, that is why they have always been soldiers." It was always up to the commander to explain that a bullet travels in a straight line at 2,800 km per second, and if you are in its path no juju can stop it from harming you. Pointing at the dead soldier's body, I would ask if the juju had helped the dead fellow.

Slowly our people started to understand the difference between machines and juju.

However, it was not easy. Later, after the bush war was over, when there was a rebellion in the north of the country, a peasant woman, Alice Lakwena, convinced many able-bodied persons who were unhappy with the "westerners' rule", to follow her. She claimed she had magic which could turn government soldiers' bullets into water while turning the rebels' stones into grenades. Lakwena's actions led to the near-decimation of the Acholi population. Still, the people continued following her until she fled Uganda for Kenya.

Explaining the science of modern weapons and how to deploy them effectively is one of the achievements of the NRA. We called it demystifying the gun.

After repulsing the first UNLA offensive, we started attacking units to acquire weapons and ammunition while, at the same time, introducing our recruits to actual combat situations. It was the best training one could undergo. We did not have war games or simulator equipment. The best war game was actual combat, which created very efficient fighters out of our raw peasants.

Our forces attacked UNLA units in Ssemuto, Singo, Sanga, Masuulita and my company, now led by Salim Saleh, attacked Kakiri for the second time. We were a company full of strong men, with some unarmed fighters whom we called commandos. They helped us carry the captured weapons. The first attack on Kakiri had taught us that it is always good to have people who would carry the captured military materials. It is never prudent to use the fighting group as carriers. The British had found it out earlier than us. That is why during the Second World War, they had the 7th Carrier Corps from Eastern Africa and the 5th carrier corps from Western Africa. The work of these soldiers, who were mostly Africans, was to carry war materials in the densely forested parts of Africa, which lacked communication, and because of the presence of tsetse flies the beasts of burden such as horses, donkeys and mules could not cope well. So the British established those carrier corps, which later constituted the core of the King's African Rifles.

The Africans who became involved in the Second World War were not recruited to do any fighting but to work as beasts of burden. In fact, in Ghana (then the Gold Coast), the motto of one of its units was "through our carriers we fight". The carriers were the black soldiers and the fighters were the whites. Their logo was on the carrying pad used by peasants when fetching water or firewood. Our commandos were mainly recruits whom we wanted to expose to battle. They would stay behind and after the fighters had overrun an enemy defence, they would rush in and carry away the needed war materials. The commandos had another tactical value. Whenever enemy scouts reported on our advance, they would report about big numbers and the enemy would panic.

Enemy reports from peasants would then be highly exaggerated. Because civilians combat uniforms and military boots when they saw a platoon of soldiers they would think it was a company, if not a battalion. A lookout person would storm into the camp and shout *Bayiye* (they have poured), meaning the enemy had poured a lot of troops in his area. When asked how many, he would answer *Buwunga* (maize). When pressed to tell how they had come, the lookout person, without shame, would say, "They have come in one or two Tata lorries with one Land Rover armed with 106 mm."

Anybody with some knowledge of the capacity of a Tata lorry would know the person was talking about one or two companies of soldiers and react appropriately.

The second attack on Kakiri followed almost the same pattern as the first one, only that this time we were more confident; we had the right intelligence information and we were better organised. The fighters had also overcome the usual fear characteristic of the maiden firefight. We had been fired upon and we had fired back for a year now, so there was no panic among us. Besides, the combatants had confidence in their comrades and in their commanders. We had assessed each other in the past skirmishes and now we knew our individual strengths and weaknesses.

Salim Saleh has always proved himself to be a good team leader. He is a highly courageous, if not a reckless fighter and the soldiers had a lot of trust in him. There is a tendency towards hero worship among troops in combat. Some commanders are able to make their troops attain unbelievable combat performance. Field Marshal Montgomery had such an effect on his troops during the Second World War. Soldiers tend to feel that, with such a leader in command, victory and survival are assured. I always felt comfortable going on missions with Salim Saleh. In all the missions we carried out together, we succeeded with the least number of casualties on our side.

The Kakiri II attack was a complete success. It was a walkover. However, it was a nasty walkover. The enemy soldiers had been killing a lot of people and they had placed bodies all around their defence lines, just in front of their trenches where other people would have prepared killing grounds and laid booby traps and mines. The UNLA were using the bodies of civilians as their fence. Even today I do not understand their aim, and if they really ever used those trenches. When we attacked at around 8.30 p.m., the trenches were empty. However, we had to wade through piles of bodies. The attack was a complete rout as had become the norm then, and we charged and withdrew without anybody following us. We passed Masuulita Girls Secondary School and marched in broad daylight back to our base. The civilian population were out in force to welcome their gallant sons.

Bukalabi disaster

Our joy and jubilation after such attacks as Kakiri would not last long. In June 1982 the UNLA, after sensing victory over UFM and being defeated in two major offensives against NRA, now reorganised for what they hoped was a major and final offensive codenamed Operation Bonanza. At the same time we were also reorganising in preparation for the enemy. The first thing we did was to call up most of our combat-tested and trained officers and men and form them into one unit designated D coy. The enemy had also deployed trained UNLA soldiers, unlike in the past when they used ill-trained NYA militias. This was going to be a test for both sides.

Earlier on, the UFM remnants who had run into our operational zone had tried to undermine the civilians' support for us on ethnic grounds. Their argument was that, since the NRA had officers from western Uganda, it should vacate Buganda for the UFM. They reasoned that, since the NRA had taught Baganda youth how to fight in the bushes of Buganda, now the NRA should start fighting in western Uganda.

In the subsequent meetings between NRA and UFM leaders which some of us combat commanders attended, Kayira demanded that the weapons rescued from the Lubiri debacle by Comrade Sonko should be given back to the UFM. After many meetings involving the elders and opinion leaders in the operational zone, Kayira's argument was defeated. He started another line of argument about ranks. Most of the former government soldiers, hence, trained personnel, were from western Uganda. The recruits were mostly local Baganda boys. Kayira's people launched a harmful propaganda. For instance, they claimed that only westerners were armed with guns and, therefore, doing all the fighting, while Baganda boys were recruits armed with sticks and doing all the cooking. It would have been irresponsible of us to arm untrained people with the few guns available in order to appease ethnic sentiments, so we talked to our recruits, who understood.

However, some of the Baganda youth were promised rapid promotion in the UFM and they started deserting with guns. One former policeman, named Bukenya, who had misbehaved at the officers' mess while under the influence of alcohol, was one of the deserters. The UFM mode of promotion was highly irregular, unproportional and unprofessional. The son of a prominent farmer, who had donated a shamba of cassava to the UFM, was immediately made a senior non-commissioned officer (NCO). No wonder then, after some deserters had stolen some rifles from my unit, and I followed them to a UFM camp to get the guns back, I was shocked by the design of their defence.

Even the camps for internally displaced people are more organised than the UFM headquarters. For starters, they did not have any defence position, no quarter guard, no trenches, no officers or other ranks and no cooking places. There were fires everywhere, since each group of two or three were doing their own individual cooking. Anyone who has ever attended an important man's wedding in the village or the last funeral rites known as *kwabya lumbe* in Buganda, can get an idea of what an UFM camp was like. We entered the camp without anybody challenging us and passed many sleeping people, while others were playing cards with portable radios playing Zairean music. It was really a disorderly picnic site. We reached some sort of officers' mess where the seniors were. Most of them were drinking *waragi* and eating roasted goat meat. They invited me to join them but I informed them that all I needed were my guns since I was really feeling insecure staying in their camp. My two escorts, Sgt. Medi and Sgt. Kakooza, had already spotted our rifles, so we just collected them and left. I was feeling really sorry for that mass of human beings who, as far as I was concerned, were simply waiting to be led to the slaughterhouse. I was not wrong because, even while we were there, they were discussing how they were going to attack the Kitala government prison. Everyone, from the cook to the commander, was aware that there was going to be a mission that night. The aim of the mission was to capture prisoners, who would be asked to join their ranks. All the details of the attack were known to us, even to those who were from a different camp.

We heaved a sigh of relief when we left that camp and sneaked back into ours. I had noticed a former comrade, Policeman Bukenya, who, because he had been a junior officer in the NRA, was now a senior officer in the UFM. When I talked to him he seemed oblivious to the danger he was putting himself in. He was supposed to be one of the leaders of the mission that night when they would attack Kitala government prison.

It had not taken long for the UNLA to get wind of this pending attack and one platoon had been dispatched to reinforce the prison warders. It was this one platoon and the few prison warders who repulsed the UFM attack. It was the last major offensive by the UFM and many people, including Bukenya, died in it. That was the end of the UFM, at least militarily.

In the NRA we continued reorganising against the pending enemy offensive. Not that everything in our camp was smooth sailing; we also had some internal rivalries. When D coy was formed, most of the senior officers wanted to command it. It was the cream of the NRA then, and the CHC had a hard task deciding who to choose to command the crack unit. Grumbling about Salim Saleh's always getting the cream of operational outfits started emerging. At first the CHC found it hard to decide because, in the first place, Salim Saleh was his young brother, hence it was easy to accuse the CHC of favouritism. Although I knew Saleh would be the ideal leader of that unit, I approached the CHC and asked for the command of D coy. My reason was that since I was junior to the others, my appointment might not raise any eyebrows. The CHC initially agreed. However, he had other plans. So, in the meantime, I was commander of D coy for the time we took to prepare for that operation. Commander Joram Mugume had started reconnoitring Bukalabi, which was the enemy unit nearest to our headquarters. He was helped by many comrades, among them an intelligence sergeant, Kasozi, who was C coy's intelligence officer. The recce was finalised but this time we were facing a different UNLA. These were trained soldiers who had been deployed in West Nile and who had been fighting Moses Ali's group. They were better trained and more disciplined than our usual NYA militias. These West Nile boys, as they liked to be called, did things unheard of in the UNLA from Central Division. As soon as they entered the area, they dug good trenches, cleared the killing ground and took up positions. No noise, no smoking, no chasing of chickens, which usually gave away the Central Brigade soldiers.

Salim Saleh led the attack on Bukalabi on 21 February 1983. The CHC had told me to stay behind after he had assessed the recce report and inspected the troops. I still do not know whether it was intuition, or maybe he did not want to put all our eggs in one basket. So Saleh, with Mugume as his second in command, and most of the senior officers and veteran sergeants, attacked Bukalabi. I have heard many stories of what transpired. Major Kakebe (deceased), who participated in the attack, tells a vivid story of how they entered the enemy killing ground without knowing it. The enemy trenches were at ground level, so by the time our people realised that they were on the enemy killing ground it was too late. It was a heroic fight on both sides and it seems both sides were equally matched in training and trench warfare. In that battle, we lost ten comrades and we suffered many casualties, among them Saleh, the commander himself, who was injured in both arms. Enock Mondo and Julius Aine of the tank hunting team were also injured. I was sitting at the CHC's command post (CP) when the soldiers carrying our dead and injured started trekking in. One can only imagine what I felt. This company comprised not only personal friends but also two close relatives, Mwebaze Rwamurinda and Mugabi Kunuda – and both had died. Here I was with the CHC and a certain old white man who was a journalist but also a former mercenary in the Congo. He was semi-senile and never knew what was happening. My old trick of reading something to divert me from ugly happenings came in handy. I had a book, *The Perfumed Garden*, which talks about the secrets of perfumes and their relationship with men's libido. Soon I was engrossed in the book and thus managed to mentally block out the groans and cries of pain of my comrades. Not only was the Bukalabi attack a disaster for us because we were not used to such heavy casualties, but the men under our command could easily lose confidence, since the very cream of the NRA had been decimated. I started thinking of who would go into battle with me next, since most of my trusted combatant friends were either dead or injured. Even Commander Fred Rwigyema broke down and wept when he saw the wounded Commander Saleh. To block out all those thoughts, I read my book. The CHC, who was sitting a little distance away, looked at me and thought that maybe I was also weeping. "Pecos," he called out to me, "what are you thinking?" I told him I was just reading a book. "Eh intellectual!" he joked. I could not suppress a smile as I imagined what he would have thought if he had known the type of book I was reading. Reading has always been a good mental therapy for me whenever I have problems. It is a good way of facing difficult situations that one has no capacity to change.

Safari 50

Apparently the enemy had not fared any better. We must have inflicted many casualties, since their offensive started melting down. In the weeks that followed, we were faced with the problem of the civilian population.

Our operational area now covered the whole of Nakaseke county, much of Singo, Busiro and Kyaddondo, with a population of about 1 million people. And yet our troops had only about 400 guns. In order to cover the inlets into our operational zone, we were forced to scatter our weapons. The landmines were becoming depleted and the enemy had now resorted to artillery driving the civilians from their homes to the rebel camps, and thus exacerbating the population congestion. The enemy's aim was to chase us from the upper part of the triangle, that is Bulemezi, which was heavily populated and which had food, to the Singo area, which was sparsely populated and had little food, as the people there were not cultivators but nomadic cattle-keepers. The CHC had earlier proposed to the members of the High Command that we should persuade the civilian population to vacate this operational zone. Even after many meetings and explanations, we, the army officers, with the support of the civilian population, had opposed him and defeated his arguments.

His reasoning was that, if the civilian population left, the battle area would be decongested and the enemy would be denied information. Our counter-argument was that we would be betraying our people if we left them to face Obote's forces without our defence. The CHC had not taken into consideration the relationship that had been forged between the NRA and the people of the Triangle. In social research this is known as localitism, when the researcher becomes so taken up with the subjects of his/her research and he/she loses the impartiality required to give objective findings. The NRA had not only become "like the people of the Triangle, they had become part of them".

There were the questions of girlfriends and personal friendships; at that time it was not easy to distinguish a guerrilla fighter from common peasants. The young women of Luweero had started asking *Luggweereki*? meaning "Why should this war end?" While anybody would think that the population ought to have been tired of the war and would have liked it to end soon, in reality, people had started to enjoy the war, strange as that may sound. The enemy continued their offensive and by May 1983 most of the population had been forced to vacate Bulemezi for Lukoola in Singo. It was a pathetic sight. Old women and men, toddlers and babies strapped to their mothers' backs, with each person carrying the few valuables that the enemy had not looted. There are many mournful songs sung about that exodus, and the people who underwent that experience are still traumatised. The enemy added insult to injury by shelling columns of fleeing peasants. Incidentally, artillery has no big effect on guerrillas as they do not have a permanent location. However, to a peasant on the run it has a telling effect. The sound of mortar fire and 106 mm guns earned the weapons names like *Siba eggugu* (Tie up your luggage). The early-morning shelling was always the unquestionable signal for civilians to tie up and take their luggage in order to run further and further towards an unknown destination.

An 82 mm mortar shell produces an unnerving noise when it is fired. First you hear the burst of the firing, then the wheezing and whistling as it sails above the trees, and then the boom! In fact, when fired upon, the old women would comment: "Ha! whatever has befallen us! You can even show it to your friend as if that friend cannot see it him/herself." The cry of all the people was "Obote!" To them whatever was happening was caused by Obote. The Luweero peasants identified the whole war with Obote's second coming. We therefore did not have to do any politicisation, Obote was doing the political work for us. It was in the middle of this chaos, of the Bulemezi-to-Singo exodus, that our recce on Kabamba Infantry School came in and it seemed favourable. Apart from the need to augment our firepower, we realised that it would also serve as a diversion from the enemy pressure.

Kabamba, which is about 200 miles (320 km) beyond our operational zone, was relaxed and not as vigilant as the units bordering the Triangle, so it was an ideal target. This time the operation was commanded by the CHC himself. We were about 1,500 in strength. Although we had carried out many such operations before, we had not yet experienced long-distance operations, which required a lot of preparation. In most cases, we would spring from our hideouts, attack the enemy camp and withdraw in less than 48 hours. This time we had to cover 350 km or more, moving in a single column and at night. Although we were nocturnal animals by then, moving 1,500 people at night was not easy.

The other main problem was hunger. We were coming from the *lukoola* where food was scarce and the only dry ration we had was boiled maize grain. Plant protein, while it may give someone a feeling of being full, is quickly digested and unlike animal protein, it has little staying power. We set off at our now usual time of 10.00 p.m., marched until 5.00 a.m., then put up defences and rested the whole day in total concealment. We had calculated that the journey of 200 miles would take us between 5 and 7 days. This was an illusion. In reality, 1,500 people who are not very well trained in night movement and who are hungry, can hardly cover 20 miles at night. Because of cases of sleepwalking due to fatigue and getting lost because of travelling in unfamiliar territory, after 15 days, we had not yet reached Kabamba, yet we had finished almost all our meagre dry rations. Instead of looking like an attacking force we looked rather like a group of malnourished refugees on the run.

The tired and hungry combatants started misbehaving. Those carrying heavy loads of weapons and bombs started discarding them whenever they thought the commanders were not watching. The worst incident was when some of our combatants slaughtered a stray calf belonging to a civilian. This was an abominable act for a guerrilla, more so in a place where we had not yet established our presence. We started meting out harsh punishments, such as fifty lashes of the cane, to the offenders, hence the name Safari 50.

After assessing the situation, the CHC summoned us, the commanders, and announced that he had cancelled the operation. It took time for what the CHC said to sink in. Here we were, just seven miles, and therefore within striking distance, of the target and the commander wanted us to abandon the mission! It was hard to accept this. We grumbled, citing how we were going to go back after all the hardships we had suffered with nothing to show for it. We had left our people literally starving, and the enemy was on the offensive and we were not going back with any better weapons than what we had left the base with. Our reasoning was that, in the first place, we had to replenish our dwindling ammunition stocks. How were we going to face the enemy?

The CHC shot down our argument with one simple reason: What if we failed to overrun the objective and were forced to withdraw in disarray? How would we be able to command these discouraged, hungry and tired troops?

It was later, after reading about what had transpired in the Sahara Desert, when the great German leader, Rommel (the Desert Fox), planned to overrun Field Marshal Montgomery's camp in order to get fuel for his tanks and was defeated, and the attack turned out to be a rout for the Desert Fox, that I came to appreciate the CHC's reasoning. However, at the time I had a hard time agreeing with him.

After a time, reason overcame emotion and we called our troops and ordered a withdrawal. It takes a lot of confidence on the part of a commander to lead people in such a situation. However, our discipline and trust in the CHC made us undertake that withdrawal. It was an orderly withdrawal, given the circumstances.

All this time the enemy was intensifying its offensive, and now they had introduced helicopters, not as combat weapons, but for spotting our movements and as a propaganda ploy. The choppers dropped leaflets pleading with the civilians and guerrillas to hand themselves over to the government forces. They were also used for CASEVAC and to drop food supplies, since the roads were no longer usable owing to our mines and ambushes. It must have been a demoralised group of NRA fighters who reported back to our bases in *Lukoola*. I was lucky enough not to be among them.

11

$\blacklozenge\!\!\!\!\blacklozenge\!\!\!\!\blacklozenge\!\!\!\!\blacklozenge$

The Katonga Bridge:
Reconnaissance

The CHC had deployed me to stay behind with one section of soldiers to consolidate the new contacts we had established in this new zone. I was also tasked to cause a diversion on Masaka road. We were not only expanding our operational area, but also fragmenting the enemy offensive.

The Kampala-Masaka road is part of the trans-African highway that connects Kenya, Uganda, Rwanda and Democratic Republic of Congo. Any attack on this road sends shivers down the spines, not only to the Uganda government, but also to the three countries — Kenya, Zaire and Rwanda — because it affects vital trade through these areas.

To the guerrilla, the Kampala-Masaka road was a tantalising target. To us it was even more tantalising, because we wanted to find ways to evacuate our civilian supporters, who had become a burden. I chose seasoned fighters, mostly former UNLA soldiers. I had people like Geoffrey Katumbuza, Fred Kashoma, Ninsima Rwamurinda, Mwebaze Kamwanamwana, Twoyem (this was a former UNLA soldier who had deserted and joined us, although he was from the east and not one of the traditional westerners and Baganda fighters. He later proved very loyal and a good commander until his death), and others. The area of Kyahi, where we had stopped in our advance on Kabamba, is not far from the Kampala-Masaka road, if one uses shortcuts.

River Katonga, which is one of the biggest rivers in central Uganda, crosses the Masaka-Kampala road at Lwera, which is a 10 km stretch of flat area running adjacent to Lake Victoria. The Katonga River forms its delta in this flat plain. There are some knolls, but it is mostly floating papyrus reed on the left of the road when one is travelling to Kampala. The east of this road offered better withdrawal routes compared to the west, which was Lake Victoria. We decided to camp on the eastern side of the road.

We set up camp in the middle of the swamp on a small protrusion of land. Finding our camp was not easy for the enemy. There were no access paths except those used by the indigenous population, who usually use these swamps for catching lungfish.

The next day, I set off with Private Kashoma on a reconnaissance patrol of the area. We were dressed casually and looked like any peasant farmer or fisherman. We were armed with only pistols and grenades concealed in our clothes. To cut the right picture, we were carrying the local herdsman's sticks, the *nkoni*. Nobody seeing us would suspect that we were up to no good. We entered Lukaya town around 10.00 a.m., stayed around a bit and started travelling along the road towards Kampala. While our major aim was to see if our presence had been noticed, I had other reasons for reconnaissance on this road. We travelled about 20 km until we reached Buwama town. This town is equidistant between Kampala and Masaka, that is 42 miles or 68 km from Masaka to Kampala and vise versa. We had crossed the Katonga bridge and it had brought back memories of our river-crossing ambushes in Luweero. I stored up that information for further use. We went back to our camp and found everybody relaxed. We had acquired some food from the peasant farmers in the area, which we had paid for.

The people were not aware of the existence of our camp. They simply sold us food, thinking we were a group of hunters. This was the season for hunting and usually peasants came together and formed gangs that hunted wild game. The people thought we were such a group. After two days we started operations on the Masaka road, around the hills on the Masaka side of Lukaya. We had tried to acquire contacts in Lukaya, but the people there were not yet sensitised enough. As Lukaya was a trading centre, the population was comprised of businessmen who could easily have reported our presence. Unlike the peasant farmers, few business people in Uganda want anything to do with politics. To them life is a rat race and what matters is how much one earns on a day-to-day basis, compared to the long-term ventures of the farmers. So the business community of Lukaya, like the inhabitants of most highway trading centres, were predominantly lumpens. We decided not to inform anyone in Lukaya about our presence.

There are two adjacent hills as one leaves Lukaya on the way to Masaka. There is a deep valley in between those hills and the road is very steep on both sides. The hills form a sort of V-shape. We started laying our ambushes on the sides of the V-shaped hills attack vehicles that are at their slowest speed trying to overcome the hill. We had the advantage of choosing which vehicle to hit. We had to be careful because there were still many civilians travelling on that road, who were not aware of the war going on. Apart from innocent Ugandan civilians, there were many innocent foreigners on that road too, such as Kenyans, Tanzanians, Congolese, Rwandan and long-distance Somali drivers, so we had to take precautions before attacking any vehicle. Above all, we were operating at the gateway to our main support. Most people in the bush had their relatives in the south-west and central parts of Uganda. It would have been counter-productive to hit a vehicle and later find out that a relative of one of our people was among the casualties.

We always took care to attack army trucks or state security vehicles only. We carried out about five missions in that area and soon information reached Kampala that Masaka road was under "bandit" attack. In those operations we captured about 10 guns. We now had 22 guns, enough weapons to arm a guerrilla platoon.

The government in Kampala would not like the Masaka-Kampala road to be closed. The Obote government reacted as we had predicted. However, as most of the troops were bogged down in the Luweero Triangle, they could not deploy massively in this new theatre of war. The government did the most logical thing, that is to intensify intelligence gathering about this group of "bandits" who were trying to spoil its good name with the international community. On our part, we thought, wrongly, that our hideout was inaccessible, so we relaxed our vigilance. After twenty days in our swamp, with successful operations and no evident enemy action, we let our guard down.

It was on the twenty-fourth day since establishing our camp that our observation post arrested a man who was on reconnaissance for the government. Later we learned that this man was a member of the local administrative police personnel and a UPC activist. He was nabbed trying to track our footprints. We had just come from a mission with two captured guns and many edibles and cigarettes when I was informed that our people who had stayed behind had arrested an enemy agent.

I summoned the man and talked to him. I ordered that his arms, which were tied at the back, should be released. After offering him tea and some biscuits, I started interrogating him. In my naivety, I could not believe that anyone from central Uganda could be against those fighting Obote's regime. This man soon identified my weakness and exploited it. He told us stories of how government troops were terrorising his village, how even he had lost relatives to the government soldiers. In my naivety I thought I had recruited a supporter, a mistake I live to regret.

We had no way of holding prisoners and we could not organise to transport the captured agent to our bases in Ngoma, a distance of 150 miles, and I could not, at the same time, order this man's execution. I had to take more precautions. After three days this prisoner became one of us. He started by doing all the manual duties like washing our clothes, cooking and doing other camp chores. Around this time I decided to report to headquarters to find out about any new developments and also to tell my bosses of the work we were doing, but mostly to get more people to handle the weapons which now outnumbered the personnel.

I set off for Lukola with one soldier towards the end of August 1983. August has always been significant in my life. I was born in August. My first child was born on 31 August 1983. I formally married Dora in August and my promotion to the rank of colonel was also in August.

The story of Caroline Nduhukire Kutesa's birth is very interesting. The enemy offensive had gone on relentlessly despite our manoeuvres to try and divert it. All our people had been hounded from the productive area of Bulemezi to the semi-arid Lukola area of Singo.

Dora was heavy at the time we were withdrawing. When she had earlier informed me that she was pregnant, I had asked her how she knew, since she had never given birth before. She just smiled at me knowingly and ignored my protestations. Now, on the night of 31 August 1983, in a camp near a tributary of River Mayanja at a place called Tweyanze, Dora gave birth. Immediately after she had given birth the enemy attacked the camp. There was a stampede as everyone started withdrawing, as was the norm. Stories abound of how one of the soldiers, while trying to carry away any useful equipment carried, a new-born baby. This soldier started running with the baby till he gave it to Jovia Saleh, the wife of Salim Saleh. Dora and Jovia, who are cousins, had escaped from the mayhem and systematic hunt for guerilla supporters in Kampala to join us in the bush.

The enemy agents had been assisted in tracking Dora's people by a letter that they had found in my pack when we were attacked in Kigogwa after we had just returned from Nairobi. I had intended to send this love letter to Dora as soon as we linked up with our people in the bush, but it had fallen in the hands of the enemy. This letter set up a chain of events that led to Dora and Jovia running away from Kampala to join us in the bush. By coming to the bush, Dora enabled me to become a father in the midst of the war.

Dora and Jovia's escape from Kampala to the Luweero Triangle is another story on its own. Unlike some of us who had used the Kyaligonza-Dampa network, the two girls had to find their own way to the bush since the whole network had been destabilised by the enemy. A number of our safe houses had been discovered and all the people were on the run. The enemy had surrounded our people in the home of one of the supporters, Mr Norman Kayonga, husband to Mrs Kellen Kayonga, Jovia's elder sister. The enemy had surrounded those people when they were about to partake of their evening tea. Most of our people were there. How they eluded the enemy bullets is a marvel even today. Mr Kayonga was wounded but he still managed to flee, inspite of his bullet wounds, to Nairobi. The others all ran in disarray.

The Dora-Jovia saga is long. Suffice it to say that they even had the courage to stay in the Mbuya barracks, the enemy hotbed, with Dora's elder sister Kanks, married to 2nd Lt. Steven Mwesigwa, whom I had talked about earlier. These two girls slept in the enemy barracks while soldiers were out hunting for them. From Mbuya they managed to go back home to Mbarara, partly by train via Kabogore. The Uganda Railways was still plying the Kampala-Kasese route. Later, by trial and error, they managed to trace us in the bush.

Now here was Jovia running with a new-born baby whose mother had taken a different direction. It took about three days for the dispersed guerrillas to reorganise. All this time the baby had not been breastfed by her mother and eventually, when they joined, she had been weaned.

I do not have any medical explanation, but this baby who was born under enemy fire and who never had the usual immunisation jabs, has never had medical problems. She is almost twenty-two as I write, and Corporal, as our Carol is fondly known, has never had any major illness. I was still on the way to Ngoma when I got the news that I had become a father. It is hard to express what I felt then. To say that I rushed to join Dora and our baby would be an understatement.

By nature I am always in a hurry in most of my activities and movements. This time I must have grown wings. I had got the news while I was in Kyahi, Maddu, in Mpigi district. How I crossed Kiboga road to the *lukoola* area is still a mystery to me. In the first week of September 1983, I saw our baby in the Ngoma area. Bearing a child must be a mystery. The pleasure I was feeling is difficult to describe. I looked at this tiny human being, my replica. I wanted to carry her. Soon I realised that the male species was never designed to carry the young. The baby, who looked tiny, was heavier than a cadet man-pack. Maybe it was in my mind, but I could not carry her for a very long time. " Corporal" was one of the first children born in the bush and so she was the darling of all the soldiers. Even today, when I meet old comrades, they always ask about their small girl, "Corporal".

Since I was a senior officer and Dora was a junior officer class two, the soldiers nicknamed our child "Sergeant" at first, until she made the mistake of crying while hiding and she was subsequently demoted to "Corporal", a rank she has held ever since.

While I was celebrating the birth of my first child, the enemy had not been sleeping. My new-found recruit showed his true character. Just two days after I had left the camp, he escaped at night and reported to his superiors about our camp. The people I had left behind had just moved the camp a few metres away but otherwise they did not take ample precautions. An enemy company, using this agent as a guide, attacked our camp at dawn. They hit an empty camp since our people had already left but they still managed to disorganise them. Our people, typical of guerrillas, just fled with the weapons they had in their hands, abandoning our harvest of about 12 guns. Luckily none of them was injured. In a guerrilla war, it is better to lose weapons than a fighter. My group reported back to base after a two-month journey on the Masaka-Kampala road.

In the meantime, our people had carried out numerous operations, attacking enemy encampments and laying ambushes. After the abortive Kabamba mission, our people attacked Kiboga on 30 January 1983, from where they grabbed 30 guns, which was a big haul. Then, on 3 July, they attacked Luweero town, which was now the enemy's tactical headquarters. They killed many enemy soldiers and captured 24 guns. However, we lost four comrades, among them a veteran fighter named Kakwenzi.

All this time the enemy was trying to use the river crossing to prevent us from going back to Bulemezi for food. We, at the same time, managed to infiltrate back slowly. The route to the outside was through Bulemezi. It was also the only place where food was available. Uganda has a wonderful climate and fertile soil, so even when people ran away and stopped cultivating the land, the food continued growing. The guerrillas would uproot the cassava plants, take the tubers for food and the cassava leaves for sauce and leave the stems lying around. Four months later those stems would have grown and would be capable of providing more food. I have always argued that instead of calling Uganda a banana republic, it should be called a cassava republic. The cassava plant is very interesting indeed. It is the only plant which is multi-purpose and, in many cases, does not need replanting. The tubers are good food, which can be fermented to produce the local gin *waragi*, the leaves can make very tasty soup while the stems can be used as firewood.

There were very many cassava battles between the guerrillas and government troops in Luweero. In these infiltration missions, we lost a valuable comrade, Captain Emmy Ekyaruhanga. Emmy was a trained army officer and a gentleman. He had served in the defunct Uganda Army. He was soft-spoken but a deep believer in the cause. He was more trained and experienced in regular warfare than most of us. At the same time, he was humble enough to take on any command. Emmy had emancipated himself from the conventional officer corps thinking and was willing to learn how to fight in an irregular war.

Most military academicians in Africa tend to try and show that Africans cannot fight a war. They introduce African candidates to sophiscated and expensive weapons. Their message is that without the help of the so-called superpowers, no African state or group can sustain a war. After this lopsided "exposure", most African officers come from training with little or no confidence in their people, their army and even their states.

While on a course at the Ghana Armed Forces Staff College, I was subjected to that type of thinking. In the course on logistics they stressed that, without the help of a "big brother" developed nation, undeveloped Third World states were unfit to engage in any war. This type of training is dangerous since it undermines the trained officers' confidence in themselves, in the troops under them and even in their very nations. In Ghana, while discussing troop movement in an insurgency-infested area which, according to the Directing Staff (DS), was known as counter-revolutionary warfare (I disagreed with this categorisation and eventually we agreed to call it counter -insurgency warfare), I had a hard task trying to explain that a battalion of troops can move 200 miles in 14 days with or without vehicles. At one time we (my syndicate) had to call my comrade Major Napoleon Rutambika, who was on the same course, to come from his syndicate to explain how he had to travel this distance from Gulu to Bibia on the Uganda-Sudan border, in 17 days, through guerrilla-infested territory.

Captain Emmy had had similar training which insisted that, in order to move one batallion, one needs more than twenty trucks plus APCs, tanks and, if possible, spotter planes. Such a movement will take at least a month. That is the type of training offered to Third World army officers.

We had a similar experience when the people of West Nile, who had fled to Zaire (now Congo), wanted to come back. The United Nations High Commissioner for Refugees (UNHCR) said they required five hundred trucks to move half a million people over a distance of 50 to 80 kilometres. We rejected that line of thinking, pointing out that at that time (1987), there were fewer than two hundred trucks in the whole country. We pointed out to the UNHCR officials that those people had left Uganda on foot when they were being harassed and that now they could walk back at their leisure, which the said people did at minimum cost.

When I say that Captain Emmy had emancipated himself from this erroneous thinking, I mean that he was ready to learn a new type of warfare, which relied more on human ingenuity than on machine superiority. Emmy gave us a lot of insight into a regular army officer's thinking. It was very sad when he was killed by an enemy patrol while he was visiting one of our local contacts. He and another junior officer, Mulondo, had left me in a camp in Ssambwe near Ndejje, not far from Bombo Road, and gone to monitor enemy movements. That was when an enemy patrol detected them and shot at them. His comrade, Mulondo,

was also injured in the mouth but he managed to run and report
to me. Emmy had always joked that the back of the human head
was the motor which drives the body, which is true. He used to
say all fighters aim to crush the backs of their enemies' heads. It
is ironical that that was the very part of his anatomy which the
enemy bullets hit. I went with some soldiers and collected his
body, which we buried in our camp. After the war his remains
were reburied with full military honours at his ancestral burial
ground in Hoima.

Monduli Cadets: *(Back row L-R) Joram Mugume, Jack Mucunguzi, Hannington Mugabi, Pecos Kutesa, Napoleon Nshambagana Rutambika; Seated: (L-R) Charles Tusingweire, John Katanaka.*

Patrick Lumumba in a studio photograph before he went to the bush.

Benjamin Muhanguzi aka "Dampa" during his clandestine days.

Lady freedom fighters. In front is Joy Mirembe, the lady who braved the dangerous route of taking fighters to the bush.

"Seven men in a boat". An artist's impression of the boat trip to Kisumu. They are (L to R) Busagwa and Paddy the boat men; Y. K. Museveni, Andrew Lutaya (to the right of Museveni); Marios Katungi (Suicide), Pecos Kutesa and Arthur Kasasira.

The Commander-in-Chief Y.K. Museveni (left) addressing A Coy. Kutesa's second-in-command, Fred Mugisha (middle ground) was then in command.

Some of the members of the NRA High Command in 1984. Left to right: Political leader Kateregga, Gertrude Njuba, Fred Bamwesigye, Pecos Kutesa, Guma Young Frank, Jim Muhwezi, Fred Rwigyema and Elly Tumwine.

Commander Fred Bamwesigye leading a patrol in the jungles of Luweero.

Gordon Rwamukaaga, an NRA combatant leading his colleagues in song. Right is Fred Mugisha, Kutesa's second-in-command, here in charge of the First Battalion.

NRA bush sickbay: An injured combatant being treated by a civilian supporter.

A Resistance Council meeting in progress. Such meetings were guarded by NRA combatants.

A destroyed agricultural estate in Kapeka. This was one of the most important infrastructures which was destroyed by the UNLA.

Some historical members of the National Resistance Council (1984): Standing Prince Jjuko, Simba, Abbey Mukwaya, Rev. Father Sseguya; seated (L to R) Kibirango, Katenta-Apuuli, Alhaji Moses Kigongo and Kahinda Otafiire.

The NRA Commander-in-Chief Y. K. Museveni seen here as a down-to-earth guerilla leader in these very humble conditions.

Attempted cooperation. Yoweri Museveni (NRA) meets Andrew Kayiira (UFM) on the right. Moses Kigongo is extreme left.

Kutesa with his wife Dora during the Masaka-Katonga siege, a few months before the fall of Kampala.

Kutesa's wife Dora with their first daughter, Carol Nduhukire Kutesa, aka Seargent. She was later demoted to Corporal for disrupting a military operation. Inset: Corporal at 8 years of age.

12

Kabamba, Masindi and Hoima Offensives

By the end of 1983 we had grown stronger and bigger. We had formed a mobile brigade out of the original mobile battalion. This brigade had five battalions, each comprising one armed company and three companies of unarmed personnel. I was the 1st Battalion commander, 3rd Battalion was under commander Patrick Lumumba, 5th Battalion under Steven Kashaka, 7th under Matayo Kyaligonza, 9th, which was the task force operating as far as Mukono on the Kampala-Mombasa highway, was under Julius Chihandae, and 11th Battalion was under Chefe Ali. My second-in-command was Peter Kerim, now a retired brigadier. This officer, who was a former Uganda Army NCO, was from Paidha, West Nile, on the border between Uganda and Zaire (now DRC). He was very good at combat and had a great sense of humour. Even now, in semi-retirement, he is still active on the Congo-Uganda border.

In February 1984, reconnaissance reports about Masindi Artillery School had come in and they were favourable. Masindi had always been a target because of its location and the kinds of arms which we knew were there. It was not in the direct war theatre, so we suspected that the troops there were relaxed.

Many recce patrols were sent out to Masindi by the CHC. Few of us were privy to this information, since we did not need to know. One of the most active people in this recce was retired Captain Kaka Bagyenda, who had joined the bush war as a civilian, but who had earlier worked as a mason during the construction of the Masindi barracks. He also had many contacts in that area. Although we had some former UA soldiers, such as Rwamukaga, Rwangira, Nyansio and others who had served in that barracks, this civilian appeared more suited for the task.

Kaka made many visits to the barracks. After some time comrades Stanley Muhangi (RIP) and John Mugume of the old Karuma Road days, were detailed to go and confirm his reports. These three comrades were courageous enough to enter the barracks through the small gates that soldiers use when escaping to go drinking. Dressed in UNLA uniforms and greatcoats, they mingled with the government soldiers and infiltrated up to the armoury. It takes a lot of courage to do what our people did during those days. These days we tease each other as to who among us could still do what we were capable of doing then. We have become bottom-heavy. Back then, a combatant was just a combatant and nothing more. The combatants now are fathers, and even grandfathers, with family responsibilities and many dependants. Not that we have lost the resolve to maintain that old discipline, but age has also set in. We are less adventurous than we were then. The final recce reports were scrutinised and deemed good enough, hence the people to be involved in the operation were briefed.

There was a big setback, though. While we had used river crossings as good killing grounds for the enemy, this time the enemy was using the same river crossings as besieging points to deny us access to the outside and to starve us in this triangle of rivers Mayanja, Lugogo and Kafu. It was an enclave that needed a lot of ingenuity for the guerrillas to break out of. We aimed to evacuate many civilian from the triangle. The enemy was aware of our aim and had besieged us.

The CHC had already been identified in the midst of the huge civilian population. There was no way of hiding his movements. In order to allow us to move with any degree of stealth, we had to make the CHC's presence as conspicuous as possible. While the CHC was using the deception of organising the withdrawal of the civilian population from the Ngoma area at the Birima River crossing, the mobile brigade set off under the command of Elly Tumwiine. As luck would have it, we had just crossed River Mayanja when enemy troops who were on a game hunting expedition, fired at an animal. The operational commander told us that our movement had been detected, so we should withdraw, back to base. We felt that it was wrong because we had left our people in a precarious situation. However, since the commander did not want us to go on, we had to obey him. Dejectedly, we withdrew. We could not mix with our people because we had already been briefed about an important mission, so we stayed put. After debriefing on 18 February we set off for Masindi, under the command of Salim Saleh. I was the leading commander of 1st Battalion with 3rd Battalion under Stanley Muhangi, 5th Battalion under Kashaka and 7th Battalion as reserve; we were 700 people with 357 guns, and the rest were unarmed "commandos".

We had to cross River Kafu, enter Masindi district and reach the barracks in 60 hours. We were helped by the burned grass, the moonlight, the fact that we were now well fed and did not suffer from the Kabamba-mission hunger syndrome.

This time we knew what we were going to do and we were able and willing to do it. We had a lot of self-confidence. We were the elite of the fighting group. We knew the government troops did not expect an attack since their attention was focused on the Luweero Triangle. Indeed, Masindi Artillery School was quite complacent about security.

We had to cover 60 km in one long march. We were also helped by the flat terrain of this river basin. We set off at around

3.00 p.m. on the 19th and spent many hours crossing River Mayanja. We were using floating papyrus reeds. Although the river was not very wide, for 700 people to cross with their weapons a mere two kilometres from an enemy detachment at Buhanku, was not an easy task. By 9.00 p.m. we had all managed to cross the river and then we re-assembled for the long march. We were lucky. In addition to the clear field resulting from the burning of grass and shrubs, there was a full moon. With my 1st Battalion in the lead, we set off at full trot towards Masindi. It is good to be young and fit, especially when one had an important mission to fulfil. One can only imagine what Phidepaedis the Greek runner was thinking as he carried the news of Greek victory over Sparta, from Marathon to Athens. The night breeze was good for long-distance running or walking. At dawn we had taken our positions around the sleeping barracks.

While Saleh, the commander of the operation, liked taking personal risks, this time he was an epitome of caution. I can understand Saleh's apprehension, having been under similar circumstances in the past. It is the leader who is, appropriately, held accountable for any mishap on a mission. Here was a major offensive which could easily have made or broken the NRA. Almost all the weapons in the NRA armoury were at stake on this mission and the most battle-tested fighters were under Saleh's command.

After the combatants had taken up positions, Saleh radioed the CHC. It was around 7.30 a.m.; broad daylight. The CHC felt concerned and wanted us to withdraw and lay siege to the barracks instead. We had not yet been exposed to the tactic of besieging the enemy, and we had already compromised concealment, which had always been a major factor in our operations. The 1st Battalion had taken up position along the Masindi-Hoima road, therefore facing the main quarter guard. All my platoon commanders were itching to open fire, when Saleh radioed me. He told me of the CHC's advice of withdrawing and laying ambushes on all roads leading into the barracks. Saleh had taken up position on Masindi hill, a prominent hill overlooking Masindi Barracks. I answered Saleh that it was impossible for me to start withdrawing as I was just within the firing range of enemy machine guns and mortars. He asked me if I was willing to take full responsibility in case I failed to take over the quarter guard. I called my commanders, Peter Kerim, my second-in-command, Fred Mugisha ("Headache") my operations officer, my company commanders, Muhanguzi and Musoke (Kyenvangunywa), who all agreed that the best option was to attack. I radioed Saleh back and informed him about our unanimous decision. Saleh also consulted other battalion commanders and they all agreed with me.

The signal for attack was, as usual, a few RPG bombs, some anti-tank grenades (ATGs) and sustained machine gun fire. My operations commander had the RPG. However, I told him to pass it over to a soldier since he would be bogged down if he became a rifleman instead of a commander. We gave the RPG to my batman and cook by the name of Katende, a soldier who had never experienced combat, leave alone fired an RPG against the enemy. However, since weapons are designed to be user-friendly, Katende found no difficulty in letting off an air burst, which was the signal for real action. "Boom!" went the RPG shell, followed by the orchestra of machine guns, rifles, occasional ATGs and the commanding tempo of the GPMGs. The music of an attack is really captivating, especially if you are on the giving end. The "rat-tat-tat" of medium machine guns (MMGs), the whine and whang of bullets hitting solid objects, the bass sound of mortar blasts and occasional grenades, if recorded, can be very exhilarating music. We were later to face better, or worse, music, when the enemy used artillery pieces and anti-aircraft guns against us. However, that day, 20 February 1984, belonged to us.

We had attacked from the lower end of the barracks, forcing the enemy to retreat uphill. We made short work of overrunning the quarter guard, the offices and the armoury, up to the sleeping quarters of the officers.

There is a wonderful feeling when you overrun an enemy objective. This feeling is heightened when you see your comrades all safe and sound. We had met little resistance apart from a Tanzanian (TPDF) instructor who at first refused to put down his weapon when I ordered him to do so. This soldier, dressed only in his pyjamas and bathroom slippers, had just jumped out of his bed, only to be met by gun-wielding guerrillas. I tried to reason with him to put down his gun but instead he rushed back inside his house. I ordered Katende to fire his RPG into the house. I do not know what befell the soldier but we did not find anybody inside the house when we entered it. I was still excitedly trying to rally my troops when I saw Saleh beckoning to me. "He has survived" was my initial reaction. There was no way I could describe how I felt then.

Saleh was more concerned with an enemy counter-attack than jubilating. He was still tense and worried while we, the people under him, were jumping excitedly up and down. We spent sometime carrying away weapons and war material from the armoury. The Masindi Artillery Training School had more arms than we had hoped for. We did not know and neither did we have time to sort out what was of immediate use. We just swept the barracks clean.

Since independence, Uganda had been importing all sorts of weapons from all corners of the world and an old barracks like Masindi had a variety of weapons. The East-West political divide had never affected the different Ugandan regimes' quest for arms. In Masindi we had, for example, weapons from Israel, bullets from Yugoslavia, mortars from Britain, bombs from China etc.

It would have taken us a month, if not more, to sort out which bullets or bombs fitted which calibre of weapons, so we just piled everything on the few trucks we had commandeered and carried away all that we could.

We had also overrun the town. However, owing to our strict code of conduct we never looted. Not that we did not carry away a few bottles of beer and whisky from the government hostel and hotel, but that is not looting, according to Ugandan standards.

We left Masindi at our leisure around 1.00 p.m. From total concealment we had overrun and occupied a major town and barracks for more than six hours. It was a major tactical and psychological victory for us. We moved about 10 km from Masindi, with most of our loot piled on the trucks being driven by our comrades, such as Drago Nyanzi and Bruce Muwanga, who knew how to drive. After reorganisation in the Kijunjubwa hills which overlook Masindi town and barracks, we found that we had lost only one commando junior officer, one Wagaba. Hence, we called the Masindi mission "operation Wagaba". Incidentally, in the local languages of central and western Uganda, *gaba* means to give. This operation had provided us not only with arms but also opened for us new avenues. It was a turning point in the guerrilla war.

Saleh communicated to the CHC and asked him to send more unarmed "commandos" to help us carry the weapons. It was during that reorganisation and weapons check that I had a nasty experience. The area where we were camped is well known for honey farming. The drivers had parked the commandeered lorries under a tree which had beehives in its branches. The fuel and fumes must have aroused the bees, which descended on me with a vengeance. It started with one bee sting, which I brushed away, before the whole swarm attacked. I tried to run towards my friends, who advised me not to come near them since they would also be attacked. Everyone started giving me advice on how to get rid of the bees, but the bees were relentless; they stung me everywhere. I tried to roll in a greatcoat, to no effect. It was Commander Kashaka who came up with a solution; he lit a fire in the grass around where I was lying and the bees left.

According to my commander, Saleh, the bees were trying to call me back to order since I was becoming too excited to control my troops. The bees had become a menace and were chasing us from our temporary camp. Worse still, they had taken over the vehicles carrying our looted weapons. Someone fired an anti-tank grenade into the beehive. This did not affect the bees in any way; in fact, they attacked more ferociously. We feared setting fire to the bushes around the tree since the vehicles could catch fire. After some time the bees settled down and we offloaded our cargo. After sorting out the most urgently needed weapons, Drago and others smashed up the vehicles by making them collide head-on. It was a big wastege. However, we felt justified since we did not need vehicles then, and after all they were the enemy's major mode of transport. By damaging the army trucks we were reducing the enemy to our level, since all of us now would have to move around on foot.

At the end of the day we had captured 765 rifles, double the number of 375 which we had used, plus lots of bullets, bombs, and some machine guns. This was the biggest catch since the war started. Among the POWs we had captured were TPDF instructors. These Tanzanians had no quarrel with us and we treated them well. Later we smuggled them out of the country with messages to the president of Tanzania, Julius Nyerere. All this time we were at pains not to antagonise Tanzania. Our belief was that Tanzania had miscalculated in supporting Obote, which would be realised and rectified in time.

It was a good thing that we treated these Tanzanian POWs well. In 1992, when I was the Chief of Training and Recruitment (CTR) of NRA, now the government army, while visiting our officers who were undergoing training in the USSR, I met one of those former POWs. This officer was very happy to see me and I learnt an important lesson. In war the common soldier is never to blame. This officer had been sent to Uganda by his government as an instructor. The Uganda civil war was none of his concern. When we met in Odessa on the Black Sea, he was an officer undergoing training and I was an official visiting my officers undergoing similar training. There was no cause for animosity between us.

When the CHC received the news of our success, he set off with the 700-man rear guard to join us. They met us at the Kafu River and we set off for our base. En route we encountered enemy groups who had come to try and make us throw away our loot. Instead we killed many of them and captured more guns from them. It was a jubilant group of guerrillas who reported back to their home ground.

The UNLA had been thrown into disarray. The attack on Masindi had unhinged their offensive plan. There was also a bigger blow to the enemy. Just three months earlier, in December 1983, they had lost one of their most able commanders, Brig. David Oyite Ojok, who had been the Chief of Staff, in a helicopter crash.

Despite being on the opposing side, Oyite Ojok was a charismatic officer respected by both his troops and even some of us. He had become involved in the war physically because he had identified the weakness of his army. David, as he was fondly known, may have had his weaknesses but he was a soldiers' soldier. No wonder it took Obote almost a year to find a replacement for him as Chief of Staff.

The day Oyite Ojok died I was with Commander Stanley Muhangi. The enemy had been deployed around the river crossings and the Chief of Staff himself was supervising the deployments. The aim of the enemy had been to block all the outlets from the *lukoola* with the aim of starving us, as there is no food in that vast flat land. The next move was to shell us using the artillery they had acquired from North Korea. The North Korean artillery instructors had been intensively training the UNLA, and had Ojok not died we would have had a rough time. It was late in the evening when two helicopters lifted off from Kyakamunywere. One was small and the other was bigger. The smaller helicopter took off before the bigger one. Then the bigger helicopter took off. It had reached cruising height when it burst into flames and disintegrated right before our eyes. Apollo Milton Obote, in his eulogy, had this to say, "Some people say it was the bandits who shot the helicopter! Others say it was a piloting error, still others say it was a mechanical fault, but from whichever angle you look at it, it was a disaster. David is no longer with us!" This was a heart-rending eulogy. Even some of us who were opposed to Obote felt touched when we heard it on the radio.

Up to now no one has come up with a good explanation of what had transpired. Recently air force officers told me that the helicopter service time had expired but Ojok had forced the pilots to go to battle. Whatever the case, Brigadier David Oyite Ojok died, and the UNLA's offensive was nipped in the bud.

It is interesting how the loss of just one officer can put the whole military establishment of a sovereign state in jeopardy. David Oyite Ojok's death had a far-reaching effect, not only on the UNLA, but the whole regime. In fact, the collapse of Obote's second government is attributed mainly to Oyite Ojok's death. During that halt in the offensive, caused by Oyite Ojok's death, we consolidated the training and reorganisation of our forces.

Hoima, June 1984

After the death of Oyite Ojok there was a power struggle in the UNLA. The surest way to fit in Oyite Ojok's shoes, according to UNLA, was to prove your combat worthiness. The first person to try to do that was Colonel John Ogole, a good soldier who lacked Oyite Ojok's charisma.

In the meantime, we in the bush were trying to get more guns and see how to move civilians from our operational zones. On 1 June 1984 we attacked Hoima. There was no big barracks in Hoima but the enemy had turned all the towns bordering the Triangle into fortified strongholds. Our attack was more of a propaganda campaign and quest for drugs and other essential needs.

The Hoima attack went smoothly but was not as dramatic as the Masindi one. We captured many guns. On top of that we raided the local bank; we just surrounded the bank and ordered the manager to give us all the money we could carry. This was not like the usual film heist but an orderly withdrawal of cash. We got sacks and sacks of Ugandan currency. We did not see any need for physical cash so all the money was treated like war booty. I do not think anyone of us was interested in grabbing that money. We saw it as war material. It was to be used to buy drugs and food for the fighters.

The only memory I have of that operation is that I had my personal turmoil. Dora had come from my village after leaving Corporal with my old mother. While there, she had contacted a woman who was known to both of us. This woman had chosen to tell ugly stories, most of them lies, about me. Dora, being young, believed this woman's tales, so when she came back she was a changed person. Until today I do not know what that woman's aim was, but she spoiled my relationship with Dora for some days. Right through our attack on Hoima, I was moving as if in a daze. Later, when I confessed my predicament to the CHC, he told me that two persons cannot always live in bliss. He said that misunderstandings do happen but as a man and an officer I should not let personal problems cloud my thinking. He advised me not to jeopardise operations because of personal problems. He pointed out that I had hundreds of soldiers who were looking to me for inspiration and many thousands, if not millions, of Ugandans who believed in what I was doing. I decided to change.

Meanwhile, Colonel John Ogole's offensive was proving to be more organised than the previous ones. He was using blockade warfare. Troops flooded the operational area and dug in. Ogole was using trained soldiers, not the usual NYA of Bazilio Olara Okello. They were more disciplined, therefore more dangerous to us. A well dug-in defence is not a good target for guerrillas, who cannot manage sustained battles. After all, there would be no arms and ammunition to loot since each soldier would be carrying his one gun.

With about 5,000 troops and artillery pieces, Ogole's men would advance a little distance, then dig in, waiting for us to attack. What we did was to ignore and bypass the dug-in troops and harass their rear bases. The war had now set in; it was becoming more difficult to operate in these circumstances, but it was a worthwhile experience. We learned how to fight against trained soldiers and not the ragtag militia who made up the biggest number of UNLA troops near Kampala.

The Koreans introduced the use of anti-aircraft guns against infantry soldiers. At one time two journalists, Tim Cooper and Ali Alison, who came to write a story about the NRA, were shocked when they found the UNLA using 14.5 mm and 12.7 mm anti-aircraft guns against us. The UNLA also introduced the 12-barrel Katyusha, best known as Stalin's Organ. It is said that, during the Second World War, when it was first introduced in battle, both the Russians who fired it and those being fired at — the Germans — ran away and abandoned the Katyusha in the battlefield.

All in all, it was a testing but instructive experience. The 14.5 mm anti-aircraft gun had the nasty effect of severing any limbs that it came in contact with. We started to have people with amputated arms. The 14.5 mm anti-aircraft gun and the Katyusha deeply scared our people. While we had become used to the 106 mm, 82 mm and 60 mm mortar bombs, which had not had any visible effect on us, these new weapons were proving to be very efficient.

Kabamba III January 1985

After Masindi and Hoima we were in an aggressive mood. Despite Ogole's offensive we continued finding ways to expand our operational area and acquire more weapons. The main thrust of the UNLA was now in the *lukoola* and Bulemezi areas. This semi-arid place was just teeming with civilians and the food situation was becoming critical. The Bahima cattle keepers of Ngoma who, from the very beginning, had supported us, now came in handy. They agreed to give us their cattle in the hope of being paid back when we captured power. The Bahima's cows, meat, now became our staple food and for three months we fed primarily on animal protein.

We started to appreciate the value of meat and milk. It is a very good diet for people who are active. In fact, the Karimojong people have always survived on this diet. No wonder that they have managed to live a semi-rebellious life with little contact with the rest of the country. Unlike plant protein, which merely fills the tummy, a meat-and-milk diet gives the person a healthy and strong body. One maintains a slim waistline; moreover, it takes time for one to get hungry. Most cattle keepers are used to long intervals between meals, so the meat diet is ideal for their lifestyle.

While the meat and milk eater has a slender body, the muscles are very well developed. After a little milk in the morning, a cattle keeper keeps running up and down with his cows till dusk, with no time to eat a midday meal. The result is that the body becomes accustomed to going for long periods without food while the muscles become more hardened. In fact, this almost caused a political problem among the fighters. The fighters from central Uganda were not used to long-distance movement without food and so they complained. It was common for an officer to be approached by a raw private with a complaint such as "You know sir, these people (the SNCOs) from cattle keeping areas do not get hungry and they never get tired."

After a time we adjusted to the animal protein diet and were very fit physically. It was because of this physical fitness that we managed to attack and overrun Kabamba Training School. This was a target that had eluded the NRA since its inception. It should be remembered that Kabamba was the first military target of the PRA when it declared war against Obote on 6 February 1981. That operation was a partial success. The next attempt had been in May 1983, when what ought to have been a Kabamba attack resulted in the infamous "Safari 50". Now we were going to Kabamba for the third time.

We set off for Kabamba towards the end of 1984. As usual, most of the fighting group, now about 1,500 in number, set off from *lukoola* area and crossed River Mayanja. As I pointed out earlier, crossing a river with 1,500 people who are heavily loaded with weapons is not easy. To make things more difficult, it had rained and the current of the river was very swift. The crossing took us a long time, and at one time the base plate of a mortar dropped in the river and we spent some time trying to retrieve it. We had planned to reach Kyamusisi, which is on the left-hand side of the Mubende-Kampala road, that day. However, we could not make it that night since dawn found us at Kiryowa. We pitched camp since our usual operational time was at night. We could not move such a big force during the day. The enemy detected our camp and tried to attack it but they were repulsed.

Around 1400HRS we held a meeting of all the operational commanders. It was decided that half the force should stay behind with the CHC as a delaying force while the rest would hurry to attack Kabamba. The CHC decoy force started moving in a very conspicuous manner, even holding rallies around the Kyamusisi and Bukomero areas. In fact, they had some skirmishes with the enemy and even managed to capture a few guns.

On 24 December 1984 we set off for Kabamba, a distance of 200 miles. The operational commander of the attacking force was Salim Saleh. The force comprised our mobile brigade. I was leading with my 1st Battalion, Lumumba with his 3rd Battalion, Kashaka with 5th Battalion and Stanley Muhangi with his 7th Battalion at the rear. Our aim was to cross the Kassanda-Myanzi and Mubende-Kampala roads in darkness.

As stated earlier, crossing a major road when one is a guerrilla is a big problem. There is a psychological fear of inhabited places when one has been under cover for long. After we had crossed the roads at midnight, it started to rain.

Moving a group of 700 people in single file in pitch darkness is no easy task. Soon we got lost. Although this time we were not as hungry as during the previous Kabamba trek, still we experienced incidents of sleepwalking. A combatant would fall asleep while moving, thinking he was still following his mates. Then he would wake up and not find anybody in front of him. In panic the combatant would dash forward and those following him would also be forced to run. This is what we called *kukata msururu* or "cutting the chain line", and it could disrupt the momentum of our movements. At times the cut-off group could be mistaken for an enemy. A lot of time would be spent in trying to identify one another, then the whole column would set off again. I think the slave traders must have experienced similar scenarios. Because of this movement, then abrupt stop, then movement again, we did not manage to cover the desired distances in time.

After some time we managed to reach the Kyahi area; the old Kyahi where the "Safari 50" punishments had been meted out, only this time we had a good reception. This area was no longer new to us and we had established contacts there. One of our contacts, Jane Komugisha, was waiting for us and she prepared food for us. In fact, she gave us two or three cows which we slaughtered and ate. Jane was an old contact of mine, we had been to school together in the early 1970s. It was a pleasant surprise when she showed me a photograph which I had taken with David Tinyefuza (now full General) and Comrade Enock Mugabirwa. The photograph was taken in 1972 and I could not believe that at one time I looked like that.

We set off from Jane's place and followed the northern bank of River Katonga through Bubanda. By dawn we were close to Kabamba. Most of the officers and SNCOs knew Kabamba Military Training School very well. We had assembled there after the Amin war, so we knew all the routes in and out of the barracks. Daybreak arrived before we had taken up position. We were all eager to attack. The 1st Battalion was assigned the quarter guard and the route to Mubende, where we expected reinforcement, 3rd Battalion and 5th Battalion were assigned the armoury and the living quarters of the enemy troops. As expected, the enemy was not in the trenches and the assault on the barracks was easy. In a few minutes I had captured my objective and taken up position facing the Mubende road. One UNLA soldier wanted to repeat what a Tanzanian corporal had done in 1981. He was advised by his comrades to let us take the guns since we were not hostile to the UNLA per se. Moreover, "he was from western Uganda and potentially friendly", according to some of the people who eventually joined us. This soldier just rushed into the underground armoury, for an unknown reason.

We had come prepared for such a move but before resorting to the last option, we tried to reason with the poor fellow. He was adamant. He took up a good firing position and held our people off. Many heroic and foolish moves were made. At one time Comrade Lumumba wanted to storm the machine gun position with two soldiers but he was held back. Red pepper was poured and burned in the armoury shells to no avail. Anti-tank missiles were fired but the soldier was protected by the armoury wall. At one time one of our very brave NCOs tried to storm the machine gun and he was shot in the thigh. Dr Kiiza Besigye, a presidential candidate, remarked sarcastically, that the wounded soldier lacked imagination. After some time an anti-vehicle mine was lowered slowly into the armoury and electronically detonated. Our main fear was that the weapons and bombs would blow up. It never happened. After the deafening boom of the mine, there was complete silence. All the same, we feared entering because we were not sure if the enemy soldier had been killed. We fired a few bullets into the armoury and received no response. Still, nobody was willing to risk his life as bait. Luckily or unluckily, one of the disorganised enemy soldiers was found loitering around. He was ordered to enter the armoury, which he did with his arms up, the international sign of surrender. He went in and we held our breath. After a time he shouted that it was safe. We ordered him to come out with a few guns. He came out holding two empty AK-47s, part of the arsenal the enemy soldier had used to keep us at bay.

Our people descended into the armoury and set about carrying out the weapons. The enemy soldier had managed to keep us at bay for at least five hours. During that time the unit in Mubende had organised and was coming to reinforce Kabamba. The soldiers of Kabamba had all dispersed. I was at the armoury admiring the weapons coming out when our OP came running and informed us that the enemy was advancing from Mubende. I immediately assembled my troops and we took up positions in the well dug but rarely used enemy trenches. The advancing enemy were not in a hurry to enter the barracks, which was under our control. They started firing ATGs at random. I can recall Comrade Lumumba rushing from the armoury side to come and reinforce me. I shouted at him to stay put as he was more exposed than I, who was in a trench, but he refused and came on. We answered the advancing enemy with some machine gun fire and they withdrew.

It was 1 January 1985. While we were still organising our withdrawal, Saleh informed us that he had become the father of Esteri. I always call the Kabamba attack "Happy Birthday Esteri". Esteri's birthday gift to us was 500-600 rifles and many bombs and a lot of ammunition. The war was now tilted in our favour. When one imagines the 40 guns with which we attacked Kakiri 1 on 6 April 1981 and now, one had to agree that the war was winnable. If we were businessmen taking stock, we would have found our balance sheet very encouraging.

The enemy was losing ground and we were gaining. Therefore we never lost hope. To us it was a matter of mathematics. If we could multiply the number of weapons and personnel, while the enemy lost, business would be good.

The withdrawal from Kabamba was uneventful except that we were too heavily loaded. The few commandos we had come with were finding it difficult to carry all the material. This time we did not commandeer any vehicles since we did not intend to use any main road. We were in radio contact with the CHC group and they were trying to come and assist us with our haul.

Birembo *Moto Wawaka*

From 1 January, when we overran Kabamba, the war equation became balanced. The enemy made desperate moves to roll back our progress. Ogole's offensive was at its fiercest. We struggled with our burden of weapons, ammunition and bombs, trying to link up with the CHC's group. We lost radio contact but eventually re-established it.

On 6 January we joined the CHC group and then we were the same group which had set off from the *lukoola*. In the whole operation we had not lost anybody but it was too early to celebrate. The enemy, now with the help of Koreans, were hot on our heels. The CHC decided that we should camp at Birembo Primary School, which was situated on a prominent hill. In conventional military tactics it is advisable to capture ground of tactical importance, but in guerrilla warfare this is a mistake. A prominent hill offers a good target for artillery and Birembo was no exception.

Birembo was positioned adjacent to another hill where the Koreans had set up their artillery pieces and Katyusha rocket launchers. They then sent out infantry probing groups which we repulsed, in so doing exposing our position.

I have earlier mentioned the music of attacking a defence, we now heard real music while we were on the receiving end. A combination of artillery, anti-aircraft guns, Katyusha rocket launchers and 120 mortars can create the most grating lyrics that only the devil can find musical. The shells started raining, first at random then in what is termed carpet-bombing; that is, bombs falling in a creeping pattern from one end of the target area to the other. It is unnerving when the bombs are fired, since the firing itself is audible, then the pregnant silence, then the whamming and whizzing sound of the Katyusha before the thud, thud, thud of the bombs landing.

We had managed to dig a few shallow shellshock, so our defence was not good enough to counter bombardment. On top of that, a Kyatyusha shell has the capability to dig deep, even in a good bunker, and blow everything outwards. In fact, when looking at the shell blasts of a Katyusha, one gets the impression that the ground itself is erupting outwards.

It was in the middle of this hellfire that I teasingly asked my Intelligence Officer (IO), now Lt. Colonel Steven Kwiringira, to move ahead and tell me how our troops were faring. Kwiringira, in his typical Kikiga style, informed me in vernacular that he was resigning from the forces with immediate effect, and if he was owed any pay he was forfeiting it. This was quite funny since Kwiringira knew there was no way he was going to leave the army when he was under enemy fire, and anyway there was no salary to forfeit. These days, when I tease him about that statement, he always answers jokingly, "What if it were you?"

In the Birembo attack we lost five of our comrades, all from the CHC escort group. In the middle of the night we left Birembo hill and moved to the Nalweyo-Kakumiro Road, where we rested.

On 12 January 1985 we crossed back to our Nkrumah zone. All this time Colonel Ogole had kept up his offensive and at one time he had attacked us but we had repulsed him and captured a few more weapons.

While on the way to our headquarters in Bulemezi, we had to pass through Kikandwa forest. Ogole's people had set up camps in Kirema School and Namirembe Primary School. The forest lies between these two hills and the enemy started shelling us from both sides. We were moving in single file, carrying weapons and other war materials, and the shells were dropping all around us. It was a miracle that we seldom lost our weapons.

The moon was shining and we were worried that the soldiers might panic. Somehow, everybody showed courage and we just continued on our way. The boys even started making fun of the whistling sound of the 120 mm bombs. We would be marching under the trees when someone would start whistling "whee". Then people would fall down to take cover to the amusement of the prankster. One can hardly imagine how people can make fun of such dire situations, but that is how we managed to keep our sanity intact in the dangerous game of war.

13

Diplomatic Offensive Starts: CHC Goes to Sweden

With the guns from Kabamba we were able to reorganise and form fully fledged units appropriate to our situation. We now had 6 battalions of 300 guns each. This was really a formidable force. Each battalion had four companies of 75 guns each and the rest were unarmed. This, compared to 1984, when we had only 75 guns per battalion, represented genuine advancement.

At the same time, the UNLA was disintegrating. There was a lot of discontent within the government forces. The replacement of the late Chief of Staff was one of the bones of contention. Obote wanted a fellow Lango, while the Acholi, being more numerous than other ethnic groups in the UNLA, felt they were bearing the brunt of the war. It is in view of the above that the CHC held a meeting of officers. He told us that the Obote regime was about to collapse, which, to us, was indisputable. He told us that it would be dangerous if Obote's regime collapsed and left a power vacuum, as the unruly UNLA would go on the rampage. In his view, there was a need for us to go on a diplomatic offensive.

It was agreed that the CHC should travel abroad to find out what the outside world thought about the war. We did not want to be left in the cold in case interesting developments were taking place. It is easy for the outside world to forget about people who are deep inside the country, fighting. Because of the government propaganda we were just a mild irritant and not people to be taken seriously.

In fact, when we decided to open the western front, Obote's people started saying on the radio that we were running away to Zaire. While, to us on the ground, it was laughable, the people who were not in the know but who supported us felt demoralised. The group to open up the western front was led by Comrade Fred Rwigyyema. It was a heroic march, reminiscent of the great trek by Mao Tse-Tung of China. This trek of mostly unarmed civilians, the sick and the elderly made a journey of about 400 km through virgin territory, and this was no mean achievement. Fred's group, accompanied by two battalions, 5th and 11th, set off on 30 March and reached its destination without losing anyone. That did not stop Obote from claiming that the whole NRA was on the run. The truth of the matter was that the main fighting force of the NRA was still in Luweero and Ogole was aware of it, hence his relentless offensive.

The CHC had to leave by our now-usual route, Lake Victoria, and my unit was tasked to escort his entourage as far from the war theatre as possible. My wife, Dora, who was expecting our second child, was in the entourage. So I had extra interest in escorting them.

The trip from Kabamba to join Kikoko, which was the last NRA unit, was tough. We went fighting all the way and, in fact, even in Kikoko, where we had to leave the CHC's group, we engaged in heavy fighting. Some combatants were injured and two comrades died. It was here that a young man, Mugerwa, referred to as a batsman, killed two enemy soldiers with just three bullets. We had set up a camp in Kikoko, which was a former defence of 7th Battalion. When the enemy attacked at around 7.30 a.m., we were in our trenches. The enemy tried to encircle us. This young man was well positioned, so when the enemy emerged from a thicket into the cleared killing ground, Mugerwa let off only three bullets and two enemy soldiers fell down dead. Despite the casualties on our side, Mugerwa became an instant hero.

The enemy was using artillery and mortar fire and our chief signaller, Lukyamuzi, now a colonel, exhibited funny antics, as he jumped up and down to the rhythm of the firing. We used to monitor enemy communications and the enemy had determined our grid references accurately, so whenever the order for "fire" was made, Lukyamuzi, who knew what was going on, felt unnerved. He knew that the enemy had the right target. Those of us who were not informed, just carried on thinking it was the usual random bombing by the UNLA. However, Lukyamuzi knew and was more scared than us who were ignorant. For those who were watching Lukyamuzi, it was fun. Whenever a bomb would be fired, Lukyamuzi would jump up, only to land back on the ground at almost the same time as the bomb. After some time, as was the norm with the UNLA, they withdrew, leaving behind some seven dead bodies, including the two soldiers killed by Mugerwa.

In the afternoon the CHC's group continued on their journey to the lake shore while we went back to our location. The journey, according to Dora, had many hazards. At one point they experienced the misfortune of getting diverted from their guide, Col. Sserwanga Lwanga, an intellectual from Ssese Islands, who had been a long-distance runner at school, and was one of the most pious and dedicated fighters. He had such a high sense of mission that he felt he had to give all for the struggle. Sserwanga was one of the most reliable couriers and at times the balance of the war depended on his capacity to deliver messages in time. His nickname was "Horse". He could run in the bush and we depended on him for useful information. It was Sserwanga who used to link us up with the outside world.

He would come with messages from outside the country, elude enemy roadblocks and deployment, pass on the message and then return to enemy territory.

Sserwanga was such an asset to us that when the enemy captured him after he was betrayed by deserting UFM soldiers, we agreed to exchange him for a Uganda Airlines plane which had been hijacked by our people to Kasese. He was such a good friend that I made him my best man when I formally married Dora.

This time Sserwanga, who was the eyes and ears of the CHC entourage, had lost contact with them. They were at a loss what to do, just as when Andrew Lutaya had got diverted from us while we were coming from Nairobi in 1981. Now Sserwanga was not in touch with the CHC group. He was the one who knew the routes and who had the contacts. One can only imagine what the group's feelings were. To add insult to injury, Dora, who was heavy with child, was moving slowly, forcing the CHC to proclaim that Dora ought to be castrated: this prompted laughter despite the precarious condition we were all in.

The CHC group later linked up with Sserwanga Lwanga and crossed Lake Victoria on a boat as we had done before. By 29 March 1985, the CHC was in Sweden and the diplomatic offensive was under way. It was on 20 June 1985 that Dora gave birth to Sankara Kutesa. The boy did not live long enough to see the end of the bush war. He died from a chest infection in December 1985 during the Katonga days. All I remember about him was that he was a healthy child with a captivating smile. He was born and lived for a short while, smiled at the world and died young. REST IN PEACE, SANKARA.

14

Birembo: The Battle That Broke UNLA's Back

The CHC had left at the height of Colonel John Ogole's offensive. We were being attacked relentlessly and were repulsing the attacks. As stated earlier, the 14.5 mm anti-aircraft gun was proving a dangerous weapon to our soldiers. The fighters' morale was ebbing, especially due to that gun's uncanny habit of amputating the combatants' limbs. We still have some of the victims of that heinous weapon with us.

We had managed to blow up one of the guns using our battery-connected mines. However, the fear remained. Peasant soldiers can easily be demoralised if they face what they conceive to be an undefeatable weapon, and despondence was setting it.

It was in view of the above that I tried with my 1st Battalion to demystify the might of the 14.5mm anti-aircraft gun. The enemy had detected our camp in Kirema and were advancing with this abominable 14.5 mm gun. This gun had raised the enemy soldiers' morale, to the detriment of our own people. I decided to lay a linear ambush along the road at a place called Kampomera. The 1st Battalion was composed of some of the best fighters the NRA had.

The enemy advanced along the road till we judged that we had a big portion of them in the killing ground. Then we opened fire. The UNLA had deployed trained soldiers who immediately took up position and answered our fire, unlike the usual NYA who would have dispersed.

Our usual operations were characterised by brief but fierce firefights followed by an organised withdrawal. This time it was not to be. The enemy took up position and we pinned each other down. Neither the enemy nor our people dared raise their heads. The bullets and bombs continued for almost an hour, which is a long time for a hasty ambush. Meanwhile, the 14.5 gun was advancing. My aim was to capture it in order to show our people that it was just like any other weapon. Despite the briefing my soldiers had received, they started making reckless mistakes. We started using fire and movement tactics modelled on those taught in training. Only this time, instead of the instructors firing over our heads, the enemy was aiming to kill. Our boys were not used to defeat and that added to our casualties. Most of us had survived firefights and we did not know why we could not survive this one. We could easily detect where the 14.54 mm gun was firing from and we were determined to capture or blow it up.

In the process we incurred an unprecedented number of casualties. One of the brave fighters who died was a young man nicknamed "Double Colour". He was shot in the chest as he was trying to crawl towards the dreaded gun. Later this soldier's body was beheaded and the head was taken to Kampala. The jubilant enemy were convinced that they had killed PECOS KUTESA. In fact, radios and newspapers in Kampala proclaimed that one notorious bandit, Pecos Kutesa, had been killed in action and one UNLA officer, Kiyongo, went ahead to tell BBC "Focus on Africa" that it was Pecos Kutesa's head since he had been with him in Monduli, Tanzania, in training. He therefore claimed that he knew me very well. One can only imagine what Dora, who was heavy with child, felt when she heard that I was dead.

The battle for the anti-aircraft gun raged on for more than four hours. I had managed to crawl near enough to see the enemy soldiers who were firing it. In fact, I had become so engrossed in the battle that I had lost all sense of command. I had become just a front-line infantry soldier. My aim was to capture this gun. Incidentally, by then my own rifle had run out of bullets. I had fired all the bullets but I did not know it, so I continued crawling nearer. I could see the enemy soldiers who were guarding the anti-aircraft gun start to withdraw and I shouted "Charge!" and tried to fire, only to hear the firing pin hit an empty chamber!

I had crawled onto the top of an earth mound, the ones they use for growing sweet potatoes in this area. By instinct or whatever unknown powers, Jet Mwebaze pulled me backwards. Jet Mwebaze was a tall, muscular, strong-boned fellow, but I believe it was the instinct for survival which gave him that mythical strength because with only one arm he tossed the whole 60 kg of me behind him like a rag. There is a phenomenal strength a person gathers when his life is in danger. One's eyesight, hearing, sense of smell and, in fact, all one's senses, act extraordinarily. How Jet sensed the next action is still a mystery, because just seconds after he tossed me behind himself, the potato mound was swept clean by the 4 barrels of the 14.5 mm gun. I can still recall the patch where I had been lying for a few minutes now looking as if a grader blade had passed over it.

In such circumstances, the adrenaline is raging. All the body functions are automated by the flow of the adrenaline fluids. I cannot recall thanking Jet or how I changed position, but soon Musoke Kyenvangunywa informed me that we had to withdraw since we had incurred many casualties and most of our people had dispersed. It was as if I was in a trance. Musoke had to drag me away from the battlefield. To me, this was very unfair. I had personally seen the enemy soldiers withdrawing and abandoning the gun which had been our primary target and here was Musoke telling me to withdraw! However, when he told me the number of our people he had seen dead, reason overcame my emotions and I followed his advice.

Of the more than 90 armed soldiers I had come with, plus the "commandos", I found myself left with only 15 people, including my second-in-command, Peter Kerim. It was growing dark. On top of that we had a casualty, a Sergeant Geoffrey Mukasa, whose arm had been shattered by the dreaded anti-aircraft gun. He had been hit in the upper arm and the bone was shattered. The arm was dangling and caused a lot of pain. We had to carry him since he could not stand and he was losing a lot of blood. One of us cut his shirt and tried to staunch the blood with that dirty rag. The most important item was a stretcher. In most of our operations we never carried stretchers, and so this time I started to appreciate its value. At such a time, one's mind works many times faster than normal.

Immediately I remembered that I had a Boy Scout knife given to me by Mr Tim Cooper who, together with another journalist, a lady called Alison Porteous, had come to witness our war firsthand. This knife had many blades and some of them were like saws. I used the knife to cut two eucalyptus saplings and, using the bark, improvised a stretcher which we then used to carry our casualty. Some time after the war, I met Mukasa, who had healed well but had a shortened arm. It is a miracle that people survive wounds in wars, which would be fatal in normal life. Mukasa's arm was not treated with any sterilised instruments, the dirty rag that was used to staunch his blood was enough to contaminate the wound, but Mukasa never developed gangrene or tetanus, nor did he suffer any other side effects apart from a shortened right arm. That is the strength of nature's healing power.

It was when we were wading through the thick undergrowth in the heavy rain with our moaning comrade, that my second-in-command asked me with his usual sneer: "Now sir, what shall we report? Where shall we say our troops are?" It may sound sadistic but Peter was trying to lighten our mood.

It was midnight when we reported to the camp. We found Saleh all over the place. He had not communicated with me for a span of 24 hours, which is a long time in the type of war we were engaged in. In the meantime, Radio Uganda was celebrating my death and our people in Kampala and Nairobi had been thrown into disbelief and shock.

Our fighters had been trekking in and, at the end of the day, we found we had lost about 12 combatants, which was one of the biggest losses the NRA had ever suffered. On top of that, the anti-aircraft gun had remained elusive. This was a big blow to the NRA but much more to me, as a commander who had led the mission. It is ironical, but the person who was in charge of the enemy attack, the current LC V Chairman of Gulu, Col. Walter Ochora, is a personal friend. He is a fat, jolly fellow with whom I had undergone training in Monduli. This Ochora is one of the people who led the rebellion against President Obote. After the NRM captured power, Ochora joined a group of rebels called the Uganda People's Democratic Army (UPDA), which later joined the NRA in 1988. Whenever we meet, we always recall the battle at Kampomera. He assures me that if I had persisted, I would have captured the anti-aircraft gun, since his soldiers had started running away. I always tell him that was a post-mortem of the battle. Whenever I ask him why he decided to lie to the Ugandan people that I was dead, he replies: "In war, the first casualty is always the truth."

The fact that the anti-aircraft gun had eluded capture or destruction by me nagged me for a long time. It was later, when I was studying that fundamental difference between fight and fright in psychology that I started appreciating the situation. Even if we had managed to capture it, how would we have towed it to our hideouts deep in the forest? Such arguments have helped my mind to settle.

After reorganisation, the 1st Battalion went on nursing its wounded and carrying out small operations. I was still in the Kikandwa area in Bulemezi, when Salim Saleh, with a large part of the mobile brigade, moved into the Singo area. Ogole continued his offensive in the Luweero Triangle. He knew that the allegation about the guerrillas running away to Zaire was not sheer propaganda. He knew that the core of the fighting force was still in the triangle, hence on 21 June 1985 there was a major encounter between Ogole's special brigade and our mobile brigade at Kambogo. This encounter was the straw that broke the camel's back. Ogole was himself in command of this brigade and our people inflicted such heavy casualties on his troops that their disorganised retreat sparked off a chain reaction, resulting in the overthrow of the Obote government. I was not in that battle, but the stories we heard were that, for the first time, the UNLA entered a well-prepared ambush which was in plain ground, where they did not expect any NRA to be. The result was that we routed the UNLA and scored a great victory.

When the UNLA reported back to Kampala, it was in a mutinous mood. The Kamboga defeat, together with another unprecedented defeat in the western sector, when our people under Fred Rwigyema attacked Rubona prison near Fort Portal, showed that the UNLA was overstretched and "the bandits" were in charge of the war. The UNLA were demoralised.

Rubona prison is about 400 kilometres from Kambogo in Singo, so the span of the front proved extremely wide. That, coupled with the enthusiasm of the civilian support for the NRA, left no doubt in the minds of the UNLA officers and me that Obote was a liability.

Fighting broke out within the UNLA ranks. The soldiers regarded the war and its subsequent casualties in terms of ethnic groups. The Acholi had always been the majority in the ranks of the UNLA, so they reasoned that if they overthrew Obote and his Langi clique, they would be accepted by the population. To

the Acholi soldiers, all the government army casualties seemed
to be from among themselves, while their cousins, the Langi,
were in offices in Kampala. The Democratic Party (DP) saw the
discontent in the UNLA as a blessing. The DP, a strong Catholic
Buganda-based political party, which lacked military support,
had always felt the need to have the army on its side. There
has always been reluctance on the part of Baganda youth to
join the army, which they viewed as a profession for failures in
education and the poor; it was mostly meant for the "foreigners"
from the north.

The Acholi are predominantly Catholics, so the DP played
their religious card, hoping, for the first time in its history, to
have a Ugandan armed force which would be an ally. On their
part, Acholi officers and men hoped that they would be accepted
by the hostile population in Kampala through the DP. Hence,
there was a marriage of convenience between the Acholi faction
of the UNLA and the DP.

The fall of Obote on 27 July 1985 found me with my troops
in the *lukoola* area, near Mr Kkaaya's farm. Mr Kaaya was one
of our staunch supporters. I can still remember Junior Officer
Rwamukaga cynically telling me that it was senseless for the
war to end while we were still alive. It is sad that Rwamukaga
died before the capture of Kampala.

Kampala city had always been our main objective. Even
in songs we used to sing *Tusonge, tusonge mpaka Kampala*
meaning "Let us move forward up to Kampala". Most of us
thought that the capture of Kampala city would mean the end
of the war. Incidentally, even the enemy thought that the end
of their tenure in office would be the capture of the capital city
and, more significantly, the capture of Radio Uganda. It is little
wonder, therefore, that when Obote was overthrown, it was an
Acholi officer who rushed to Radio Uganda to announce their
coup d'etat.

The first announcement by Okello Kolo Boom, a businessman who was an army hanger-on, and Lt. Col. Walter Ochora, called upon Mr Yoweri Museveni to report to Parliament. A circus as looting reminiscent of Idi Amin's fall started in Kampala. Only, this time, there was not much to loot since the people had very few things to be looted.

The coup against Obote originated from Gulu, the home area of the two Okellos, Tito Okello-Lutwa and Bazilio Olara Okello. More precisely, it was organised and blessed by Father John Scalabrini, an Italian priest who commanded a lot of respect among the Acholi population. Father Scalabrini was the rector of Lacor Seminary. He had developed a great love for the local Acholi community. While the southern part of Uganda had been introduced to cash crop farming, the north had been kept as a manual labour reserve. Hence, the northerners were more involved in the forces, railways and harbours and sugar plantations.

Father Scalabrini introduced the sunflower crop, which does well in northern Uganda. Not only did he offer the peasants sunflower seeds, he also established an oil extraction plant. Father Scalabrini had become a saviour to the civilian population of both Gulu and Kitgum districts. He would lend the sunflower seeds to the peasants, then mill the flower seeds, sell the sunflower oil and pay them. He did not only stop at giving them value for their labour and land. He also helped quite a number of young people to go to school. He had acquired the status, not only of a benevolent community chief, but also a demi-god because of his priestly cassock.

I was later to become a personal friend of Father John when I was put in command of Gulu. He became very friendly and he is the one who told me how the anti-Obote coup was planned. Father Scalabrini told me that, when disagreement broke out within the UNLA ranks, the top Acholi commanders ran back to their home base of Gulu and found sanctuary in his residence. "His people" were good but lacked leadership. He believed the

Acholi were "his people". He continued, "Look young man! These generals were hiding under my bed, till I asked them whether or not they were soldiers. I also asked them why they were running away from Obote. I asked them to go ahead and overthrow him." It was owing to Father Scalabrini's prompting that the Okello junta marched on Kampala.

The coup was a fiasco, because the civilian population did not experience any change. It was the same rogue troops now marching into the city, with the clenched fist (the DP symbol) on one hand, and firing in the air with the other. The civilians were not impressed. The new UNLA troops were chanting DP! DP! DP! but the reception of the civilian population was chilling, to say the least. It was that feeling of unacceptability that forced the new leaders to appeal on Radio Uganda for all the forces opposed to Obote to come out and work with them.

As stated earlier, there were more than twenty groups opposed to Obote from the beginning but, by the time of the coup five years later, only four could be accounted for. These were the FUNA in the West Nile region, the FEDEMU, the UFM and the most noticeable opposition group, the NRM. Now the Okello group was sending out radio appeals for all of us to join in their fiasco. Those of us in the NRA just laughed at the junta's thinking. They thought that the sole aim of going to war was how gaining part of the political cake. As far as they were concerned, all of us had taken up arms because only the Langi clique of UPC was "eating". What a fallacy! We had gone to the bush, not only to change the status quo, but also to sweep away the entire system. When the late Rwamukaga was joking about Obote's ouster, at the back of his mind, he knew that the war was far from over.

When the Acholi faction of the UNLA was advancing from their base in Lacor Seminary, they had to pass through our area of control, that is the Kampala-Gulu highway. We had a tactical agreement with them and, in fact, Comrade Lumumba, with a few soldiers, went up to Bombo barracks to meet Gen. Tito

Okello-Lutwa, before he became the fifth president of Uganda. General Tito was the designated leader of the Acholi/UPC/UNLA clique that had overthrown Obote. Nobody had any ill-feelings towards the grandfatherly figure who could not communicate fluently in any language besides Acholi. Being from the Second World War King's African Rifles (KAR), he had seen it all and had no ill intentions towards all the *bijana* — grandchildren — as he envisaged us. To him, all of us were just misguided youth. He had no quarrel with any of us, whether UNLA, FUNA, FEDEMU or NRA. We were his grandchildren. The politicians tried to use him. However, with his native intelligence and experience, he resisted manipulation.

From 27 July 85, there was a lull in activity on both sides. That was the time of the infamous peace talks, *"pich toksi"* according to General Okello-Lutwa and "pistol talks" according to us, the fighters. During that lull, there was a lot of informal contact between us, the NRA, and some UNLA elements. Again the UFM caused problems for us following the announcements on Radio Uganda by General Tito's faction and subordinates, like (retired) Col. Walter Ochora. This group, which had been out of action for some time, now emerged and declared themselves the leading anti-Obote fighters. The UFM was followed by another group, FEDEMU, and other splinter groups. These people were quickly assimilated into the UNLA and given some sectors to control.

The UFM combatants knew most of our routes and supporters. They were later turned into informers by the Okello junta. It was the UFM boys at UNLA roadblocks who betrayed Sserwanga Lwanga. These UFM operatives, nicknamed "computers", easily identified "Horse", while he was on his sojourn from Kampala. They cynically addressed him as *Afande,* a Kiswahili word meaning "Sir", and challenged him to deny that he was senior officer Sserwanga Lwanga of NRA. Sserwanga had no ready reply and was made a prisoner of war.

Later Sserwanga Lwanga was exchanged for a plane that Capt. Innocent Bisangwa had hijacked, but the damage had already been done.

In the course of the Nairobi talks, a ceasefire was declared. However, the UNLA continued their atrocities. There was very little control over the UNLA troops and the killing and abduction of suspected NRA supporters continued. While the CHC and the political wing of the NRM/A were talking of political compromise, in the bush we were only interested in a military compromise. The UNLA naively believed that the NRA fighters were tired of war and so all they had to do was promise us high ranks and we would desert the cause. To some of us this thinking was laughable. Some of us had a lot of contempt for the high-sounding formal ranks. In fact, during the introduction of formal ranks after the capture of power, I was opposed to being called a colonel, general or brigadier like the UNLA dinosaurs in Kampala. However, I was convinced that, in a national army, which we had become after Declaration No. 1 of 1986, we had to have regular ranks. I had argued that the Chinese army did not have those ranks but my argument was shot down, and I accepted the reasoning of the army leadership known as collective responsibility.

The Okello junta made a fundamental mistake. After realising that we were not easy to lure with promises of ranks, they approached former Uganda Army elements from West Nile. Their reasoning was that the people of West Nile were ethnically closer to them. Gen. Okello added that the stubborn NRA people were the Baganda and 'Nyarwanda', the latter being a derogatory term the UNLA used to refer to Uganda's southerners. This move and reference angered not only indigenous Ugandans but also Julius Nyerere of Tanzania who, at that time, still wielded a lot of influence.

As talks were still going on in Nairobi, planeloads of former Amin soldiers were landing at Entebbe. As if that was not

enough, the UNLA embarked on what they termed the final
phase of the war, looting and killing in the Luweero Triangle.
The fragile peace talks were tottering, hence we continued
training and carrying out recces on the UNLA camps near our
positions. It was during this period that we received some arms
and ammunition from Libya. These weapons were dropped
by llyushin planes in the *lukoola* areas. I had been given
instructions to light bonfires to guide the pilots. We did not
need to bother. The pilots of these planes knew the *lukoola*
very well and it was a pleasant surprise when, at dawn, these
planes started flying over the Ngoma areas dropping parachute-
borne weapons.

We spent an exhausting day chasing the white parachutes
and retrieving the precious cargo. All in all, we got about 800
rifles and about 800,000 rounds of ammunition. This was a
very big morale booster. The only disappointment was that
most of the guns were unique. At that time, we were not very
conversant with Uzi guns. Also, their maintenance is much
more difficult than their handy counterpart, the AK-47. Since
beggars cannot be choosers, we soon mastered the use of the Uzi
guns and they played a big part in the subsequent battles.

In all wars, it is prudent for belligerent forces to capture as
much ground as possible and to become more prepared both
for a better bargaining ground or a better fallback position in
case peace talks failed. That is what both we the NRA, and our
adversary the UNLA, were doing.

15

Fighting the Okello Regime

The peace talks chaired by Kenya's President Arap Moi continued in Nairobi on shaky ground, failed and on 24 August 1985, the CHC, Yoweri Museveni, sent an advance order to us in the bush to attack or force the surrender of all UNLA forces near our locations. General Tito Okello had told Ugandans in an address, that the war was over since he had rendered the "big snake" (Museveni) toothless. Kampala city was a replica of Beirut. The city of seven hills was divided into a city of five army camps, each with its own agenda and command structure. Civilians in the city had difficulty identifying which faction was in control of which area.

All sorts of groups were setting up their tactical headquarters around the city. There was the original UNLA, then FUNA, then UNRF, FEDEMU and UFM. Each faction had occupied one of the hills of Kampala and they were staying in the few good hotels available.

When the order was given for the NRA to move, each unit advanced on its nominated target. Comrade Patrick Lumumba and Bamwesigye moved on Busunju, another group moved to Luweero and another unit to Matugga.

My 1st Battalion, with Mugisha "Headache" as second-in-command, surrounded Kiboga town. We moved in broad daylight and took up positions around the administrative buildings where the UNLA unit was camped. I dispatched a civilian to go and tell the unit that they were under siege, and that if they were willing to give up, they should inform us, or if they preferred fighting, we were in a position to do so.

My officers urged me to order the attack as Lumumba, with whom we were in radio communication, had done in Busunju. I restrained them because I felt there was no need for unnecessary bloodshed. The UNLA soldiers, who numbered about 2 companies, were not even dug in, they were just waiting for orders to return to Kampala, because according to them, the war was almost over. I was sure of my move because the commander of the group in Kiboga was Lt. Okecho Okecha and his second-in-command was Lt. Kakooza, and both officers had trained with me in Monduli, Tanzania. I knew they would not fight. The fighting spirit of the UNLA was at its lowest ebb. I am happy that my prediction proved true after an exchange of emissaries. The UNLA commander agreed that we should meet. Around 10.00 a.m. I left my unit under the charge of "Headache" and entered the enemy defence.

Comrade Santos Okecho Okecha, who later proved himself a good fighter when he joined us, welcomed me with an open heart. He called all his troops to order and told them what was going on. I gave the soldiers two options: those who wanted to join us could do so and those who wanted to go to Kampala were also free to do so, provided they left their weapons behind. At first there was a slight reluctance. However, when they saw Mugisha's troops taking up positions, they agreed. The government troops put their guns down and started boarding their trucks. They had four lorries and a water tanker. Okecho Okecha, best known by comrades as Kanyogoga, had a hard time making a decision. At first he refused to open up his improvised armoury, insisting that he first had to get orders from his seniors. I told him that at that moment he was on his own and that communication to Kampala could not save him and his troops. Lt. Okecho Okecha, later Lt. Col. in the NRA/

UPDF, made a momentous decision on that day, 24 August 85, my 29th birthday. He decided to join the guerrillas and save the lives of his more than two hundred soldiers.

The UNLA boarded their trucks under the command of the second-in-command Lt. Kakooza, who is now LCV Chairman, Mubende. Kakooza's last remark, after getting a movement order from me, a guerrilla, was that I should join him and go to Kampala, since by the time I left the bush, he would have taken over all my girlfriends. Of course, we laughed over that.

The Kiboga mission proved that, between us soldiers, there is never any deep-rooted hatred. We do our job to the best of our ability. War is just like a match, with losers and winners. It is the politicians who have the time to harbour hatred and resentment since they have to justify the wars, which are usually political anyway and in many cases unjustified.

Our troops had overrun Matugga, Busunju and Luweero with different degrees of success. After reorganisation, we found we had captured many weapons with few or no casualties on our side. From Kiboga, we had not only got weapons without firing a bullet, but also acquired a good future combat commander. Most significantly, a message had gone out to the belligerent troops that the guerrillas were not killers or inhuman or detractors as the government propaganda had tried to depict us.

Many people started deserting the UNLA and joining the NRA during this time. Rumours were also wreaking havoc on the morale of the enemy. Soldiers who passed through our hands had to justify their failure, so they came up with all sorts of myths about our military might. The civilian population added to the myths about the guerrillas by concocting stories about all sorts of miracles performed by the guerrillas. The people who had been cowed by the vicious UNLA actions started thinking differently about the the UNLA. They started doubting Okello's propaganda when they saw the dejected disarmed government troops withdrawing from the front line. The tide had started turning.

The message from the NRM to the Okello junta was simple. It was a warning that, if the junta was serious about peace, they should try to discipline their troops or else we would continue with the war, something we were fully capable of doing. Many of our people failed to understand why we were willing to go on fighting. Obote was gone, there was no need to fight.

There was the misconception that the sole reason for our going to war was to overthrow Obote and start sharing the loot with the remaining UNLA. This was very far from the truth. Even the lowliest of our comrades knew that there could never be peace in Uganda as long as the UNLA stayed in control of the army. Many of our Ugandan supporters were of the view that all we needed to do was capture Radio Uganda, broadcast an announcement, and then the suffering of our people would be over. I can forgive these Ugandans since all the changes they had ever experienced since independence were through the capture of Radio Uganda. They were also aided in this misconception by the myth about our strength, created by the withdrawing UNLA soldiers, and our own excited supporters. However, we were aware of our real strength and we were not yet ready to take over power.

The other group pushing for the winding up of the war was the international community. Since Obote was now gone, they did not understand why we could not work with the Okellos. In fact, at one time during the peace talks in Nairobi, Mr Robin White, a BBC African Service correspondent, had the cheek to ask Yoweri Museveni whether he was delaying the war in order to be president of Uganda. Mr White had imagined that he would score a journalistic scoop by making Museveni lose his head, as was the norm among African leaders when subjected to Mr White's witty and cynical interrogation. The CHC had the presence of mind to ask Mr White about the importance of the presidency of Uganda in 1985, compared to, say, the mayorship of London. The result was that the momentum of Robin White's attack dissipated quite quickly.

The only international leader who understood our stand then was Julius Nyerere of Tanzania. He alone knew that the problems of Uganda could not be solved by the mere exit of Obote. After all, the Okello clique was inviting former Idi Amin's soldiers back. To President Nyerere, that was unacceptable; "the very big snake" *(nyokapango)* he had chased away from neighbouring Uganda was now coming back from the Sudan, where he believed it ought to have been buried. President Nyerere's disagreement with Amin was based on principles and not merely sentiment. Now the Okellos, whom Nyerere had supported while under Obote, had shown their true character. Nyerere started supporting the NRA openly.

We reorganised and waited for the outcome of the peace talks. Meanwhile, the UNLA continued to ravage the country.

On 12 September 1985, the CHC gave the order to NRA to advance on UNLA positions. The western axis overran Fort Portal and all the UNLA detachments advanced on the Mbarara military barracks, which is the major barracks in the West. This force was under Commander Fred Rwigyema.

The mobile brigade under Commander Salim Saleh attacked and overran Mubende and advanced on Hoima and Mityana towns, capturing them both. In Mityana, we captured many Ministry of Agriculture motorcycles. Our bush comrades, whose knowledge of riding did not go beyond bicycles, now became excited about these motorcycles. Many accidents happened and a few good comrades died. A young man would sit on a motorbike and rev it up. However, once the clutch was released, the motorbike would fly into the air, and in most cases our amateur riders would hit the tarmac with the backs of their heads, which proved fatal in many cases. I can still clearly recall when we commandeered a Uganda Electricity Board (UEB) Land Rover, which we proceeded to nickname *Ndege ya chini* (ground plane). These young men would drive at high speed in front of my vehicle, pretending to be a presidential motorcade outriders. It was fun, but any slight mistake could have ended in an untidy pileup.

It was in Mityana that the 5th Battalion under commander Steven Kashaka (now military attaché to Tanzania) inflicted many casualties on Karimojong warriors. In their mobilisation exercise the UNLA had not stopped at recruiting former Uganda Army personnel. They had secured the services of some Karimojong, who are traditionally cattle rustlers. These young men were deceived that there were many cattle up for grabs in southern Uganda. When they were thoroughly beaten by the 5th Battalion and forced to withdraw, not only suffering many casualties, but also going back without a single cow, their honeymoon with the Okello junta was over.

From Mityana, we advanced on Masaka, the fourth largest town in Uganda, then home to the Masaka Mechanised Regiment. This is also one of the biggest military barracks in Uganda. Before advancing on Masaka Road, we passed through Kyenjojo on to Fort Portal, where we met our other forces and the whole of our rear was now safe.

In the meantime, our western axis under Fred Rwigyema and Julius Chihandae advanced from Fort Portal and attacked Mbarara. This attack was not successful. The enemy had detected their movement and withdrawn to another location. Our people took the town and immediately entered the barracks. There was little resistance in the barracks and our people made the fundamental mistake of going straight to the armouries and capturing the big guns without adequate preparation against a counterattack from the enemy. Since I was not in that battle, I cannot authoritatively tell what transpired. I can recall, however, the sense of euphoria we experienced in after entering the Mbarara barracks. The enemy, under the command of my former cubicle-mate at Monduli, Lt. Col. Santansio Constantine Otto, counterattacked and took our combatants completely unawares. It was a disaster on our part. We lost 45 comrades, among whom a personal friend, Mugerwa, a young officer who had been my ADC, then an ADC to Commander Fred Rwigyema. This young man had developed a kind of hero-worship for me, because I had led him successfully on many missions. He used to tell his comrades *Huyu hana barah* (That one has no misfortune). He died on 12 December 1985 in that infamous Mbarara attack. Rest in peace Comrade Mugerwa.

Our people did not abandon Mbarara completely. Instead, they moved away from the town centre and the barracks. They established themselves on all the hills overlooking the town and barracks and dominated all the routes leading into Mbarara. The siege of Mbarara had begun.

After linking up with our other troops in Fort Portal as a mobile brigade, we advanced on Masaka through Kamwenge and Ibanda, then joined the Mbarara-Masaka road at Kibega near Sanga, where we met a group of UNLA soldiers whose intention was to rescue their comrades in Mbarara. We repulsed and chased them up to Masaka.

The attack on Masaka Mechanised Regiment was not a success although it was not as disastrous as the one on Mbarara. Our forces, led by Salim Saleh, with commanders such as Patrick Lumumba and Geoffrey Taban, now a brigadier, tried to assault the barracks. However, the perimeter fence was heavily mined and their advance was thus checked. Although our losses were minimal, we suffered some casualties from anti-personnel mines and the enemy did put up a good defence. They had well-dug communication trenches, bigger guns than we had and a well-prepared defence. This made it foolhardy to assault the Masaka barracks at that time. We also decided to lay siege to the barracks.

These were two big siege operations against well-established government barracks. In military terms, this was a great achievement; in political terms, it was a tremendous success because we had managed to cut off the whole of the western part of the country. We had established a pseudo administration over a very large part of the country bordering Tanzania, Rwanda and Congo. The area under our control covered the whole of Bunyoro, Kigezi, Ankole, Toro, Masaka and a big part of Mubende. This territory covers about two thirds of Uganda; it happens to be the most productive and is more heavily populated than the rest of the country, excluding Buganda and Busoga. We had now under the NRA command about 8 million people, out of a total population of about 19 million in Uganda.

Our next step was clearing our backyard. We set out on this task by clearing all the enemy detachments in the area under our control with the two barracks under siege. The population under our control was jubilant. In fact, one of the lasting impressions of that time was what we noticed when we entered Fort Portal. The sense of joy and relief from the feeling of siege by the UNLA was so high that it seemed to me that even the trees and buildings were drunk. The people of Toro are well known for their love and enjoyment of life. This is because they knew that they could now start enjoying genuine freedom. They really went out of their way to express their appreciation of our work. The feeling of arrival I had experienced in 1979 during the war against Idi Amin was now tripled. The people of Toro felt a sense of redemption beyond their wildest dreams.

It was not only the people of Toro, but the entire population under the command of the NRA/NRM that felt they had been given a new lease of life. The political wing of the NRM started putting up a new administration by creating resistance councils (RCs) from the parish up to district level. Our task was to defend the borders of this new state within a state.

The UNLA soldiers in Mbarara could only get reinforcements through Masaka, and in order to effectively control our area of operation, we had to cut off our zone from Kampala. That was when the control of the Kampala-Masaka-Mbarara highway became imperative. After occupying the so-called ground of tactical importance, in both the Mbarara and Masaka sieges, and having made sure that the UNLA soldiers were confined to their barracks, the next task was to cut off the only access routes to the enemy headquarters in Kampala from their besieged troops.

The 3rd Battalion under Commander Patrick Lumumba carried out the siege of Masaka. The enemy mines helped him since even the enemy themselves did not know the mine layout and were thus confined to the main road as the only access to the outside world. The enemy was well entrenched with bigger weapons than Lumumba's people. However, those weapons were stationary and could not be moved easily. On his part, Lumumba had the control of the Masaka Technical School hill, which directly overlooks the Masaka barracks. Lumumba also had the entire town and the support of the population. Our people occupied strategic hills like Bwala, Kako, Kitovu and Kyabakuza.

Masaka barracks was sealed off tightly. It was just a matter of time before physical needs forced the besieged soldiers to surrender. All that time, we were monitoring enemy messages both from Mbarara and Masaka to Kampala. Our people continued bombarding the besieged UNLA, who in turn retaliated with heavy mortar and anti-aircraft guns. The siege of Masaka, which lasted three months, was a test of will between us and the besieged enemy.

Field Marshal Montgomery one time stated: "When all conditions are equal, it is the willpower of the one belligerent commander over his adversary that determines the course of the battle."

It was a battle of willpower between us, the besiegers, and the besieged UNLA forces. One of the messages from the second-in-command of Masaka, then Captain Olanya Ojara, who later became a lieutenant colonel, and was my second-in-command when I was Chief of Training and Recruitment in the NRA, which we intercepted, was hilarious, to say the least. Capt. Olanya Ojara had taken over command when the garrison commander, Major Tebandeke, had died after he was hit by our anti-aircraft gun. Capt. Olanya Ojara sent a message to his headquarters empowering them to use any weapon at their disposal, even those not allowed by the Geneva Convention, to enable him to break out of the siege, since Mbarara depended on him for its survival. Later when I showed Olanya Ojara his message, we had a great laugh about it.

The Katonga bridge

In order to effectively control the area under NRA/NRM and to prevent enemy reinforcements reaching the Mbarara and Masaka garrisons, we had to control all the access routes from Kampala to south-western Uganda. River Katonga offered us the best natural barrier and the Katonga bridge was a godsend to us, the defenders of the territory under our jurisdiction.

It was the 1st Battalion, with Fred Mugisha as my second-in-command which had blocked the bridge. The 5th Battalion under Stephen Kashaka and Ahmed Kashillingi were told to man the southern side of the road.

As I had already intimated, the bridge which I had earlier reconnoitered reminded me of the Kalongero bridge of Luweero Triangle. We immediately set up position a few metres from Lukaya town and moved onto the bridge where we dug in our defences.

Effectively, we had cut off Masaka and the whole of southern Uganda from Kampala. This was a very provocative action on the part of the NRA/NRM. The Okello junta could not stomach such an insult and so the famous Katonga bridge battles were set in motion.

The Okello troops, with the help of former Uganda Army soldiers, made many attempts to cross that bridge. It offered us a good killing ground and served as a tantalising objective on the part of the enemy. After Commander Salim Saleh, I was the next most senior officer in the Masaka siege and the Katonga bridge buffer zone. The Masaka battles were enjoyable because we did not incur many casualties and the people were very supportive. We also had access to many facilities that we had never had for a long time in the bush.

The NRA embarked on a massive recruitment exercise and many able-bodied young men joined. It was easy to recruit since the recruiting people had a lot in common with the civilians in that area. There were no language barriers or cultural differences, instead all of us were sons of the same soil.

Men encouraged their sons to join the army, which was a new phenomenon in western Uganda, but especially in central Uganda, where aversion to the profession of soldiering was legendary. We had recruited a big number of youth from Toro, especially Bundibugyo and Bwamba, which are on the slopes of Mt Rwenzori. The Bakonjo are by nature short but stout people. These young men were nicknamed *Kyamukwese* from a revolutionary song they had introduced among our many marching songs. They were very good fighters.

One of the most memorable battles with these young men under my command was when the enemy, for the first time, used the papyrus reed floating fields in the western part of the road and tried to encircle us. This was the very papyrus float I had earlier used as my hideout when I came on my first Masaka- Kampala Road sojourn. This move would have been very dangerous if the enemy had been well-trained. However, the UNLA was recruiting mostly untrained youth from the north.

Most of our senior soldiers and NCOs were from Buganda and they could only communicate in Luganda and a little Kiswahili, while our comrades from Bundibugyo could only communicate in Rukonjo and some English. On their part, the Okello soldiers understood only Luo and some English.

Usually, when under stress, people tend to revert to their mother tongues. It was not different when we met in battle. What transpired was the rebirth of the Tower of Babel. At the end of the battle, it was one of my NCOs, Sergeant Semakula, who described the scene vividly. He told me that the war had reached an interesting stage. "*Afande,* this war is making me crazy," he complained. I asked him why. "You see *Afande,*" answered Semakula, "our people understand and talk only in Rukonjo and English, which most of us, their leaders, do not understand. And the *adui* (enemy) talk only in Luo and English, which we do not understand. In fact the whole battlefield is *katogo*". *Katogo* is a meal, a Ugandan delicacy, prepared from a mixture of foodstuffs like matooke, cassava, beans, greens, meat etc. It was a veritable mixture of languages. However, all is fair in love and war. Usually it does not take much verbal communication for someone to express their love. So in battle a lot of action is carried out by signals and the people in battle understand much faster than they would do in normal circumstances. Some UPDF soldiers have married Congolese girls and are living happily, even though few of them understand each other's language. In fact, when the NRA, now the UPDF, soldiers went on a peacekeeping mission in Monrovia, Liberia, it is said they left behind some 200 offspring, the result of a sign language called love.

So in this battle involving sign language, our Baganda NCOs and junior officers commmanded their Batoro and Bakonjo recruits successfully. It was a bad battle for the enemy who lost more than thirty soldiers. They were buried in shallow graves, all around the battlefield.

The other big battle on the bridge was commanded by my second-in-command, Fred Mugisha Headache. When the enemy attacked us this time, I had left the camp for other missions. They came with an old armoured personnel carrier (APC). This piece of hardware was of Second World War vintage and was reminiscent of the Kampala-Matugga-Bombo road tank. Our peasant soldiers shot at it with their rifles but the huge thing kept on advancing. Apprehension was setting in when Mugisha showed his generalship. He told the combatants to concentrate on the soldiers covering the APC's flanks so that the APC would eventually advance alone. In fact, the APC advanced, crossed the bridge and continued up to our very trenches. That was when the driver and the soldiers in the APC realised that they had advanced alone, since all the covering troops had either been shot by our people or had run away.

Mugisha had managed to control our people and they had not panicked. I still hold Fred Mugisha (RIP) in high esteem because he saved the day; and not only that, whenever we were in battle with him, he always showed the kind of presence of mind and courage which I can never boast of possessing.

After the APC driver and his operators realised that they had been abandoned on the battlefield, they jumped out and fled towards Masaka, leaving their machine stranded at the bottom of the hill. After the Katonga bridge, Mugisha decided to set the APC on fire, which he did by lighting a fire under its fuel tank. The shell of the derelict APC remained where it had been burnt as a mark of Mugisha's bavery, long after the war. When the government ordered that all war scrap be collected, it was removed. However, some of us still treasure that battle scene. Mugisha, who had fought heroically throughout the war till the fall of Kampala, died in 1991 from injuries inflicted by Karimojong cattle rustlers' bullets in 1988. After the APC episode, the UNLA's momentum was checked. However, they never rested. Every morning a group of UNLA would come to the bridge and we would repulse them. Katonga, just like Kalongero, had become a bridge too formidable to tackle for the UNLA.

In the meantime, the enemy in Masaka had begun to feel the strong pangs of hunger. After one month, their rations had started drying up, so the enemy soldiers tried to break out of their siege, not to fight but to forage for food in the plantations near the barracks. Our people had a field day sniping at any soldier trying to break out. The poor fellows had it really rough. Not only did they have to contend with the 3rd Battalion snipers but their own anti-personnel mines and other obstacles, which also wreaked havoc on them. One of the stories our soldiers like telling is about an enemy soldier who, after crawling through the minefield, managed to break a young bunch of bananas and, while trying to get back, was hit in the leg by a mine. His cries for help attracted his friend, who tried to carry him away, only for the friend also to step on a mine which blew off his leg. Neither our people nor the enemy could venture to assist them, not even to perform the merciful *coup de grâce*. The cries of those two mortally wounded soldiers went on for about three days before they became silent; merciful death had taken over. These and many such bizarre stories are still being told by both the besieged soldiers and the besiegers.

I had maintained my Land Rover, which had been commandeered from UEB in Mityana. This vehicle, with its driver, Deus, a young man from my own village area, who had been driving since he was about 10 years old, was not only the command vehicle, but also the supply vehicle for the frontline. This vehicle, whose top we had sliced off so that it came to resemble a jeep, could fly to our headquarters in Masaka and back with bullets and bombs in a span of 40 minutes. From Katonga to Masaka and back is about 72 miles (115 kilometres).

I can still recall sending radio messages in the middle of battle to Commander Salim Saleh on Kisunzu hill, his tactical headquarters in Masaka town. The message stated that I was sending Deus to him for more bullets, only to be told that my emissary was just entering the headquarters camp. It was classic driving on the part of Deus, and the young man enjoyed it a great deal. People in Lukaya town would cheer him on as he drove through the town at 120 kph on his way to Masaka, and even when coming back. The UNLA had maintained their regular way of fighting and usually the battle would be over by 3.00 p.m. By 6.00 p.m. we would be in Lukaya town painting the town red.

The battle at Katonga bridge was a decisive turning point during the war. It was at that point that the backbone of the UNLA was broken. The UNLA massed all their troops and put all their effort in trying to dislodge us from the bridge, but in vain.

It offered all the belligerent forces a good opportunity for a decisive pitched battle and luckily the war was in our favour. Although our forces made some mistakes, the balance sheet on our side was good. The UNLA soldiers in both Masaka and Mbarara continued to starve and send out desperate messages as their casualty rate rose.

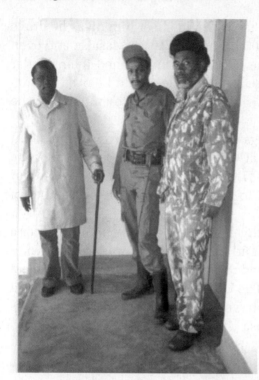

Pecos Kutesa (middle) with Mzee Lt. Col. Izaruku Amin (left) and Mzee Lt. Col. Barihona in Masaka before the fall of Kampala.

Two comrades who made a difference at the battle front with Kutesa: Salim Saleh aka Caleb Akandwanaho (left) with Fred Mugisha aka Headache/General.

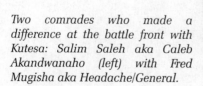

The Nairobi Peace talks: the government side at the talks of 1985. Left to right, front row J. Bugingo, Major Kiyengo, Sam Kuteesa, Oketcho, Paul Semwogerere, Olara Otunnu and Brigadier Toko.

The NRM side: Front row left to right: Eriya Kategaya, Matthew Rukikaire, Zack Kaheru, Sam Male, Gertrude Njuba, Kirunda Kivejinja. Back row are Grace Ibingira, Abu Mayanja, Ruhakana Rugunda; extreme right standing is James Tumusiime.

The Nairobi Peace Talks concluded. Yoweri Museveni (centre) signs as Tito Okello-Lutwa looks on (seated right), 17 December 1985.

The National Resistance Army combatants enter Kampala, 25 January 1986.

Yoweri Museveni was sworn in as President of Uganda on 26 January 1986.

Meet the Press: Yoweri Museveni addressing a press conference after being sworn in as president on 26 January 1986.

Top NRA officers after the first Army Council, State House, Entebbe 1986. Front row from left to right: Tadeo Kanyankore, Elly Tumwine, Yoweri Museveni, Fred Rwigyema and David Tinyefuza. Pecos Kutesa is in the second row third from the left.

Kutesa and Dora's wedding day: left is the best man Serwanga-Lwanga "Horse".

Above: After the war, Pecos Kutesa returned to one of the Lake Victoria islands to reminisce about the boat journey made by seven men in 1981.

Pecos Kutesa in 1994 campaigning for the Constituent Assembly seat for Kabula County, which he won.

Constituency Assembly Delegate. Pecos Kutesa (right) as Constituent Assembly delegate for Kabula County contributing to the deliberations in 1995. Left is Sam Kuteesa representing Mawogola County.

16

The UNLA Surrenders

"All things being equal," wrote Field Marshal Montgomery, "it is the willpower of one belligerent commander over the other that decides the course of the battle." No truer words have ever been said about war. At the Katonga bridge each belligerent commander tried to give of his best and the battle of willpower was stretched to breaking point.

The UNLA tried their best to rescue their besieged troops. They resorted to all sorts of tricks, even using the few transport helicopters at their disposal to drop food and drugs in the barracks. Although our air defence was not very sophisticated, we forced the helicopters to jettison their cargo far from the intended target, hence breaking the morale of the beleaguered troops. At one time, the helicopters tried to drop some bombs using these non-combat helicopters (these bombs were scary, especially to the civilian population). We had acquired some shoulder-fired missiles, but throughout the war at Katonga we did not bring down a helicopter. The helicopters would discharge their cargo and return to Entebbe. The battle raged on for three months but the government of Uganda failed to dislodge us, the "bandits", as they called us.

Indecisive battles are always costly for all the parties involved. It would have been good if one party had the means to end the war. However, in the case of the UNLA and the NRA, it was an impasse. The CHC at one time compared the two groups to a one-eyed man fighting against a blind enemy.

Masaka was a good battleground for some of us. Personally, I was born, grew up and went to school in Masaka. I knew all the routes and quite a number of people in town. One of them was Haji Ggaanya, who was married to a young girl from my home village, and he had been an NCO in the Uganda Army. Somehow he had managed to get into the barracks and win the commanding officer's confidence. Later, when the barracks surrendered, he told us many interesting stories. In history, we read about Magellan and how his sailors resorted to eating the ship mice after being without food at sea for a long time. Now in Masaka, rats became an endangered species. Fights even broke out among soldiers over this new-found delicacy. Haji Ggaanya told these and many more bizarre stories about the soldiers' behaviour when they were hungry. Soon all semblance of order was gone. The age-old ethnicism and sectarianism that has bedevilled Uganda for so long surfaced. In their hour of danger the troops started clustering along ethnic lines. Sectors of command and arcs of fire were now manned on an ethnic basis. Instead of feeling a sense of belonging, given the fact that these poor fellows were in the same boat, the soldiers from one sector would not feel sympathy for their comrades when an NRA mortar bomb landed in the "other" ethic group's sector.

The chain of command started breaking down. A private would only respect an NCO or officer from his own home area. The contingent of former Uganda Army soldiers started viewing the other UNLA soldiers, who were predominantly from Acholiland, with hostility. There was no love lost between the two groups of comrades-in-arms. The soldiers from other tribes were looked upon with suspicion. The new commander (now Lt. Col.) Olanya Ojara tried to rally his troops but it was difficult. All this time, we monitored Olanya's messages, which, although desperate, conveyed a sense of his dedication to his army.

In the meantime, we continued recruiting and training while the political wing went on establishing a new administration in the areas under our control. The peace talks in Nairobi were going on, but we were more interested in winning battles, if not the war.

By 2 December 1985, a few hungry soldiers started breaking rank and surrendering. We also started sending probe teams into the barracks. Maj. Kaka Bagyenda (retired) was one of the first people to enter the barracks; this was the old Kaka of the Masindi attack. We started sending messages to the members of the enemy force known to us. One of the people in the barracks was Sergeant Kakuru, an intelligence officer (IO). Kakuru and I had grown up together. I sent him messages encouraging him to desert and he informed me through my couriers that he and many others who were from the "wrong" districts, according to the UNLA thinking, were virtually under arrest or at best under constant surveillance.

On 10 December 1985, Masaka barracks capitulated. I moved with a few escorts up to the formerly fearful quarter guard. Instead of being fired upon, I received salutes from all directions. It would have been an exhilarating moment for me, but when I looked at the shrunken-eyed, emaciated bodies of the enemy, I could only feel sympathy for those fellow Ugandans who, a few days earlier, had been gallant Ugandan soldiers but now looked like cancer patients just released from hospital.

The first person I met was Capt. Olanya Ojara who was the commander. He welcomed me with open arms and hugged me. His first request, amazingly, was if I had a drink on me. One would have expected Olanya to ask for food as the most immediate need, but he asked me for a sip of Uganda Waragi which I happily gave him. Up to now, Olanya reminds me of that sip of Waragi. We are still good friends.

Masaka Mechanised Regiment surrendered with officers and men together with all their weapons. Fortunately, we had enough recruits to handle the weapons. The first thing Capt. Olanya wanted to know was whether they were POWs and, if that was not the case, whether they would be allowed to move through our lines to what he called "our own FEBA (forward edge of the battle area)". It took me long to convince this regular army officer that in the type of war we were fighting things like FEBA did not exist. The soldiers in the barracks were more interested in the most basic needs of man, food and water. We converted my former school, Masaka Senior Secondary, into a holding ground for our captives. After a hearty meal, the former enemies started identifying with us. We kept guard over them but mostly for their own protection, since none of these former besieged soldiers and officers had any intention of trying to escape. The whole area was filled by a hostile population. So they were willing to stay put. Later, I was to learn that it is known as the syndrome where the captured person identifies with and starts depending on his captor for survival. In fact, most of these captured soldiers wanted to join hands with us and fight their former comrades. At that time we did not readily use captured soldiers, but later we used them very effectively. In his book *The Prince*, the great philosopher Machiavelli claimed that: captured enemy troops sometimes fought harder than other soldiers since the captured soldiers have to prove their loyalty.

After the fall of Masaka, we had to turn our attention to Mbarara. The Mbarara barracks had not suffered as much as the Masaka barracks. The soldiers under siege in Mbarara had a lot of freedom of movement. Unlike their Masaka counterparts, they still held part of the town and neighbouring villages. On top of that, they knew they had inflicted a heavy blow on us and they feared our revenge. The commander, my former cubicle mate in Tanzania, Lt. Col. Santansio Constantine Otto, was a very ambitious and committed UPC stalwart. He was very dedicated to his cause and he felt any loss of ground on the part of the UNLA as a personal loss. The difference between Lt. Col. Santansio Otto and the UNLA NCOs of Masaka was that Otto knew most of us the NRA officers opposing him. To him, this was a personal challenge and he went ahead to resist determinedly. To Lt. Col. Santansio Constantine Otto, it was a source of personal humiliation to surrender to me and others whom he had trained with. He knew our weaknesses and strengths. In his book, which depicts Uganda's military history from pre-colonial days to the 1980s when political power in Uganda lay in the barrel of the gun, Olara Otunnu Amii calls that "familiarism."

It is, therefore, little wonder that even with the combined effort of the besiegers of Masaka and our other troops, it took up to the beginning of January for Mbarara to surrender.

Physicist Albert Einstein talks of the law of relativity. In battle one day is equal to months, if not years of peace time. The delay of the surrender of Mbarara, while to any causal observer was a mere one month, to us the fighters, and the expectant civilian population and international community, was a long time. This law of relativity has played itself out for some of us who have seen what happened in Uganda. When one imagines that some politicians have been in the opposition since before we were born, one should feel for them. The five years we spent in the bush seem longer than the twenty or so years we have been out of the bush. In fact, at the back of the minds of most of us, it seems like it was only yesterday that we captured Kampala.

Lt. Col. Otto (RIP) delayed the course of the war for another month because of his stubborn faith in his cause. As an individual, I pay tribute to people like the late Otto. In the meantime, the peace talks were going on in Nairobi, slowly, until a paper agreement was signed on 17 December 1985, merely to please the convenor, President Arap Moi of Kenya.

17

The Fall of Kampala

The final assault

Even after the fall of Masaka and Mbarara, the Katonga bridge continued being very active. This bridge acted like a light which draws flying insects to their death. The UNLA, in their wisdom, continued trying to cross this bridge. We, on our part, continued repulsing their assaults with high casualties on their side. However, like in all battles, we did not get off scot-free. Once, after the 1ˢᵗ Battalion had repulsed the enemy, our 5ᵗʰ Battalion, under Commander Ahmed Kashilingi, tried to ambush the retreating soldiers at the Equator. The soldiers managed to overwhelm us and we lost a number of comrades, among them Ninsima Rwamurinda, my cousin with whom we had reunited at the Katonga bridge one year earlier. He was the second son of Mr Ezekyeri Rwamurinda; the first son, Mwebaze, had died in the Bukalabi attack. I had to take the body home for burial. This was the second body I was burying in our home area within a period of two months. The first was our son, Sankara Kutesa, who had died when he was barely five months old.

Life in our liberated zone was going on normally. There were weddings, births, baptisms and deaths. In fact, some of our comrades were so overcome with the euphoria of visiting their homes that they almost abandoned the war. This is the bane of a "people's" war. The fighters do not envisage anything beyond their immediate families and environs. To them the whole war is about liberating themselves and their immediate families.Matters relating to national consciousness are usually treated as secondary issues.

On 15 January 1985, when the CHC chaired a meeting of combat commanders and ordered a final assault on Kampala, most of us were exhilarated. This was what we had waited for all those years. We had the illusion that the war in Uganda would end with the capture of Kampala, so everyone was psychologically ready to reap the fruits of his sweat. Almost immediately every person became a brave and unfailing fighter, at least in words. The mood of the meeting was high animation, even chief cooks were ready to attack Kampala using their knives and pans, the chronically ill, were miraculously healed, forgotten battle songs were remembered, the tempo of our movements and speech was marked by a rare briskness and everybody was jovial. All wrongs among us were forgiven, everybody started viewing everybody else as a bosom friend. It was the mood of a winning team.

The plan was a multi-pronged advance on the city. The 1st and 3rd Battalions continued on the main road, while the 5th and 7th Battalions advanced on the left flank. The 9th Battalion had advanced further and attacked a UNLA/UA defence at Kammengo, not far from Mpigi town. In that attack Comrade Santos Okecho Okecha proved a very brave and resourceful combat commander. The combination of UNLA/UA was dislodged, leaving behind many casualties. In that battle, we started hearing long-forgotten names of former Uganda Army officers, the very people who had attacked our people in Bondo in 1981. The names of people like Alai Tata and even the infamous Isaac Maliyamungu floated around. One cannot be sure whether the Okello junta might have floated those names to rally support from the political north. Our fighters were not in the least impressed by those high-sounding names of self-styled generals. After all, we had seen them running away when the Tanzanians attacked Uganda in 1979. The Tanzanians had simply swept the whole lot away from their defences. The advance had started on 17 January and by 22 January we had half-encircled Kampala city. While the 1st, 3rd, 5th and 11th Battalions from Mbarara led the frontal attack from the direction of Masaka, the 7th Battalion was advancing from Hoima Road through Kakiri and had already reached Nansana. River Rubiji encircles the southwestern part of Kampala and would have offered good positions for a determined defending force. However, the UNLA did not use it to its full value.

The defenders of Kampala, with the help of Korean experts, had positioned their artillery pieces on Summit View, one of the highest hills in Kampala. On our part, Comrade Kasirye Gwanga (now a brigadier), who was in charge of our heavy artillery, positioned his weapons on top of Mutundwe hill. Mutundwe hill dominates Kampala. In fact, when you are on top of this hill, Kampala looks like a broad sheet map or a city seen from an airplane porthole. Those two, Summit View and Mutundwe, are good for target practice when using medium-range artillery, and Kampala is in the valley between the two hills.

The two major roads leading out of Kampala, that is the Masaka-Mbarara highway and the Mubende-Fort Portal road, start at the Busega roundabout. The UNLA had placed anti-aircraft guns and other artillery pieces at this road junction and they thought that they had effectively stopped our advance. It is a good tactical defence position but that is all it is — tactical — and not necessarily a strategic defence for a whole city.

Feeling acutal fear

Our people have a saying that "the water pot usually breaks at the door steps", meaning that even a well-executed plan can run into jeopardy in the final phases, or that "a boat can capsize near the shore after enduring high seas." These and similar thoughts must have been going through my subconscious as I looked at Kampala city and all its grandeur. I developed goose pimples immediately. I started shivering and running a high fever. This was the sight of my long-term goal which now appeared to be within my grasp and which ought to have increased the flow of adrenaline. Instead, I was getting goose pimples. In fact, I developed fear, which was uncalled for. Throughout the war, I had never experienced fear at all. The CHC must have sensed my discomfort when I told him that I thought I was developing tuberculosis. Even today I tease myself about why that malady was the first to come to my mind. The CHC told me to stay at the tactical headquarters while my second-in-command Fred Mugisha, continued. We were in a meeting on 24 January 1986, when we received information that the enemy had withdrawn from the Busega roundabout without a fight. My "tuberculosis" disappeared just as miraculously as it had started.

Our people advanced at high speed. The 1st Battalion, now under Fred Mugisha, advanced towards Republic House (Bulange), then the UNLA headquarters, while 3rd Battalion under Patrick Lumumba advanced on the Lubiri barracks. The UNLA had used the former army shop as an ammunition dump but how it caught fire is anyone's guess. Soon bombs started blasting off. I was with the CHC when the sound of bomb blasts and smoke engulfed Kampala. The CHC at first thought that the UNLA was using BM rocket launchers to bombard the city. I had to point out to him that the bombs were air burst from the ground up but were not incoming shells.

It was getting late when the CHC directed me to go to Catholic Cathedral at Rubaga, the headquarters of the Roman Catholic Church in Uganda, which was now under our command. He gave me some telephone numbers. He wanted me to call President Julius Nyerere of Tanzania, to inform him that we had entered Kampala. This shows the high degree of respect the CHC had for the old man. The CHC instructed me to request Emmanuel Cardinal Nsubuga, who was the head of the Catholic Church in Uganda and a staunch supporter of the NRA, to allow me to use his phone to ring President Nyerere.

On the way, we found many civilians curiously watching this new group which had captured Kampala. Kampala people had been used to seeing one group of soldiers overthrowing another group and announcing a new government. It was not a new phenomenon to Kampala residents, right from the 1971 coup of Idi Amin, the 1979 takeover led by Tanzanians, to the then recent 1985 coup of Okello Lutwa. They had been accustomed to coups and to them ours was no exception. The only divergence was that these new coup-makers were talking the local language and their physical features resembled those of the local people. We did not look or act intimidating. We looked just like everybody else, not like "soldiers" in the Ugandan context. They were asking themselves: "When will the looting start?" They told us: "We warmly welcome you, but now what new rules have you got for us? Should we show you good shops to loot from?" and things of that nature.

One of my cheeky sergeants informed all and sundry that we, the new liberators, had three cardinal rules we wanted the people to follow religiously:

Rule No. 1: No looting or grabbing anything which does not belong to you.

Response: "Ah, you mean no looting, sir?"

Sergeant: "Yes, no looting. Anybody caught looting will be shot."

Rule No. 2: Do not harbour any enemy soldier or abandoned weapon. Report all immediately.

Response: "That is very well sir, just allow us to get our hands on them. All you will find is ashes."

Sergeant: "Please no extrajudicial killings."

Response: "Mmm, but they have been killing us."

Rule No.3: No girl or young woman should have knickers on.

Response from ladies: "Now what have our knickers done?"

Rule No. 3 was of course a crude joke contrived by the sergeant. It had nothing to do with army rules or the ladies for that matter.

Nevertheless, to the law-abiding residents of Kampala, these were taken as a serious departure from the norm, but rules which had to be followed to the letter.

When we reached the cardinal's place, we found our fighters surrounding the place. The person in charge was Musoke Kyenvangunywa, the Musoke of the Kampomera anti-aircraft episode. He told me that everybody had run inside except a few brave nuns. I talked to the nuns. I told them that I would like to use the cardinal's phone to make an important call. They said they were tired of the pseudo-liberators and reminded me that a few years earlier the UFM people had used the same Rubaga hill to provoke the UNLA, then they (the UFM) had run away and left the cathedral people to face the music. I insisted that we were different from the UFM, but they would not buy my argument. To put the message across more emphatically, Musoke fired a mortar shell from the compound of the cathedral. The nuns and priests all ran inside and hid themselves in the basement of the place. There was little I could do. So that important message from the CHC to President Nyerere was never sent. It was becoming dark, so we just dug in around the cardinal's place and waited the night out.

In the meantime, the battle for Republic House was raging on but the most furious fight was at the Lubiri barracks. This Lubiri, at the time the former palace of the deposed Kabaka of Buganda, has a fortification wall. It was the 1966 storming of the Lubiri by Idi Amin, then colonel, under orders ostensibly from President Milton Obote, that led to the occupation and conversion of the palace into an army barracks. This place is of historical significance in Uganda.

Comrade Lumumba's 3rd Battalion stormed Lubiri. The enemy soldiers put up a determined defence. When one recalls Kayira's UFM attack on Lubiri, it seems the UNLA expected a repeat of that fiasco. However, our fighters were more serious than the UFM. Our combatants were using real 60 mm mortar bombs and not RPG shell air bursts. The combatants tried to scale the wall, but it was hard, so they sieged it and poured in bombs, grenades and sustained machine gun fire. When I met the Kenyan contingent of the monitoring group of officers, they told me that the sustained machine gun fire frightened them badly. GPMGs and anti-aircraft guns produce a very unnerving sound if one is on the receiving end. When we later talked to these officers, who were senior in rank and service, they asked me in Kiswahili which types of weapons we were using? These officers, who had been in the army longer than me, had never had weapons fired at them with the intention of killing them. If anything, they had fired weapons at targets, on range grounds. Now they were witnessing actual combat. The 3rd Battalion continued sustained fire on Lubiri barracks till morning.

In the meantime, the 1st Battalion had overrun the army headquarters (Republic House) and continued to Radio Uganda. In the 1980s the battle for the capture of the one and only national radio in any African country was the ultimate aim of any belligerent force. National radio stations signified the only link between the leaders and the led in Africa. All one had to do was capture the national radio station, and then announce a regime change.

The Okello junta and their cohorts put up a spirited defence of this radio station but our people were more than determined to capture "power", which in Africa then was symbolised by the capture of the national radio station.

While all this was going on, Commander Kasirye Gwanga kept the enemy's heavy artillery occupied, while 11th Battalion under Comrade Chefe Ali was moving on foot and climbing up Summit View. The Korean experts and UNLA artillery officers never quite knew what hit them. While all their attention was on Mutundwe hill, they found themselves surrounded by infantry soldiers who ordered them to put up their hands. Although it is said that all is fair in love and war, I think a member of the artillery personnel feels betrayed when he is captured by a mere infantry person because, despite the artillery person's fire superiority, an infantryman sticking the barrel of his small firearm in your face and telling you to give up, renders your fire superiority worthless. A person with just a pistol can capture someone behind a BM 40 mm rocket launcher.

That is what the 11th Battalion infantrymen, under Chefe Ali, did to the UNLA artillery people. They just sneaked up on the UNLA's artillery positions and disarmed the soldiers. They then radioed Kasirye Gwanga's people to stop firing. Thus there was a lull in artillery fire but small arms fire continued throughout the day. At around 3.00 p.m. the enemy abandoned Lubiri and comrade Lumumba's people entered the one-time headquarters of hell in Uganda.

Fred Mugisha had carried out most of the fighting for the capture of Republic House (Bulange). He went on to storm Radio Uganda. Many UNLA soldiers believed that losing Radio Uganda meant losing power. They put up a spirited defence and the battle for Radio Uganda was consequently tough. However, 1st Battalion under Fred Mugisha emerged victorious.

The conglomerate of factions which had partitioned Kampala among themselves started fighting one another. The first casualty we saw was Captain Nkwanga, the leader of FEDEMU, whose body we found lying on the roadside near Silver Springs Hotel on Ggaba Road. Apparently, the Okello clique had invited him to the hotel together with other faction leaders for a meeting, but it seems that when he went to attend that meeting he was shot in cold blood by Bazilio Olara Okello. The FEDEMU people started joining us individually and not under any central command. On our part, we welcomed any deserter from the more than five groups that had held Kampala for the six months the junta was in power.

The 5th Battalion under Ahmed Kashilingi was supposed to capture Entebbe International Airport. However, they encountered a bigger force. Apparently, all the former UA personnel and a big group of UNLA had converged in Entebbe. While the 5th Battalion was advancing towards Entebbe town, they met this big force of the enemy, who were trying to vacate the town. Apart from Lake Victoria, there is only one outlet from Entebbe, the Kampala-Entebbe road. Our people met a force of more than 1000 enemy soldiers at Kisubi, about 20 km from Kampala. The enemy broke through the 5th Battalion ranks and advanced towards Kampala.

By then the CHC had set up his tactical headquarters at Bulange, the former Republic House. It was a tense moment since the enemy was now advancing from our flank. The 3rd Battalion under Patrick Lumumba, which had captured Lubiri, was dispatched to hold off the advancing soldiers. It was late, so after a little firefight both sides took cover to wait for morning. The civilian population was very hostile to the withdrawing government forces. In fact, a number of UNLA/UA soldiers were captured and lynched by the civilians. This was the fate of one Lt. Ojok.

This young man had been with us in Monduli, Tanzania, for cadet training. Officer Cadet Ojok had had a rough time during training because he was a stubborn young man, although the Tanzanian instructors tried very hard to break him in. Frequently, when we were in class after back-breaking exercises, an NCO would request the officer in charge of the class to release Officer Cadet Ojok to him (the NCO) for extra duty. *Afande nakuomba* Officer Cadet Ojok Fok Fok (Sir, I request to have Officer Cadet Ojok Fok Fok for a minute) was a common request throughout our training. If there is any punishment during training that Ojok did not do, then it has not yet been invented in military training. I might add that Ojok Fok Fok did twice the amount of training all of us did in those nine months in Tanzania. Now the poor fellow was captured by angry civilians and burnt to death.

Ironically, this happened in the very same area where a former UPC lady chief had earlier on staged the infamous roadblocks. If there are ghosts, then that place, Kitubbulu, about two kilometres from Entebbe town, must be haunted. The place has always been a withdrawal outlet for government soldiers whenever a coup took place in Uganda. The Libyan soldiers who had come to Uganda in 1979 to beef up Amin's troops lost many comrades at that location. When Okello overthrew Obote many UNLA soldiers were killed there. Now the withdrawing UNLA soldiers met the same fate there. Even the commandant of Entebbe Air Base, a captain, was gunned down there while withdrawing from Entebbe in his brand-new Mercedes Benz. His car was looted and then set on fire. The charred remains of that captain and his five bodyguards remained on the roadside for days.

The 3rd Battalion had linked up with the 5th Battalion in Najjanankumbi, just five miles from the Kampala city centre, and they had taken up positions in order to advance at daybreak. I had also linked up with my 1st Battalion and we were meant to advance along Jinja road. We passed through the town and while in Bugolobi, a suburb of Kampala, I remembered our people who were in Luzira Maximum Prison. A group of our soldiers, with the now long-gone Dampa as their guide, had been captured at a roadblock as they tried to escape to join us in the bush in 1981. This group had been travelling by pickup to our rendezvous in the bush. However, they were captured at a roadblock with all the evidence of deserting soldiers — weapons and uniforms, which had been disguised as luggage. Dampa evaded capture and reported to the bush. This group had been in the condemned section of Luzira Prison for the duration of the war. Among them was Lt. Napoleon Rutambika who had been with us in Monduli. Napoleon was later to serve under me and attend Ghana Armed Forces Staff College (GAFSC) in 1990.

This time I decided to go to Luzira and rescue him, together with 14 or so other privates who were with him.

I left my unit under Fred Mugisha and took along a platoon in order to advance on Luzira Prison. Members of the police and prison services in Uganda are civil servants par excellence and they are never bothered about political changes in the country. Regimes have come and gone but the police and prisons have always been left intact. This time it was no different. The prison officers were ready at the prison quarter guard to salute whoever had become the new leader in Uganda. To the prison officers, their routine was not to be changed an iota. I was saluted smartly by a potbellied prison officer, then asked politely to fill in the quarter guard master book. Then I was escorted courteously to the prison gates. Here we were asked to surrender our weapons to the soldiers outside. No weapon except that of the prison officers is allowed into the cells. I had the capacity to open the prison gates and allow all the inmates out but I did not. I had great respect for the police and prison services, despite the fact that I had been a rebel for five years. I told the prison officers that I only wanted Lt. Napoleon Rutambika and his group.

There is an unsettling feeling when one enters a prison cell. Huge padlocks are opened, then you enter and immediately the gates are slammed shut behind you. The place was silent and the atmosphere calm. After passing through three gates my two escorts and I were told to stop. We could see many people peeping at us from behind bars. The prison officer called out the name of Napoleon and he came forward. Only Napoleon could explain what he felt when he saw me, but on my part I was speechless. He did not appear as emaciated as I had expected him to be, but in all respects this was a very changed Napoleon. He did not in any way look like the Napoleon Rutambika whom I had known since 1979 and with whom I had trained in Tanzania. All the same, he had maintained his sense of humour. The last gate was opened and Napoleon embraced me, and for some time we just hugged each other without speaking. Then I teased him as to how he, a soldier, could be kept under guard by prison warders, but he just laughed. I told him that I had come to rescue him and the people under his command who were in prison, as well as anybody else. He gave the prisons officers the names of his comrades and they were called out one by one.

Before we left he reminded me of two other prominent NRA supporters who were in prison. These were Lt Col Bigo Byamugyenyi (retired), who had been in charge of formal education in the then Uganda Army. This old man, a relative of mine, had joined the army in the 1960s and was one of the few educated officers in the Uganda Army. That is why he was in charge of formal education till the fall of Idi Amin, when he was locked up as a prisoner of war throughout the time of the Military Commission, the Obote regime and the Okello junta. The second person was Ephraim Rwakanengyere, former commissioner of local police, who had earned himself notoriety during the first Tanzania-based guerrilla invasion of Uganda in 1972, by posing with captured guerrillas and telephoning President Idi Amin while standing at full attention. I added these two gentlemen to the 14 comrades together with Napoleon and took them out of the prison. I had to sign for their safety, which seemed ridiculous. I could not imagine why the prison officers thought that their former detainees felt safer in prison than outside in freedom.

I took the former inmates to Republic House (Bulange) where the CHC's tactical headquarters was. I handed them to the CHC, who was happy to see them. However, he advised me to return the two gentlemen, Rwakanengyere and Lt Col. Bigo, to Luzira since they had civil cases to answer which had not yet been resolved by the judiciary. I drove these two gentlemen back to Luzira. All the same they were very grateful to me for having secured their release no matter how brief their freedom had been.

That evening the UNLA soldiers in Entebbe started surrendering to us. On 26 January 1986, the troops who had surrendered numbered about 900. The battle for Kampala had ended. It was a dramatic end to an interesting war. The people were overwhelmed; we, the soldiers, were exhilarated. We were fully armed and on full alert, but the atmosphere of euphoria was almost unbearable for most of us. I was lucky to meet my former friends, Mr Tim Cooper and Ms Alison Porteous, the very ones who had filmed me in action in the Luweero bushes. I met these two people at Imperial Hotel. It was an exciting reunion after about three years since the filming. They asked me how I felt and I answered genuinely, "Nothing succeeds like success, I feel on top of he world!" It had been a war worth fighting, even though we had lost many useful people.

18

The War Beyond Kampala

We had left two withdrawal routes for the UNLA. One was Jinja Road towards the Kenya border and the other was the Kampala-Gulu road. My unit advanced towards Jinja, the second biggest and formerly main industrial city of Uganda. I spent the night in Kampala and continued the advance in the morning. When we reached the boundaries of Jinja town, we met many former FEDEMU and UFM soldiers, who immediately joined us. There was no battle for Jinja at all because all the soldiers we met, even in the barracks, just laid down their arms. When I entered the officers' mess I met the boss of a team of British instructors. This tall, imposing fellow stood up, saluted me and threw his cap on the ground. I still do not know what that gesture meant.

Jinja town was calm and the people were happy to meet us. Immediately, the authorities summoned people for the first NRA rally on the Jinja Municipality grounds. The people of Busoga region were a bit apprehensive, since they did not know what to expect. The NRA did not have many home boys from Jinja then. Now I was called upon to address the people. In all my life I had never addressed such a big gathering. The people of Busoga are more populous than most Ugandan ethnic communities. There are also many very highly educated people in Busoga society.

I stood on the dais and faced what to me appeared a sea of faces. The people were all seated, tightly packed on the ground, the size of two football pitches. They waited patiently to hear what this young man from the bush had to say. Like their Kampala counterparts, the people of Jinja had witnessed all the changes of government in Uganda. Jinja has been the withdrawal route for the routed government troops and the first port of call for the new, conquering people. Right from the first coup of Idi Amin, through the ouster of the Amin regime, the fall of the Obote II government, up to this new group of people who had taken over power in Kampala, these people had seen it all. When a person is in opposition to the government, he becomes more informed than other people in towns and villages. While the common person is interested in the day-to-day chores of life, the person in opposition, especially if it is armed opposition, is always eager for any fresh news and information.

The people of Jinja were surprised when I addressed them in relatively good English and talked about international affairs off the cuff. They did not expect a "bush boy" to be so well informed. On my part, I was happy to see the formerly passive faces now break into an enthralled and attentive mood. Meanwhile, in Kampala our people were grappling with electrical power failures and communication breakdowns. The CHC was not yet sworn in. Unlike in the past, when the first person to capture Radio Uganda would announce a change of government, our people were delayed because the communication system in the whole country was in a shambles.

After addressing that mammoth rally in Jinja, I tried to follow up the main group of my battalion, which had advanced along the Jinja-Malaba road. It was evening and I was getting reports that the advance was still smooth despite some uncoordinated rear-guard action by the looting and withdrawing UNLA troops. I was sitting in the front passenger seat of the command Land Rover with Deus driving and Dora and three soldiers as rear passengers. I do not know where the bullet came from but it passed clean through one of my bodyguards, Pte. Rutaitsire, and I was struck on the right temple. The bullet sliced through my ear and lodged in the temple just above the right eye. I remember shouting that we had been hit, and Dora pulling me onto her lap while I bled profusely. I did not lose consciousness immediately because I remember Deus reversing the Land Rover and racing back to Jinja. I had been shot seven miles from Jinja town, just before Kakira.

I lost consciousness for a time but when we reached hospital I pleaded with Dora not to let the staff put me on sheets which might contain other patients' blood. The CHC had told us about AIDS and we had seen a number of AIDS victims during our stay in Masaka. The hospital staff were very professional and efficient. I received the best treatment that they could give. On 27 January 1986, when the CHC was sworn in as president of the Republic of Uganda, I was still in Jinja Hospital. I heard him live on Radio Uganda when he promised Ugandans that what had just transpired was "not a mere change of guards but rather a fundamental change". Up to now I recall that statement with nostalgia. I still tell my friends that what NRA did was an irreversible reaction, not a reversible one, unlike a chemical reaction.

The people of Uganda heaved a collective sigh of relief which could be heard even across the boundaries of the country. Uganda had achieved a rare feat in Africa. It had created its own guerrilla army with little help from the outside world, and most importantly an army with no links to any of the countries belonging to either side of the then East-West bipolar divide. When asked whether the NRA was pro-East or pro-West, the CHC, now H.E. Yoweri Kaguta Museveni, the President of Uganda, told all and sundry that the NRA was neither pro-East nor pro-West but that it was pro-Uganda.

Kampala had fallen. A new president had been sworn in. Control of the whole country by the NRM/A was still uncertain and many people were waiting for the army to intervene. My unit, the 1st Battalion, now under Fred Mugisha and Musoke Kyenvangunya as his second-in-command, continued eastwards. After two days, Dr Ssenkatuka, an old surgeon, removed the bullet from my head. This old gentleman did a fine job; today you cannot tell that I had an AK-47 bullet in my head. I have always told people that I have concrete inside my head, and that that was why that bullet simply bounced off. For purposes of convenience, I was placed in Nytil Jinja Guest House where I was accorded all the hospitality befitting a conquering hero. The whole town leadership offered whatever help they thought I wanted. Most of us were not materialistic in our outlook on life, thanks largely to the lessons we had learned as anti-government forces.

The management of the Nytil textiles industry offered bundles of cloth worth 300,000,000 Uganda shillings! I asked them the purpose of the material that they had offered me, since I was neither a tailor nor a trader. They were surprised at my naivety. Later I learnt that all one needed in those days was a chit from a political bigwig requesting essential commodities such as sugar, beer, cloth, etc. Then all one had to do was to sell the chit and pocket the proceeds. The buyer of the chit would purchase the merchandise then sell it on the open market. That was the accepted mode of distribution and the government had put a fully-fledged Cabinet Minister in charge of essential supplies.

The Ugandan people had a hard time teaching the naive "bush people" how things worked in Uganda at that time. One episode of tragicomedy is best recalled by the current First Secretary in the Ugandan Embassy in Washington, DC, who was the company secretary for Nile Breweries then. The management of Nile Breweries offered a full lorry of beer to a group of soldiers to go and celebrate their victory. After looking at the lorryful of beer, the officer asked for somebody who knew how to drive. One soldier saluted and said, "I know how to drive, sir!" "Okay," said the commander. "Here are the keys. Turn this vehicle around and drive to the officers' mess, right?" "Right sir," replied the soldier, who immediately jumped into the driving cabin, started the lorry and drove it straight into River Nile. Up to now, neither the driver nor the lorry and the beer have ever been recovered. To the First Secretary, that signified the soldiers' mentality. Such and other similar bizarre deeds were what the population of Uganda saw their liberators doing.

The next task that the new government faced was building a new national army. There were many groups of armed people who had to be absorbed into the army. The NRA policy was to incorporate anybody willing to cross over, provided he did not have a criminal record and was fit for military service. It was an enormous task. The different factions had different backgrounds and ideologies. Most of them were semi-trained while some had undergone military courses at diverse colleges. Uganda's policy, even in the days of the East-West bipolar divide, was to have its soldiers train in whichever country offered training facilities. This tradition has persisted to date. Here we had officers trained in Cuba, Sandhurst (Britain), Liven (North America), Russia, Libya, and Tanzania, to name but a few. These officers and men who had different training and cultural backgrounds had to be merged into one national army.

This did not present much difficulty but discipline was lacking among these groups and therefore they could not meet the NRA standards and the expectations of the civilian population. Here were former Uganda Army officers and men, former UNLA soldiers, and psuedo-military gangs such as FEDEMU, UFM and other anti-government groups, all formed around their ethnic or regional areas. In fact, in the early days, we even absorbed a group called Baruli Freedom Fighters. Baruli are a minority community found in central Uganda. There were many such groups of "freedom fighters" joining us as we captured more territory. At first, we had tried to distribute them among our existing formations but after some time, we just kept them as they came without even changing their commanders. We, however, told them to follow our operational code of conduct, which was designed to change the perception of soldiers among the Ugandan civilians.

The policy might have seemed risky but we were in complete control of all the troops by August 1986 when formal ranks were introduced in the NRA. People started identifying with us because of the discipline the NRA had shown. That put a new face on the profession of the military in Uganda. Unlike in the past, Ugandan soldiers were now viewed as "our boys" and not as "those soldiers".

One exception was the 35th Battalion created out of UFM. Because of its undisciplined background, they wanted to avenge themselves against the people of Acholi, something reminiscent of the attitude of the Acholi militias towards the people of West Nile in 1979. This unit, which was under my command, was immediately disarmed and disbanded. Otherwise the policy of integrating captured or volunteering enemy soldiers worked smoothly.

A big number of my former compatriots from Monduli, Tanzania joined us. My former cubicle-mate, Lt. Col. Santansio Constantine Otto, who had surrendered in Mbarara, was happy to get in touch with me. However, the poor fellow was already quite weak with AIDS-related diseases. When I wanted to hug him as a lost-and-found friend, he told me that he was very weak, as I could see. Getting together with my fellow cadet officers took place in Kampala.

After recovering sufficiently, I did not join my former 1st Battalion immediately. Instead I was made Brigade Commander of the 157 Brigade, which was tasked to hold Kampala. Hence,

I was the first NRA Brigade Commander in charge of the city. It was in my capacity as the officer in charge of Kampala and Jinja that I got to meet many of my former course-mates, among whom Lt. Kagata Namiti (RIP). This officer had been with me in section 1, platoon 1 D coy in training. He was more of a politician than an infantry officer. Even Corporal Chacha, a Tanzanian instructor who had given his assessment of us while on a field exercise, had told us that Namiti would end up as a politician, which turned out to be the truth.

The process of integrating former opposing forces into the NRA went on smoothly, and for some time it seemed sanity had returned to Uganda. The police force, though not having participated in the war, was still a weak force. None of the former governments had viewed the police force as a necessity, therefore recruitment and training in the Uganda Police Force was still at a low level. The new army was deployed to do many police-related duties. One operation I carried out was rounding up the many unregistered vehicles in Kampala. Uganda had always imported used Japanese vehicles and when there was a breakdown in law and order, many people imported these used cars without bothering to register them. Operation Nagoya, as we termed it, took many people unawares. We applied our knowledge of the city paths and shortcuts to place roadblocks in and around the city in one night.

The next morning, the whole city was sealed off to check for unregistered vehicles. The people in Kampala were very surprised about our intimate knowledge of the city. They could not believe how these "bush boys", as they called us, could know Kampala so well. Although people are averse to paying taxes and detest delays in their movements, they were all the same happy with the humane way in which we handled them. People started saying that we were not soldiers in the Ugandan sense. This confirmed Prof. Mahmood Mamdani's assertion that "civilians in Uganda had got angry enough and shot the soldiers off the streets of Kampala."

This operation was an eye opener for both the civilians and the fighters, because it created an atmosphere in which we started understanding each other. It was during that operation that the Kampala population for the first time passed through our roadblocks and were surprised when few or no bribes at all were solicited.

The people of Uganda had never seen soldiers who did not demand *chai*, the local term for tea but which also refers to a bribe. Not that there were no black sheep among us, but the sense of control then was still high. We, the fighters, were individuals who identified ourselves with a common cause. We were not mere army numbers but sons and daughters of the people among whom we were operating.

It was this sense of belonging and identification with the people that earned us a huge welcome and support in all the towns we captured, except for a few such as Gulu and Kitgum. These were the home towns of the Okello junta leaders, so this was expected. Still, when I was posted to Gulu in mid-1986, I found the place peaceful and the people hospitable. That is why, when I married Dora formally in 1986, it was in Gulu that we had our after-party and honeymoon. The people in Gulu pledged to support our marriage with 50 head of cattle. They were very excited about the wedding of the first NRA commanding officer in their own Acholi Inn, then the only government hotel in Acholiland. It was a confidence-building party and the people of Gulu started believing that the NRM was not bent on revenge, as they had feared in the beginning.

The withdrawing UNLA officers had told the people that the NRA would carry out revenge against the Acholi people because of the heinous atrocities the UNLA had visited on the people of Uganda in general and Luweero in particular. When they saw our behaviour and observed our humility, they were pleasantly surprised and they started being open to us.

Although the honeymoon between the NRA and the Acholi was short-lived, in those days we had identified with the civilian population of Acholi and we made many useful friends. Among the many steadfast friends I made are Major General Oketa and Lt. Col. Walter Ochora, now LC V Gulu. These two and many others are still my very genuine friends.

Postscript

A s already mentioned in the introduction, this book is the story of Uganda's revolution from 1979 to 1986, when the NRA captured power and paved the way for political and economic reconstruction. My aim in telling the story "how I saw it" is to give a firsthand testimony of the events in which I was one of the principal agents in the country's revolutionary process. However, since this book is being published twenty years after the NRA capture of power, the story would be incomplete without briefly summing up the gains and shortfalls of Uganda's revolution since 1986. In any case, 1986 actually marked the beginning rather than the end of the revolution. The capture of political power gave the NRM government an opportunity and the challenge to translate the convictions and promises of the NRA's five-year armed struggle into reality. The purpose of this postscript is to update the story, to highlight what the revolution has achieved or failed to achieve without deviating from "how I saw it" criteria that I set myself in my original conceptualisation of this narrative.

At the personal level, my participation in the post-1986 events has not been as spectacular as my role in the armed struggle from 1979 to 1986. In September 1986, at the youthful age of thirty years, I was appointed the first commander of the Gulu-based NRA 4th Division in charge of Gulu and Arua districts – a territory that is about one-sixth of the whole country. This meant that I had to shift from the mindset and work methods of an anti-establishment guerrilla or bandit into a servant of the new NRM government, operating in a new bureaucratic framework. As 4th Division commander from 1986, my greatest challenge was to battle a succession of insurgencies from the Uganda People's Democratic Army (UPDA) to the Holy Spirit Mobile Forces and its successor, the Lord's Resistance Army (LRA). These insurgencies were defeated and in 1988 thousands of UPDA rebels surrendered and were integrated in the NRA. Their leaders, including Charles Alai, who became a junior minister, and Col. Walter Ochora (now Gulu District LC V chairman) took up leadership positions in the NRM government as part of the process of national reconciliation.

Apart from my security responsibilities, I had to do political work by initiating confidence-building measures to win over the population of a region which was still in a state of shock after the rout of their sons by a southern-dominated army. Through the good offices of Rev. Father John Scalabrini of Lacor Seminary, I got in touch with two elders – Otema Allimadi, an Anglican Protestant and the prime minister in the second Obote regime, and Andrew Adimola, a Roman Catholic and the DP's Secretary General – and brought them together for lunch. These old rivals, who had never seen eye to eye, shook hands and I hoped that their handshake would mark a new beginning in the politics of a society that had hitherto been torn apart by religious cleavages and prejudices. Of course, it was too much to expect that a decades-long religious divide could be bridged overnight.

Also, as part of my public confidence-building strategy, my wife and I decided to hold our after-wedding party at the former Acholi Inn in 1987. Local dignitaries and a cross-section of the public were among those invited to the party. We deliberately kept the presence of bodyguards thin around the inn and entrusted our security to the local community. Our invitations to the party and the deliberately contrived low-key security detail pleased the local community, symbolising the growing solidarity between the NRA and the Acholi community. Indeed, the Acholi went out of their way to give us 50 head of cattle as a token of appreciation for our new friendship. Unfortunately, we lost all the cows to the Karimojong rustlers the following day, proof that the Karimojong warriors had no respect even for the cattle of a "whole" brigade commander, let alone those of ordinary citizens! Nevertheless, for all the ravages of the Karimojong rustlers and the efforts of the insurgents to sour the NRA-Acholi rapprochement, by 1988 our confidence-building strategy was beginning to pay off.

In 1988, the NRA leadership introduced formal ranks of general, brigadier, colonel, major, captain etc., into the army. More in tune with the more egalitarian title of "commander", which made us proud in our guerrilla army and made us look with contempt on the so-called decorated professional UNLA soldiers, I was among those comrades who were not so keen on these high-sounding ranks. In my view, adopting the new ranks was tantamount to reducing our victorious army to the contemptible levels of Field Marshal Amin, General Tito Okello, Maj. Gen. Oyite-Ojok, Brigadier Bazilio Okello, Captain Ageta etc., whom we had outshined on the battlefield. Anyway, we had no choice but to accept the decision of our leadership, justified on the grounds of converting the NRA from a rank-less guerrilla force into a regular, hierarchical professional army on a par with other national armies the world over. So I was promoted to the rank of colonel, which I have held since then. Of course some junior officers, many of whom never went through the baptism of fire, have overtaken me along the way and obtained higher ranks. But that is life where, as on the road, we move at different speeds to different destinations. Therefore, I still cherish my rank in the army almost twenty years down the road.

In 1990, I was recalled from the 4th Division and sent to Ghana for training at its Armed Forces Staff College (1990-91). In the course of training, I came to appreciate the gulf that exists between a guerrilla force and a professional army.

While the guerrilla with his rifle is a foot soldier par excellence, the professional soldier without logistics, transport and sophisticated communications is like a sitting duck. Where the guerrilla soldier improvises and very much depends on his wits and devices, the professional one is prone to stay put, awaiting directives from above. Thus, through the training in Ghana, I can now understand why we, the bandits, frequently outmanoeuvred the UNLA, even when the odds were stacked against us. When I returned to Uganda from Ghana in 1991, I was appointed Chief of Training and Recruitment in the NRA (1991-94) with the brief to professionalise the army, and I would like to believe that I performed my duties to the satisfaction of my superiors.

In the meantime, the constitution-making process in Uganda had been in progress since the appointment of the Benjamin Odoki Constitutional Commission in 1989. I was determined to play my part in this historic exercise. Therefore, when plans were under way to elect delegates to the Constituent Assembly (CA), I was granted leave of absence by the NRA leadership to contest the position of Kabula County delegate in Rakai District, which was one of the 214 directly elected CA delegates in the country. I easily won the contest and, as a result, I had a rare historic opportunity to participate in the CA debate on the Odoki draft constitution, culminating in the promulgation of our current constitution on 8 October 1995. Much to my disappointment, my efforts to secure the constitutional recognition of the Bahima people as an ethnic entity by including them in the constitution as such did not appeal to the sentiments of the majority of the delegates. During the CA deliberations, I came face to face with the intrigues, manoeuvres, opportunism, duplicity and even treachery of the political class and I must say that I felt greatly relieved when the CA exercise was done with. So instead of contesting the 1996 parliamentary elections, I chose to report back to the safety of the army – henceforth renamed UPDF

(Uganda Peoples Defence Forces) under the 1995 constitution – because I did not have the stomach for the rough world of parliamentary politics.

When I reported back to the army in 1996, I resumed my assignment as Chief of Training and Recruitment until 1998, when I was once again granted leave of absence to join Makerere University for a degree course in Social Work and Social Administration. I had always dreamed of acquring university education and I really looked forward to my course as a new intellectual challenge that deserved utmost energy and concentration. I must say that my three-year course at Makerere (1998-2001), specialising in psychology, was challenging but intellectually refreshing and rewarding. The course enabled me to conceptualise my experience in soldiering, including my reflections on the meaning of life and death, within a wider theoretical framework. Unfortunately, since I completed my degree course, I have not had the opportunity to try out my intellectual skills in psychology in dealing with the day-to-day challenges in military service. However, I have had ample time to reflect on what has happened to my life and my country since that fateful decision to join the struggle for freedom and democracy in 1976 after being subjected to repeated humiliations at roadblocks.

Since I left the 4th Division in the north in 1990, I have not had the opportunity to command operational actions on the battlefield in the various military challenges facing the NRA and its successor, the UPDF. I have thus missed out on action in successive operations against our enemies, not only in northern Uganda and southern Sudan, but also in the Rwenzori Mountains and the Democratic Republic of Congo. For this reason, I feel I would not be the person best placed to relate NRA/UPDF exploits in the 1990s and early 2000s. I have confined myself to telling the story I saw and "how I saw it". I challenge my comrades to push the story of the aftermath of Uganda's revolution forward by recording their direct operational experiences in more recent years, so that the history of Uganda's revolution can be used to inform the present and the future.

When we joined the struggle for freedom and democracy, most of us were in our teens or early 20s. We were full of energy, idealism, enthusiasm and sense of adventure. We were angry enough to take on what we saw as an iniquitous and oppressive system, regardless of the dangers, risks and sacrifices involved. We had a sense of purpose and mission, a mission we managed to accomplish in 1986. We are now, more than a quarter of a century down the road, approaching or even on the other side of 50 years of age — old enough to be grandparents. In the intervening period, we have seen and learnt a lot about life and death, about human nature and motivation, about hopes and realities, about heroism and betrayal and, above all, about the theory and practice of power. In the process, our initial youthful enthusiasm and idealism have been tempered by a sense of realism and pragmatism about what can and cannot be done. As one French statesman once remarked: "If you are 20 years old and you are not a radical, there is something wrong with your head, but if you are forty years old and you are still so radical, then you have learnt nothing from experience." I now agree with Karl Marx that every synthesis – every revolution, including our own – is invariably pregnant with new contradictions.

So, looking back down memory lane, twenty years after the event, what can be summed up as the balance sheet of Uganda's revolution? What have been the gains and losses of the revolution? What needs to be done to ensure that the revolution remains on course, in accordance with the imperative Mao Tse-Tung once called the permanent revolution? Without going into details, which, in any case, would be outside the scope of the core of this book, I am proud to say that Uganda's revolution has impacted tremendously on the military, political and economic spheres of national life since 1986. But, at the same time, the revolution has encountered many challenges, which were either not anticipated or could not have been predicted.

On the military front, the NRA/UPDF has been transformed into a national army, reflecting the demographic character of our country. After 1986, the NRA absorbed and integrated disparate rebel movements that had fought the second Obote regime, without compromising its historic mission and discipline. Since then, the NRA/UPDF has continued to absorb ex-rebels who have surrendered but still opted to pursue a military career. The post-1986 national army, the jewel in the crown of Uganda's revolution, has generally upheld human rights and dignity (roadblocks are no longer points of humiliation), observed the rule of law, defeated successive enemies of the NRM regime and their foreign backers and defended the territorial integrity of Uganda. Of course, there have been blemishes here and there along the way, such as reports of widespread corruption, ghost soldiers, junk helicopters, erstwhile comrades turning into renegades, etc. But, compared to its predecessors, the Uganda Army and the UNLA, the NRA/UPDF stands in a distinguished class of its own and its reputation of discipline and patriotism is still beyond reproach. The only challenge that we did not anticipate was the AIDS scourge, to which many of our best officers and comrades have lost their lives. Indeed, over the years, the pandemic has proved more deadly than the bullets of our successive adversaries.

Politically, Uganda's revolution ushered in the era of participatory democracy, the rule of law, constitutionalism and the sanctity of human rights and civil liberties. The resistance councils (RCs), which originated in the Luweero Triangle, spread to the rest of the country after 1986 and became a platform for participatory democracy. In 1992-93, the RCs became the pillars of the policy of decentralisation and when this was enshrined in the 1995 constitution, the RCs were transformed into popularly elected local councils (LCs) in accordance with the Local Government Act of 1997. The path to constitutionalism began with the appointment of the Odoki Constitutional Commission, through the debates of a popularly elected Constituent Assembly, culminating in the promulgation of the 1995 constitution. Since then two general elections have been held at local and national levels and two referenda have been conducted to settle contentious constitutional issues. Also, the constitution has been tested in courts of law and recently it was revisited and amended amidst heated debate and controversy, which, I think, is healthy for democracy.

Related to constitutionalism has been the widening horizon of the freedom of the press. Uganda's revolution paved the way for the mushrooming of privately-owned electronic and print media. Many FM radio stations and several TV networks, as well as many newspapers, have been set up since 1986. The advent of the Internet has also opened Uganda up to the flow of ideas from all over the world. All these electronic and print media have been platforms for the articulation of diverging and conflicting ideas and have been building blocks for the consolidation of democracy in Uganda. Recently (in 2004), the political space was opened up to allow for the revival of multiparty politics that were frozen under the Movement system an opening which should make it possible for various political forces to contend for power in a constitutional and peaceful manner. But while the freedoms of press and association have flourished, there is plenty of room for improvement in the sphere of freedom of assembly. It is also imperative for the electronic and print media, as well as all registered political parties, to exercise their freedoms in a responsible, civilised and mutually tolerant manner, to allow for informed moulding of public opinion and enabling the sovereign people of Uganda to make informed choices.

In the economic sphere, the tremendous gains of Uganda's revolution transformed Uganda, from the pauperised laughing stock of the world into a relatively prosperous African country (by African standards) that has recently escaped from the rank of the poorest of the poor countries around the world. In 1986, the NRM government inherited a shattered *magendo* economy with rampant triple-digit inflation where "chasing the line" and "the economics of allocation" were the order of the day. Since then the *magendo* economy has been thrown in the dustbin of history, the shops are overflowing with goods and inflation has been tamed, reduced and kept down at single-digit levels. The Uganda shilling has become fully convertible and the spectre of the elusive "Mr Foreign Exchange" no longer haunts our country. Also, the economy has grown at the respectable rate of 6.5% since the early 1990s and the manufacturing and construction sectors have been booming at even higher, double-digit growth rates. Moreover, Uganda has successfully coped with the social costs of structural adjustment and privatisation and embarked on ambitious programmes of poverty reduction, free primary and secondary education, modernisation and industrialisation.

However, the building of an independent and self-sustained national economy, which was one of the goals of Uganda's revolution, has so far remained an elusive dream. On the contrary, instead of realising an independent and self-sustaining national economy, Uganda has become more and more dependent on donor largesse and budget support, making us vulnerable to external pressures and dictation. The architects of Uganda's revolution did not anticipate this turn of events. The promised modernisation of agriculture is yet to be achieved and the economic gains of the revolution have not evenly trickled down to the peasantry, which is the backbone of the NRM regime. Many of our people, especially in northern Uganda, remain trapped in abject poverty and backwardness, which means that the mission of Uganda's revolution was not fully accomplished.

When the architects of Uganda's revolution captured state power in 1986, they did not anticipate some of the challenges that, in due course, slowed down the momentum of the promised "politics of fundamental change". For example, the advent of rebel movements in northern, eastern and western Uganda in the late 1980s and the 1990s was not expected. Although all the rebel movements were defeated by the NRA/UPDF, they diverted the nation's meagre resources from the task of post-war economic reconstruction, impoverished the insurgency-affected areas, displaced millions of people and, especially in the case of northern Uganda, led to the rise of the controversial internally displaced people's camps. Secondly, in retrospect, the architects of Uganda's revolution either overlooked or did not appreciate the magnitude of the northern-southern social and political divide.

My experience as 4th Division commander in northern Uganda taught me that the perceptions and attitudes of the people in northern Uganda are profoundly different from those of the people in the southern half of the country. Take land tenure, for example. While southerners have embraced individual land tenure, in the north the consequencies of the shift from communal to individualised and privatised forms of land ownership would be too ghastly to contemplate. That is why rumours of the plots by "foreigners" to grab land in Acholi and to develop individual private estates have been used to scare the people in that region into sustaining the LRA. If people living in the same country cannot see eye to eye on something as basic as land tenure, imagine how difficult it is to bridge the north-south divide in the complex areas of politics, economic management and democratic governance. Yet, without bridging the north-south divide, the architects of Uganda's revolution will not achieve its dream of forging national unity and banishing sectarianism from the politics of our country.

Despite the shortfalls of Uganda's revolution, its balance sheet looks very good indeed. On the whole, the revolution has remained on course and its mission has been accomplished. As I close this book, Uganda is a much better country than it was back in 1986. But as we pat ourselves on the back and move into the future, we need to look back and take stock of where we have come from in order to map out where we are going. We had the courage and conviction to take on a sitting government that was oppressing and humiliating our people. We won. We should, therefore, have the same courage to admit our shortfalls, correct them and learn from them. As we face the future and pass on the baton to the next generation, let us not take the gains of our precious revolution for granted. Let us jealously guard them, enrich them and sustain them for the sake of a better Uganda and a promising future for our children and their offspring.

Index

Acholi community, 18, 206, 260

Adimola, Andrew, 260

Alai, Charles, 260

Ali Chete, 12, 175, 244

Ali, Moses, 97, 127

Allimadi, Otema, 260

Amin, Dada Idi, 1, 6, 11, 16, 18, 19, 42, 48, 93, 206, 215, 242: his fall 248; his regime, 18, 79, 251

Arusha town (Tz), 17, 33, 93

Bakiga tribe (Ug), 32

Basoga tribe (Ug), 32

Besigye, Kiiza (Dr), 191

Binaisa, Godfrey (fr. pres. Ug.), 97

Birembo attack, 192-194

Bushenyi town (Ug), 44

Cadet training – Tanzania, 24-37

civilian population and its importance in the struggle, 124

Constitution, 1995 (Ug) 263, 265

Constitutional Assembly (CA), 61, 262, 266

Dampa, Benjamin, 55, 56, 115

Democratic Party (DP) 53, 205, 207

Democratic Republic of Congo, 16, 86, 156, 175, 263

demystification of the gun, 144

diplomatic offensive, 195, 198

East African Community, 93

East African Railways, 86, 87

elections, general 1980 (Ug), 49, 136

Entebbe International Airport, 37, 60, 86, 108, 245

fall of Kampala, 237-249

FEDEMU, 207, 208, 211, 244, 250, 254

Field Force Units (FFU) Tz, 5

first combat mission (Kakiri), 60-72

Former Uganda National Army (FUNA), 51, 98, 66, 208

Front for National Salvation (FRONASA), 6, 12, 18, 21, 22, 32, 40, 41, 43, 49, 53, 55, 64

Ghadafi, Muamar, 85, 126, 127

Guma, Frank, 37

Habyarimana, Juvenal (Fr. pres. Rwanda), 65

Jinja Military Academy, 22

Kabamba III attack January 1985,

187-192: Masindi and Hoima offensives 175-194; training school (wing), 20, 25, 51, 53, 64, 153

Kafu river, 84, 124, 176, 177, 183

Kagame, Paul, 65, 67, 68

Kakiri II walkover, 142-146; *see also* second attack

Kasirye Gwanga, 239, 244

Kashaka, Steven, 175, 177, 189, 220

Katabarwa, Sam 40, 92, 93

Katera attack, 73-82

Katonga bridge, 220-225; reconnaissance, 156; river 124, 157, 190

Kayira Lutakome, Andrew, 57, 98, 126, 127, 147

Kerim, Peter (Brigadier), 175, 179, 202

Kigongo, Moses, 109, 110, 111

Kikosi Maalum,17, 18, 20, 21, 32, 40, 41, 42, 43, 44, 49

King's African Rifles, 144, 208

Kisumu port (Kenya), 19, 92

Kony, Joseph 141

Koreta, Ivan 12

Kyakabale, Anthony 62

Kyaligonza, Matayo 55, 56, 57, 58, 83, 113, 175

landmine warfare, introduction to NRA/PRA, 113, 114

Lakwena, Alice 143

Lord's Resistance Army (LRA) 141, 260, 268

lukoola (savannah flatland), 76, 77, 78, 80, 152, 153, 155, 160, 162, 183, 187, 188, 192

Lule, Yusuf (fr. pre. Ug.), 13, 97, 99, 100

Lumumba, Patrick, 48, 55, 175, 189, 190, 191, 207, 211, 217, 219, 240, 243, 245

Lutaaya, Andrew, 44, 58, 83, 89, 92, 108, 109, 198

Lutaaya, Ssonko (Lt. Col.), 130, 131, 132

Luttamaguzi, Onesimo, 83

Luwero Triangle, 20, 84, 121, 123, 141, 159, 161, 177, 204, 220, 265: consolidation of NRA defences in – by 1982, 141, 142, 156; operational zone in –, 141, 147, 151, 187

Magara, Sam, 40, 64, 65, 66, 112, 117, 118

Masindi Artillery School, 177, 180, 181

Mayanja river, 124, 135, 160, 176, 177, 178, 180, 188

Mbabazi, Amama, 92, 93

Mboijana, Chris, 96, 97

Military Commission (Ug.), 45

Mobile Brigade, 120: 181; under Tumwine, Elly, 114, 181, 208, 219

Mande, Samson, 139

Monduli Military Academy, 22, 24, 38; *see also* National Leadership

Academy (NLA / CTU), 34

Moses, Ali, 97, 127

Mubende Training Wing, 20, 25

Mugume, Joram, 112, 149, 176

Museveni, Janet, 93, 94

Museveni, Yoweri Kaguta (pres. Ug) 8, 12, 17, 31, 45, 51, 65, 81, 83, 87, 89, 96, 100, 105, 107, 108, 112, 206, 211, 214, 252: as chairman of High Command, 116, 119

Muwanga, Paul, 32, 109

Mwanga (Kabaka), 83

Mwebaze, Jet, 123

Moi, Arap Daniel (fr. pres. Ky) 211, 236

Nairobi journey, 86-95: return from – 105-122

Nakasongola training school, 45, 48, 51

National Resistance Army/ Movement (NRA/M); *see also* PRA 4, 22, 42, 55, 82, 119, 144, 146, 147, 178, 203, 204, 207, 208, 209, 212, 218, 232, 233, 250, 252, 254, 255, 256, 257, 259, 260, 261, 262, 263, 267, 268: code of conduct of – 120, 137: formation of – 97-104; government of 259, 260; introduction of formal ranks in – 261; struggle heroes of – 131

National Security Agency (NASA) Ug. 54, 56, 58: operatives of – 54, 57, 59, 110, 119

Njonjo, Charles 96, 97

Nsubuga, Emmanuel (Cardinal) 241

NYA (Not yet alloted Army number) militias, 135, 146, 149, 186, 200

Nyerere, Julius (fr. pres. Tz), 31, 37, 42, 182, 215, 240, 242

Organisation of African Unity (OAU): Charter, 86, 94; conference, 16.

Obote, Milton, 42, 45, 46, 79, 97, 107, 109, 152, 153, 184, 195: his regime/government II, 43, 49, 83, 86, 94, 119, 126, 195, 204, 207, 215, 246, 248, 260: his return, 43, 44; the fall of his government, 205, 214, 215, 251

Ochora, Walter (Col.) 203, 206, 208, 258, 260

Odoki, Benjamin Constitutional Commission (1989), 266

Ojok, Oyite David (Brig.) 31, 32, 47, 57, 136, 184: his death 183, 261

Okello, Olara Bazilio 58, 83, 111, 186, 206, 245

Okello, Tito Lutwa, 83, 209, 215, 259; his junta 26, 207, 208, 209, 214, 215, 216, 220, 243, 244, 246, 248

Operation (s) Bonanza (UNLA), 1982, 146; safari 50, 151-155

peace talks (Nairobi), 209, 214, 215, 227, 228

political education; *see* cadre 122, 123

re-organisation and preparation for Nairobi – NRA / NRM, 82-84

Resistance Councils (RC) system; *see* Local Council, 121, 218, 265, 266; *see also* local councils or people's governance

Rurangaranga, Edward, 110

Rwanda Patriotic Front (RPF), 83

Rwigyema, Fred, 14, 64, 65, 68, 83, 116, 121, 151, 215, 216, 217

Salim Saleh, 12, 17, 52, 113, 121, 144, 145, 149, 150, 151, 204, 217, 224: as commnder to Masindi 178, 179, 180, 189, 192;

Serwanga Lwanga (Col.), 197, 198, 208

Ssese Islands (L. Victoria), 89, 90

State Research Bureau and Public Safety Unit, 1, 2

Tanzania People's Defence Forces (TPDF), 12, 17, 35, 42, 43, 62, 73, 182

Tinyefunza, David, 190

Tumwine, Elly, 64, 73

Uganda Freedom Fighters (UFM), 56, 75, 98, 126, 127, 130, 146, 147, 149, 207, 208, 242, 243, 250, 254, 255: attack on Lubiri by –, 126-130; end of – militariry, 149; harmful propaganda by –, 147

Uganda Patriotic Movement (UPM) 40

Uganda Peoples' Congress (UPC), 43, 54, 56, 82, 207, 235: government/regime of – 49, 51, 53, 55; headquarters of 57; youth wingers, 81, 110; chairmen, 44, 81, 109

Uganda Peoples Defence Forces (UPDF), 141, 222, 262, 263

Uganda Nations High Commissioner for Refugees (UNHCR), 165

Uganda National Liberation Army/ Front (UNLA/F), 4, 21, 22, 44, 51, 135, 184, 204, 207, 208, 211, 212, 213, 237, 238, 239, 240, 246, 245, 249, 250, 251, 254, 257, 262: massacres/atrocities of – 122, 129, 141, 209

Walugembe, Alderman, 79

War beyond Kampala, 250-258

West Nile, 18, 19, 49, 51, 151, 207, 209